America's War in Vietnam

America's War in Vietnam

A SHORT NARRATIVE HISTORY

Larry H. Addington

Indiana University Press
BLOOMINGTON AND INDIANAPOLIS

This book is a publication of

Indiana University Press
601 North Morton Street
Bloomington, Indiana 47404-3797 USA

http://iupress.indiana.edu

Telephone orders   800-842-6796
Fax orders   812-855-7931
Orders by e-mail   iuporder@indiana.edu

© 2000 by Larry H. Addington

*The paper used in this publication meets the minimum
requirements of American National Standard for Information
Sciences—Permanence of Paper for Printed Library
Materials, ANSI Z39.48-1984.*

MANUFACTURED IN THE UNITED STATES OF AMERICA

Library of Congress Cataloging-in-Publication Data

Addington, Larry H.
    America's war in Vietnam : a short narrative history / Larry
H. Addington.
        p.   cm.
    Includes bibliographical references and index.
    ISBN 0-253-33691-0 (cloth : alk. paper). — ISBN 0-253-
21360-6 (pbk. : alk. paper)
    1. Vietnamese Conflict, 1961–1975 — United States.   I.
Title.
    DS558.A33   2000
    959.704'3373—dc21   99-41326

3   4   5   05   04   03   02   01

Contents

Maps

Preface

This work is intended to be a short, narrative history of America's war in Vietnam: its origins, course, and outcome. I have written it in hopes of making clearer to students and general readers alike, without exhausting their patience in the process, what happened to Americans in Vietnam and at home during the war. As explained in the acknowledgments, I have drawn heavily from my experience in teaching the history of the war to both graduate and undergraduate students, and, as almost every teacher knows, one learns as much from student reactions and contributions as from course preparation about what to teach and how to teach it. I have tried to make this book benefit from that experience.

For readers who struggle with foreign names and terms, I have provided some guides to pronunciation in the index, though these should be treated as functional rather than as definitive. I have also included a list of abbreviations at the front of the book for quick reference so that the reader will not drown in the "alphabet soup" that is inevitable in military and political environments. As the literature on America's war in Vietnam has become so voluminous, the bibliography indicates only some of the works consulted, but it will provide a starting point for readers who wish to delve more deeply into particular aspects of the story.

As America's war in Vietnam cannot be really understood without some knowledge of Vietnam's earlier history, I have devoted the opening chapters to Vietnam's historical evolution, the effects of the French colonial presence there in the nineteenth and twentieth centuries, America's alliance with Ho Chi Minh in the Second World War, and the events and politics that led up to American involvement in the French Indochina War (1946–1954). As I also believe that an understanding of the motivation and tenacity of Ho Chi Minh and his followers is essential to understanding both that war and America's war in Vietnam, I have tried to give some insight into the origins of Vietnamese communism.

Finally, I have tried to place the Vietnam experience within the framework of the American perceptions of the larger Cold War, perceptions that so powerfully influenced American involvement in what was essentially a civil war among Vietnamese, Laotians, and Cambodians. And although I have given some description of French, American, and communist military operations in respect to tactics and strategy, in the main I have selected a few particular military events to illustrate military trends, problems, and turning points. Wars are, after all, conducted by fighting, and in my view too many texts give too little attention to the sequence and impact of military events.

On a personal note, throughout the war years I was a professor of history in a military college far away from Southeast Asia. Yet I could not escape some of the war's more direct effects. Among these was the loss of former students whom I remember as fresh-faced cadets but whose fate it was to die as fighting men in a faraway land. But my greatest personal loss was a friend, a professional army officer, whom I had known since childhood. Therefore, I have taken the liberty of respectfully dedicating this book to the memory of Captain Don York, U.S. Army, killed in action in June 1962 while serving as a military adviser to the Army of the Republic of Vietnam. His death was among the first four hundred of nearly sixty thousand Americans deaths in the longest, as well as the most controversial, war in American history.

LARRY H. ADDINGTON
CHARLESTON, S.C.

Acknowledgments

In writing this book, I owe a great debt to the many veterans and non-veterans who addressed my class on America's war in Vietnam at The Citadel, the Military College of South Carolina, over the years before my retirement. Directly or indirectly, they influenced the account given in this work, but space allows for only a few to be mentioned by name. Though many people made a contribution for which I am grateful, I alone am responsible for the presentation and interpretation of events.

My special thanks extend to Colonel Myron Harrington, USMC, Ret., whose account of his company's experience in the eye of the storm in the battle for the Citadel at Hue in 1968 was riveting; to the late Larry Dring, Army Special Forces, who informed us about his experiences in fighting alongside the Montagnards; to Brigadier General Larry Wright, USAF, Ret., for his account of fixed-wing air transport in Vietnam and, humorously, the problem of carrying a white buffalo by air to appease a Montagnard chieftain. And to General William Westmoreland, USA, Ret., who was seated next to me at a dinner long ago and who informally answered my questions about his estimates of communist strength in South Vietnam just prior to the Tet Offensive.

I also owe thanks to my former colleagues in the History Department, including Colonel David White, USMCR, for reading the manuscript, relating his experiences in the siege of Khe Sanh, and putting at my disposal extensive papers regarding the episode; to Professor W. B. ("Bo") Moore Jr., who read parts of the manuscript relating to events in America during the war, who made useful suggestions, and who provided a "Baby Boomer" perspective; to my former student Colonel J. W. "Bill" Gordon, USMCR, who shared with me his experiences of serving in Vietnam as a company-grade officer; and to Jane Bishop, who gave my classes the perspective of an anti-war protester. I also owe thanks to Bob Sloan, my sponsoring editor at Indiana University Press, who originated the idea for this book. And, finally, my gratitude to my wife Amanda, who was again made a "computer widow" while I struggled with research and composition, and who has patiently and supportively borne it all.

Some Abbreviations Used in the Text

AA	Anti-Aircraft
AAA	Anti-Aircraft Artillery
AFFV	Army Field Force, Vietnam
ARVN	Army of the Republic of Vietnam
CIA	Central Intelligence Agency
CIDG	Civilian Irregular Defense Group
CINCPAC	Commander-in-Chief, Pacific
COMUSMACV	Commander, U.S. Military Assistance Command, Vietnam
CORDS	Civil Operations and Revolutionary Development Support
COSVN	Central Office, South Vietnam
DK	Democratic Kampuchea
DMZ	Demilitarized Zone
DOD	Department of Defense
DRV	Democratic Republic of Vietnam
FANK	Forces Armées Nationale Khmer
GHQ JGS	General Headquarters, Joint General Staff
GHQ MACV	General Headquarters, Military Assistance Command, Vietnam
ICCS	International Commission on Control and Supervision
JCS	Joint Chiefs of Staff
KIA	Killed in Action
KIA/BNR	Killed in Action, Body Not Recovered
KR	Khmer Republic
LPDR	Lao People's Democratic Republic
MAAGI	Military Advisory and Assistance Group, Indochina
MAAGV	Military Advisory and Assistance Group, Vietnam
MACV	Military Assistance Command, Vietnam
MAF	Marine Amphibious Force
MIA	Missing in Action
MR	Military Region
NLF	National Liberation Front

NMW	National Mobilization against the War
NVA	North Vietnamese Army
OSS	Office of Strategic Services
PAVN	People's Army of Vietnam
POW	Prisoner of War
PRC	People's Republic of China
PRG	Provisional Revolutionary Government
PRK	People's Republic of Kampuchea
RDP	Revolutionary Development Program
ROV	Republic of Vietnam
SAC	Strategic Air Command
SOG	Special Operations Group
SOV	State of Vietnam
SRV	Socialist Republic of Vietnam
TZ	Tactical Zone
VC	Viet Cong
VNA	Vietnamese National Army
VMLA	Viet Minh Liberation Army
VPLA	Vietnamese People's Liberation Army

America's War in Vietnam

1.

The Geography of Vietnam and Its History to World War Two

The Physical Setting

Vietnam has been likened to two rice bowls at the opposite ends of a carrying pole. The rice bowls represent the Song Coi (Red River) delta in the north and the Mekong River delta in the south, and the carrying pole represents the long, narrow territory in between. The country uncoils from its frontier with China, at approximately the 26th parallel, in an elongated "S" that stretches southward for more than 1,200 miles to a point below the 9th parallel, where the Ca Mau peninsula separates the South China Sea from the Gulf of Thailand. In all, Vietnam's borders encompass 127,300 square miles, or a land area slightly more than that in the state of New Mexico. For much of the distance from north to south, the Truong Son (Long Mountains) provide a natural frontier between Vietnam on the one hand and China and Laos on the other; the mountains near the Chinese border attain elevations as great as 10,000 feet, while those along the Lao frontier have elevations from 4,000 to 6,000 feet. This mountainous frontier gradually runs out along Vietnam's border with Cambodia in the Mekong delta. Though Vietnam's coastline is not much shorter than that of the eastern seaboard of the United States, the country at its widest point is no more than about 250 miles across, and it is only about 20 miles wide at its narrow waist at the 17th parallel.

In 1960, Vietnam's two largest cities were Hanoi (population about 600,000) in the north and Saigon (population about 1.6 million) in the south. The two cities, opposing capitals during America's war in Vietnam, are situated almost exactly seven hundred miles apart, and are respectively located in the alluvial plains of the Red River and the Mekong River—the chief, but not the exclusive, rice-growing areas of Vietnam. At the narrow waist of the country are Danang and Hue, with populations of 240,000 and 140,000 respectively in 1960. In this region, offshoots from the Truong Son reach nearly to the sea, and this geographical circumstance has left semi-isolated but heavily populated rice-growing deltas along the coast of central Vietnam.

In contrast to the crowded coastal deltas of Vietnam, the Central Highlands of southern Vietnam are relatively thinly populated. Most of the population here is composed of tribal peoples whom the French called Montagnards, or "mountain peoples." Found throughout the Long Mountains of northern and southern Vietnam, the Montagnards divide into eighteen tribal groups. Some tribes, such as the Hmong, have communities that sprawl across the frontiers of Vietnam, Laos, Burma, and even China. All Montagnards tend to identify with clans and tribes rather than with the countries within whose borders they happen to live.

Thus, because of geographical, agricultural, and demographic circumstances, of the approximately 30.5 million people living in Vietnam in the early 1960s (16.5 million north of the 17th parallel and 14 million south of it), close to 29 million people lived on only about 20 percent of the national territory. The remaining 1.5 million people—most of them Montagnards—lived in the more than 100,000 square miles of mountains and plateau. If the same situation existed in the continental United States, over 95 percent of the American population would live between the eastern seaboard and the Appalachian Mountains, while fewer than 5 percent would have the rest of the country to themselves. These peculiarities of geography and demography greatly affected the strategy, and arguments over strategy, of America's war in Vietnam.

THE HISTORY OF VIETNAM TO 1802

The Indochinese peninsula as a whole—which besides Vietnam, Laos, and Cambodia, technically includes Thailand (Siam)—was originally populated by an Austro-Indonesian population, most of whom lived in what is today Thailand and Cambodia. About 2,000 B.C., Thai and Khmer invaders from the northwest pushed these aboriginals aside, and some of the Khmers settled in the Mekong delta. Sometime later, seafaring peoples from ancient India settled in what is today central and south-central

Vietnam and founded there the kingdom of Champa. Finally, the Viets, a people akin to the Chinese and the ancestors of the modern Vietnamese, migrated from China to settle in the Red River delta.

According to tradition, the Viets were descended from a group of fifteen tribes called the Lac Viet, who created a kingdom in the Red River delta that they called Van-lang and that the Chinese called Au Lac. Apparently they were independent until 208 B.C., when, during the Han dynasty's rule in China, a Chinese warlord named Trieu Da used his forces to conquer the Viet kingdom. Trieu Da turned the Viet territory into his personal fiefdom and called his state Nam Viet (South Viet). Then in 111 B.C. the Han empire extended its direct rule over Nam Viet and renamed it Gia Chi, a term corrupted later by Westerners into "Cochin" as in "Cochinchina." Still later the Chinese empire renamed its Viet territory Annam, meaning "Pacified South." In modern times, these name changes, and more to come, would lead to confusion in the West as to the national identity of the Vietnamese.

Regardless of names imposed by China, the Viets never lost their sense of a national identity separate from the Chinese. Though they borrowed the Chinese system of ideograms for writing, the Chinese version of the Buddhist faith, and the mandarin traditions of Chinese government based on the Confucian code, they were never long quiescent under Chinese rule. For more than a thousand years after the first Chinese occupation, their history is replete with revolts for independence, so many in fact that they almost made a mockery of the term "Pacified South."

The first recorded Viet revolt against Chinese rule occurred in A.D. 40 and was led by Trung Trac, a titled Vietnamese lady. She had become enraged when a Chinese commander ordered her husband executed, and she was joined by her sister in arousing the disgruntled Viet nobility and population into action. Under the leadership of the Trung Sisters, the Viets drove the occupying Chinese army from Viet territory, and briefly the Sisters ruled the country as co-queens. When the returning Chinese overthrew their government in A.D. 38, the Sisters committed suicide rather than surrender. Down to the present day the Vietnamese conduct ceremonies honoring the Trung Sisters as Vietnam's first national patriots.

As Viet history unfolded, there were more revolts against Chinese rule, but none were successful until A.D. 938. Even then Viet independence was repeatedly imperiled by more Chinese invasions, three of them under the Mongol rulers who had earlier conquered China. Much of the time, the Viets were too weak to fight the Chinese or Mongols in pitched battles, and they turned to the techniques of guerrilla warfare, gradually wearing

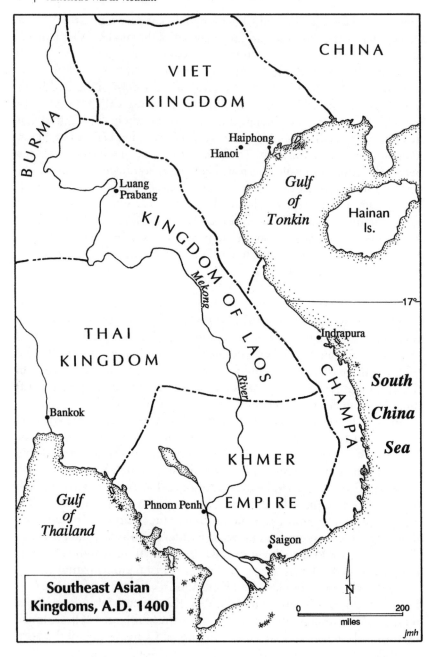

CHINA

VIET
KINGDOM

Haiphong
Hanoi

Gulf
of
Tonkin

Hainan
Is.

BURMA

Luang
Prabang

KINGDOM OF LAOS

Mekong

THAI
KINGDOM

17°

Indrapura

River

CHAMPA

South

China

Sea

Bankok

KHMER

Gulf
of
Thailand

Phnom Penh

EMPIRE

Saigon

N

**Southeast Asian
Kingdoms, A.D. 1400**

0   200
miles

jmh

down their foes with "little war" until they had enough strength to expel them from the country. Thus, by the time of America's war in Vietnam the waging of "protracted war" by irregular means already had a long history among the Vietnamese.

The final Viet overthrow of Chinese rule occurred during the reign of the Ming dynasty early in the fifteenth century. In 1418 Prince Le Loi raised the banner of revolt, and by resorting to a guerrilla-style warfare that was becoming second nature to the Viet people after generations of fighting a stronger enemy, his forces managed to isolate the Chinese garrisons within the Viet cities. When Le Loi's forces were finally strong enough to risk a decisive battle at Tot Dong in the Red River valley in 1426, they so routed the Chinese army that two years later China effectively recognized the Viet kingdom's independence by granting it the status of a tributary client state. Apart from an abortive Chinese invasion of Viet territory in 1788, the Chinese have not attempted another permanent, full-scale occupation of Vietnam to the present day.

As the Viet emperor, Le Loi named his kingdom Dai-Viet (Great Viet State) and established his capital at Tong Kinh (a name later corrupted by Westerners into "Tonkin"), a city on the Red River about seventy-five miles from the coast; it was subsequently renamed Hanoi. ("Tonkin" survives to the present as a name for the northern part of the country and the Gulf of Tonkin.) Dai-Viet's territory extended from the 23rd parallel to the 17th parallel, and occupied roughly the same area as that of the (communist) Democratic Republic of Vietnam from 1954 to 1975.

The Viet "golden age" commenced under Emperor Le Thanh-tong, who ascended the throne in 1460 and ruled his country for the next thirty-eight years. During Le Thanh-tong's reign, he established a political and bureaucratic structure that was to survive largely unchanged for generations. Subject to the will of the emperor, six ministries shaped policy and passed on imperial decrees to thirteen province chiefs. They, in turn, transmitted the decrees through district offices to some eight thousand communes. Each commune was governed by a village chieftain or mayor selected by its inhabitants, and its internal affairs were largely left to the discretion of its members.

The mandarins, an elite class of Confucian scholars, provided the Viet kingdom its civil service at large. To become a mandarin, a Viet had to master the complex and demanding code of Confucius, the Chinese sage of c. 500 B.C. whose teachings had become the basis of Chinese government. Entry into its corps was by examination, and in theory class did not bar anyone from applying. Himself a scholar in the Confucian tradition, Le Thanh-tong devoted much of his energy to the advancement of his people's learning on all levels of society. Thanks in part to his efforts, the Viets enjoyed a high level of literacy in his time and for centuries afterwards.

Le Thanh-tong also maintained a standing army of almost 200,000 men and officered it with those who had passed rigorous examinations in order to enter its officer corps. He used a nationwide draft to keep the ranks filled. The excellence of the army gave him the means to launch successful wars of expansion against the kingdom of Champa, the Indian-based civilization south of the Viet border, and what is now central Vietnam came under Viet control after the capture of the Cham capital at Indraputra in 1471. After Le Thanh-tong's time, the Viet kingdom continued to expand southward, but it became ever harder to rule these expanding southern territories from the north.

Early in the seventeenth century, the single Viet kingdom split into the Trinh kingdom in the north and Nguyen kingdom in the south. The Nguyen emperors continued the program of Viet expansion to the south, and they finally penetrated into the Mekong delta. Here bitter struggles ensued with the Khmers (Cambodians) who had lived there for generations, but early in the eighteenth century the Nguyen Viets finally drove the Khmers from much of the eastern delta. During the "Long March," as the long-time Viet expansion southward to the Ca Mau peninsula is termed, the Viets demonstrated formidable powers as warriors. And between them, the two Viet kingdoms rounded out the frontiers of Vietnam largely as they are today.

Meanwhile, in 1612, Roman Catholic missionaries from France reached the Viet kingdoms. The Viet emperors largely tolerated their proselytizing, and Monsignor Alexandre de Rhodes undertook to transliterate the Viet language into a written form, using the Roman alphabet. This form, known as *quoc ngu*, is still used today. And though the vast majority of the Viets remained Buddhists, a significant Viet minority were converted to Christianity. In consequence, the influence of the missionaries on the indigenous Roman Catholic population became another factor in the Viet political and cultural equation.

A key turning point in Viet history was reached when both of the Viet kingdoms were swept up in the Great Tay Son Rebellion (1772–1802), one that derives its name from the mountains in south-central Vietnam where it commenced. Though its causes are not entirely clear, they surely involved the Mandate of Heaven, a Confucian concept. Under the Mandate, the subject owed absolute obedience to the ruler, but that obedience was conditional upon the ruler's observance of tradition and law and upon a perceived harmonious relationship with the universe. The mandarins, the emperor's civil servants, were supposed to ensure harmony, the legal niceties, and a just rule over the emperor's subjects, but a major misfortune—ranging from military defeat to mandarin misconduct to acts of nature—could result in the perception of the emperor's subjects that he no longer had the favor of heaven and its mandate. In those circumstances, revolt was justified. Even today "revolution" is still expressed by a Vietnamese term that roughly translates as "change the Mandate."

After three years of fighting, the Tay Son rebels overthrew the Nguyen kingdom in the south, and in 1775 they marched north to overthrow the Trinh kingdom. But Prince Nguyen Anh, a survivor of the deposed Nguyen dynasty, refused to give up the struggle in the south, and for years his ragtag army of loyalists managed to hang on in remote bases in the watery maze of the Mekong delta. In the process of seeking to restore his dynastic fortunes, Nguyen Anh discovered an ally in Monsignor Pierre Pigneau de Bahaine, the head of the French Catholic missions.

Pigneau spent years vainly seeking outside aid for Nguyen Anh's cause, even making a trip back to France to seek assistance from the government of Louis XVI. He finally secured help from French traders in India, who, in return for future trading rights in the Viet kingdoms, provided Nguyen Anh with munitions, a small corps of mercenary soldiers, and officers to train Nguyen Anh's soldiers. The French aid helped to change Nguyen Anh's force from a ragtag body of loyalists into a disciplined body of 50,000 European-trained and mostly Catholic troops. With this reformed army, Nguyen Anh first drove the Tay Son rebels from the Mekong delta and then defeated them at the battle of Qui Nhon in 1799 for control of the central part of the country. Though Pigneau died of natural causes on the eve of that victory, Nguyen Anh and his army went on to extinguish the last of the Tay Son resistance in the north in 1802. Thus, after centuries of division, the land of the Viets was reunited at the beginning of the nineteenth century.

Nguyen Anh's military success gave strength to his claim that he enjoyed the Mandate of Heaven, and his remaining task was to ensure that his country would remain united under his dynastic successors. Accordingly, he took the title of Emperor Gia Long; he proceeded to rename his country "Vietnam" (literally Viet South), and by extension his Viet subjects became redesignated as the Vietnamese. He placed his capital at Hue in central Vietnam; in imitation of the Forbidden City in Beijing, he caused to be constructed there the Citadel, a great masonry fortress along the banks of the Perfumed River, and within its confines he located his Palace of Perfect Peace. The Nguyen dynasty that Gia Long founded would survive to almost the middle of the twentieth century.

THE CATHOLIC PROBLEM AND
THE ARRIVAL OF FRENCH IMPERIALISM

Because Gia Long owed his final success against the Tay Son rebels in no small measure to the support of the French Roman Catholic missions and their Vietnamese converts, his relations with them were amicable to his death in 1819. But there was also potential trouble in the presence of the Catholic Vietnamese. They owed fealty to a faraway Pope in Rome and to his priests in Vietnam, yet they were subjects of an emperor who ruled by the authority of an abstract Mandate of Heaven unrelated to Christianity. The emperor also exercised his power through a system of powerful mandarin officials, who resented the presence of Catholic priests and who were distrustful of the mixed loyalty of their Vietnamese converts. Under these circumstances, relations between the imperial government and the Catholic minority deteriorated after Gia Long's death.

In 1825, Emperor Minh Mang issued edicts circumscribing the activities of the Catholic missionaries and forbidding more missionaries to enter Vietnam. Matters hardly improved under Emperor Thieu Tri, who ordered the arrest of Father Lefèbvre for meddling in Vietnamese political affairs, whereupon the Catholic missions appealed to France for protection. In March 1847, a French warship bombarded Danang, called Tourane by the French, in order to compel the emperor to release Lefèbvre. After still another dispute over the treatment of Catholics with Emperor Tu Duc in 1856, the French again bombarded Tourane in order to have their way.

In the late 1850s, Bishop Pellerin, at the time the head of French Catholic missions in Vietnam, proceeded to France and lobbied the government of Emperor Napoleon III and French business interests for a far-reaching intervention in Vietnam. Pellerin made the case that Vietnam should be brought under French control both for the protection of Roman Catholicism and for the commercial advantage of France. He also could point to the fact that he had even secured the blessing of the Pope for the enterprise. Anxious to gain the approval of his subjects in France, most of whom were Roman Catholic, Napoleon III found his excuse to act against Vietnam when Father Diaz was put to death in 1857 for interfering in Vietnamese politics.

In August 1858, a French fleet put troops ashore at Tourane. The troops pushed up the Perfumed River to seize Hue and impose France's will on the emperor, but the expected easy victory over the Vietnamese army did not happen. Though the imperial army was technologically backward compared to the French forces, it put up a formidable resistance that, combined with the effects of tropical disease and heat, finally caused the French to abandon their effort and even to abandon Tourane.

The French then redirected their effort toward the less well defended Mekong delta in the Nam Bo (South Country), which they invaded in February 1859. The French forces succeeded in capturing Saigon, then a small fishing village, in August 1859, and then proceeded to occupy the four adjacent provinces. After they had seized still more territory in the south, in 1862 they compelled the imperial government to sign a treaty of peace that gave the French formal control over a colony in the south that they dubbed "Cochinchina." And in 1863, French forces moved up the Mekong River to Phnom Penh and established a "protectorate" over the kingdom of the Khmers (Cambodia).

After the Third French Republic succeeded Napoleon III's Second Empire, it proved as imperialistic as its predecessor. Ten years after the establishment of the Cambodian protectorate, French naval forces seized the port of Haiphong at the mouth of the Red River in northern Vietnam, and subsequently French vessels and troops moved inland to occupy Hanoi and to open the Red River as far as the border with China. From Hue, Emperor Tu Duc retaliated for the French invasion with a campaign against the Vietnamese Catholics, whom he claimed collaborated with the invaders. Years of unresolved conflict followed, and by 1883 the French had to decide either to withdraw from northern Vietnam altogether or to launch a major effort to dominate the whole country.

The die was cast in May 1883, when the French parliament approved the establishment of French protectorates over the northern and central parts of Vietnam. The timing could not have been worse for the Nguyen dynasty, for Emperor Tu Duc died in July, even as French forces were gathering to advance up the Perfumed River. The mandarins at the imperial court at Hue were divided over which of the royal princes should succeed him and how to deal with the French threat. Finally, with a shaky claim to the Mandate of Heaven, the Emperor Hiep Hoa assumed the throne in August. After barely a show of resistance to the French, he signed a humiliating treaty on their terms.

The treaty converted central and northern Vietnam into French "protectorates," and to these parts the French attached the names "Annam" (central Vietnam) and "Tonkin" (northern Vietnam) respectively. Henceforth, French officials had the right of approval over all actions of the imperial government in either territory. And, of course, as Cochinchina was a colony rather than a protectorate, it did not fall under even the fictional authority of the emperor. The French also abolished the use of the terms "Vietnam" and "Vietnamese," and depending on where a Vietnamese lived, he or she was officially designated by the French as Cochinchinese, Annamese, or Tonkinese. Like the Chinese before them, the French sought to erase the Vietnamese national identity by substituting bogus identities suitable to their interests.

In 1885, a palace coup engineered by mandarins replaced Emperor Hiep Hoa with the thirteen-year-old Prince Ham Nghi. Under mandarins hostile to the French, the new emperor disavowed the treaty made in 1883 and refused another. The French were enraged and, in retaliation, their troops carried out a bloody sacking of the Palace of Perfect Peace. The young emperor and his counselors eluded capture by fleeing west to the mountains, but there Ham Nghi was betrayed by Montagnard tribesmen into French hands. He was subsequently sent into permanent exile in French Algeria. The French supplanted him with Emperor Dong Khanh, a more compliant member of the Nguyen royal family, whom they surrounded with obedient mandarins and officials.

In 1887, the French created the French Indochinese Union—comprising Cochinchina, Annam, Tonkin, and Cambodia—and in 1893 they added the kingdom of Laos to the Union as another protectorate. Though Laos was an isolated, land-bound kingdom with only a small population, it was strategically located on the borders of Vietnam, Cambodia, Thailand, China, and Burma (now Myanmar). As the British and French agreed to leave Thailand as neutral territory between their respective Southeast Asian empires (the British included Burma and Malaya), the annexation of Laos completed the French empire in the region. Collectively, the French designated their possessions in Southeast Asia as "French Indochina." They settled down to exploit their Indochinese territories to the fullest extent possible, and Vietnam's ordeal under the French would last well into the twentieth century.

VIETNAMESE RESISTANCE

Though the French claimed that peace had been established in former Vietnam with the institution of a compliant emperor and court at Hue in the mid–1880s, in fact fragmented resistance to their rule continued here and there across the country for years. The most distinguished figure in the resistance was Phan Dinh Phung, one of Ham Nghi's mandarin advisers who had urged him to defy the French in 1885. After Ham Nghi's capture, Phan formed a guerrilla army in the mountains adjacent to the coast in central Vietnam, and from its mountain strongholds it harassed the French in Annam until Phan's death in 1896. A subsequent and relentless French

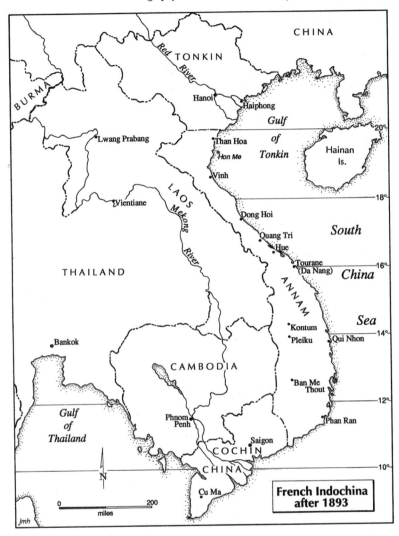

repression largely ended significant armed resistance to their rule by the beginning of the twentieth century.

As armed rebellion flickered out, Vietnamese nationalists turned to other means to alleviate Vietnam's condition. One of the most important of these modernizing nationalists was Phan Boi Chau. Originally a radical monarchist, he thought for a time that with Chinese and Japanese help an assertive Vietnamese emperor might crystallize opposition to French rule.

Eventually, he abandoned that hope for another. Inspired by the career of Sun Yat-sen, founder of the Chinese republic after overthrow of the Manchu dynasty in 1911, Phan dreamed of establishing a free and democratic republic in Vietnam and formed the Viet Nam Duy Tan Hoi (Association for the Modernization of Vietnam) to that end. But in 1925 the French arrested Phan on grounds of sedition and sentenced him to house arrest for life. By the time of his death in 1940, Phan's career had demonstrated that modern political ideas without a coherent strategy for revolution made little impact on a Vietnam under the French boot.

Five years after Phan Boi Chau's arrest, a return to violent resistance to French rule was marked by the emergence of the Viet Nam Quoc Dan Dung (the Vietnamese National Party or VNQDD), an organization with ties to China. Its agents sometimes engaged in assassinations of French bureaucrats and pro-French Vietnamese, and in 1930 it stimulated a revolt by native troops at Yenbay, a town near Hanoi. Though the French army promptly crushed the rebellion, they took vengeance not only on members of the VNQDD but on villages near Yenbay even suspected of sympathizing with the rebels. Their excessive repression sparked some popular peasant uprisings in both Tonkin and Annam, but these revolts were too disorganized to last long. The Yenbay episode demonstrated that while there was great revolutionary potential in the peasant population, they needed a leader with the right political program and revolutionary strategy to mobilize them. Within a decade, one such leader would appear in the person of Ho Chi Minh.

FRENCH RULE TO THE EVE
OF THE SECOND WORLD WAR

Paul Doumer, the first civilian governor-general of French Indochina (1897–1903), set the course of French rule in Vietnam that lasted to the eve of the Second World War. From the French administrative capital at Hanoi, he favored the business and investment interests of the French and the Hoa, the Chinese minority living in Vietnam, over those of the Vietnamese. (Eventually, the Chinese living in Vietnam had an investment in the colony's businesses second only to that of the French, a situation that made the Chinese less than popular with most Vietnamese.)

Doumer sought to make French colonial rule in Indochina as self-supporting as possible, and Vietnam was clearly the most valuable part. He undertook to pay the French administrative and military expenses there by making state monopolies of salt, alcohol, and opium. By 1903 opium sales represented a third of the colonial government's income from Vietnam.

Hmong tribesmen in Laos were encouraged to cultivate the opium poppy, and its extracts were sold to the colonial government in Indochina at bargain rates. Heretofore, drug addiction had not been a serious problem among the Vietnamese, but with the French deriving revenues from opium sales and encouraging its use, it became an increasing problem. Alcoholism among the Vietnamese also rose with French stimulation. Salt was essential to Vietnamese food preparation, and although natural sources of salt were plentiful in Vietnam, the Vietnamese were forced to pay artificially high prices to the French for the ingredient.

The French also suppressed traditional Vietnamese schooling above the village level, and the Vietnamese educational scene became dominated by *lyceés* established for the children of the French *colons* (European colonials) and for the education of Catholic Vietnamese. Only one *lyceé*, located in Hue and founded by a Vietnamese, was established expressly for the education of non-Catholic Vietnamese. Admission to French schools was difficult for anyone without wealth or the right connections, and relatively few rural Vietnamese got much education at any level. A consequence of the French educational policy was that though a high degree of literacy had characterized even the Vietnamese peasantry before the coming of the French imperialists, by 1939 only 20 percent of the population could read and write.

Another consequence of French educational policy was that although small numbers of Vietnamese—mostly from the wealthy and middle classes—managed to acquire educations above the level of the *lyceés* at the small University of Hanoi (which had a student population of around seven hundred by 1940), whenever possible the wealthier Vietnamese sent their sons and daughters to France for their higher education. But even those Vietnamese fortunate enough to receive university degrees found little employment for their talents in their homeland. Such conditions became a natural breeding ground for dissent among Vietnamese intellectuals and the well educated.

Still, the wealthier Vietnamese, and especially the Roman Catholics and the Chinese, managed to profit by the French presence to a degree. By subservience to their colonial masters, they were often allowed to escape the more crushing burdens and discriminations imposed on other Vietnamese, and opportunists were willing to serve as French interpreters, as go-betweens for the French and Vietnamese village chieftains in enforcing labor quotas, and as lackeys in other ways that might profit them. So much corruption marked the government in French Indochina that one senior French official is quoted as saying that the only Vietnamese friendly to the French were the Christians and the crooks. Although the French legacy in

Vietnam included industries, roads, railroads, improved ports, and increased sanitation in the cities (Saigon, which grew into a major city, became known as the "Paris of the East"), very few ordinary Vietnamese benefited from these improvements.

A principal complaint of the rural Vietnamese against the French was their practice of exporting much of the rice produced in Vietnam to other countries. Rice was the main food staple of the peasantry, and in some years all that was harvested was needed for food by the native population. In consequence, when the harvest was poor and the French continued to export rice, many Vietnamese peasants suffered from hunger. By the 1930s, 70 percent of the peasantry in Vietnam had been reduced to tenant farming, and the rest of the peasantry had their private landholdings so reduced that they could no longer feed their families from their production. The French shifted surplus labor from private or village farming to their many enterprises, and peasants were put to work in the mineral mines in the north or on the French rubber plantations in southern Vietnam. Often riddled by malaria, dysentery, and malnutrition, the workers, especially on the rubber plantations, died in huge numbers. Even by the standards of other European overseas colonies before 1939—and those standards were none too high—Vietnam earned the unenviable reputation as being the "Colony of Cruelty."

2.

THE CAREER OF
HO CHI MINH TO 1939

THE MAKING OF AN ASIAN COMMUNIST

The man who would become famous under the name Ho Chi Minh ("He who enlightens"), and who would also become America's chief antagonist in America's war in Vietnam, was born in Annam on 19 May 1890 under the name of Nguyen That Thanh. Little is known about his mother except that she was a concubine. Nguyen Sinh Sac, his father, was of peasant origins, but through assiduous study of Confucian philosophy, he had risen to the lower ranks of the mandarins and to a place at the court at Hue. The emperor's subservience to the French led to his disillusionment, and he gave up his post at court to become an itinerant village school teacher.

Still, Ho was more fortunate than most Vietnamese in that he was enabled to pursue his formal education as far as the *lyceé* at Hue, though it ended there when, at age seventeen, he quarreled with a teacher and left school. After a stint as a village school teacher, he headed south to the port of Saigon, where he signed on as a stoker and cook's helper aboard a French vessel. In signing on, he used an alias, the first of many he would use over the course of his lifetime. When he sailed from Vietnam in 1911, he would not see his homeland again for thirty years.

Ho's shipboard experiences carried him to British India, French North Africa, France, and, in 1913, the United States of America. He visited the seaports of Boston and San Francisco, and he left the sea for a time to settle in Brooklyn, New York. During his sojourn in America, he ventured into black Harlem, observed the American attitudes on race and class, and acquired a working use of Americanized English. (Besides Vietnamese, French, and English, he would eventually speak Russian, Siamese, and three dialects of Chinese.) While not all that he saw in America was flattering to the country, he was impressed with the great optimism among its immigrants, and his ambivalent attitude toward America may date from this time.

The First World War commenced in Europe in the summer of 1914. In 1915 Ho worked his way back across the Atlantic to England, and then left the sea to become an assistant pastry chef in a London hotel. But Paris beckoned. Some 100,000 Vietnamese were employed by France as soldiers and laborers on the Western Front, and the Asian quarter of the French capital was burgeoning. Toward the end of the war, Ho moved to Paris and adopted a new alias: Nguyen Ai Quoc (Nguyen the Patriot). He established a small photographer's shop as a means of making a living.

In Paris, Ho spent his spare time reading, joining debating societies, and even writing *The Bamboo Dragon*, a play that attacked the Nguyen dynasty for its collaboration with the French colonialists. But when the Paris Peace Conference convened at Versailles in the spring of 1919, he attempted to deliver a petition to the conference on behalf of Vietnam. Ho had been greatly impressed by Woodrow Wilson's announced principle of national self-determination as one of those upon which the peace should be based. (Actually, Wilson was thinking of the white peoples of eastern Europe yearning to be free of the former empires of Germany, Austria-Hungary, and Russia. He was not thinking of the colonialized peoples of color in Asia and Africa.) The petition asked for reforms in Vietnam that included constitutional government, democratic freedoms, and an end to the colonial exploitation of the Vietnamese people. Though the petition went no place, the effort made the name Nguyen Ai Quoc widely known to Vietnamese in Paris. The future Ho Chi Minh began to emerge from obscurity.

Ho's flirtation with Wilsonian liberalism ended with the disappointing reception of his petition, and he began to look in new directions. In 1920, he attended a meeting for the organization of the Socialist Party of France, but again he was disappointed. Most French socialists seemed in no hurry to address colonial questions and instead focused on the plight of the working class in France. But some socialists were inspired by events in Russia, where in November 1917 a revolution had propelled V. I. Lenin and his Marxist Bolsheviks into power. In 1921 they formed the Communist Party of France. Ho joined the party though, as he admitted later, he knew little about communism at the time except that it was opposed to colonialism.

Only after Ho entered the French communist party did he learn much about Karl Marx (1818–1883) and his theories of industrial capitalism as contained in *The Communist Manifesto* (1848), his multi-volume study *Capital* (the first volume was published in 1867), or his other publications. Marx taught that a crisis in industrial capitalism was going to be the inevitable result of fewer and fewer people in the West owning wealth and the major means of production and more and more people being pushed into the ranks of the exploited proletariat (i.e., the industrial working class in the cities). This tendency, Marx thought, would at some point create a critical mass of misery in industrial societies that would finally explode into proletarian revolution and the overthrow of capitalism.

None of Marx's writings was very relevant to Ho or the situation of the Vietnamese under the French boot, but something else in the communist literature was highly relevant. What really excited Ho in the communist literature was V. I. Lenin's *Thesis on the National and Colonial Question*, written in 1915 while Lenin was in exile in Switzerland. The *Thesis* gave a new twist to Marx's theory of class warfare and made Marxism relevant to Ho's colonial concerns and his world outlook.

In his essay, Lenin modified Marx's analysis with his own theory that the great wave of Western colonial overseas expansion in the late nineteenth century was proving to be a relief valve for the capitalist system. That wave had mostly affected Africa and Asia, and Lenin argued that by exploiting the peoples, resources, and markets in undeveloped parts of these continents through colonialism, the Western capitalists had postponed the day of crisis in industrialized societies. In addition, Lenin's thesis supported the idea of revolution among native peoples as the means of fighting imperialism in colonialized countries.

For Ho, Lenin's thinking was a revelation, for it forged a vital link between Ho's personal experience of colonial oppression and Marxism-Leninism. The link would play a large role in Ho's thought, as it did in the thinking of many Asian revolutionaries early in the twentieth century. As Ho would see matters, communism, anti-colonialism, and Asian nationalism were natural allies. The combination became Ho's ideology.

HO, THE ASIAN COMMUNIST MISSIONARY

Once converted to Marxism-Leninism, Ho wrote articles for the French communist newspaper *L'Humanité,* and he became the editor of *Le Paria* (The Outcast) in Paris. In one of his pamphlets, he scorned the symbolic figure of French Justice with her scales and sword, claiming that on the way to Indochina she had retained the sword while losing the scales of justice.

Ho's writings, smuggled into Vietnam, not only made him better known inside the country among literate Vietnamese, but also served to familiarize them with the idea that social revolution and anti-colonial resistance were inseparable.

But the pseudonym of Nguyen Ai Quoc also found its way to the lists of the French security services, and in 1924 Ho left Paris for Moscow. Lenin had died in January of that year, setting off a power struggle between Joseph Stalin and Leon Trotsky to be his successor as communist leader in Russia and head of the Communist International (Comintern). Ho was too preoccupied with attending the so-called University of Oriental Workers (actually an academy for training Asian insurgents) to be much involved in Soviet Russia's internal struggles, but Stalin's final victory over Trotsky in the late 1920s was to have important consequences for Ho later.

After finishing his instruction in Moscow, Ho left for China, where he ostensibly served as an interpreter to Mikhail Borodin, then Soviet adviser to General Chiang Kai-shek, a major figure in the Kuomintang (Nationalist Party) and head of the Whampoa Military Academy. In order to make his movement more broadly representative, Sun Yat-sen, president of the fledgling Chinese republic, had admitted the Chinese communists to the Nationalist Party in 1924, though the admission had heightened tensions within the party between right and left. Ho used his time in part to enlist Vietnamese students and exiles in southern China in his Revolutionary Youth League, a precursor of the Communist Party of Vietnam, and he seemed on his way to building a base for revolutionary activity in Vietnam.

But Ho's promising start in China was destroyed when, after the death of Sun Yat-sen in 1925, Chiang Kai-shek took his place and in 1927 launched a blood purge of the left wing of the Kuomintang in a surprise betrayal. As civil war erupted between Chiang's nationalists and the Chinese communists, Ho fled China. A year later, he turned up in Thailand, where he sought converts among the Vietnamese population in the northeast corner of the country, but some time later he moved clandestinely to British Hong Kong.

While in Hong Kong in 1930, Ho founded a small covert Communist Party of Vietnam, a first step toward fomenting peasant revolution in his homeland. But under pressure from the Stalinist-dominated Comintern, he was forced to change his party's name to the Communist Party of Indochina (CPI) and to adopt an official program that called for proletarian revolution in the cities rather than peasant revolution in the countryside. While outwardly conforming to the Comintern's dictates, privately Ho kept his faith in peasant revolution.

Ho's differences with Stalin hardly mattered in the short run, for soon after the founding of the CPI a British crackdown on dissident organizations in Hong Kong resulted in Ho's arrest and his subsequent imprisonment for nearly two years. Either before or during his imprisonment, Ho contracted tuberculosis, but in a curious way the disease came to his aid. While confined in a prison infirmary for treatment, he induced a hospital employee to report him as having died of TB, and then he escaped undetected into China. For a time even the ever-vigilant French security services believed that he was dead.

During the rest of the 1930s, Ho was a wanderer. Chiang Kai-shek's offensive in the south of China forced the Chinese communists, led by Mao Tse-tung, to carry out the "Long March" in the middle of the decade to China's hinterland in the north, and thus it became more difficult for Ho to find communist support near the borders of his homeland. Ho was reported to have been in many places during this decade, and on one occasion he trekked for five days across the mountains of central China in order to reach Mao's stronghold in the caves of Yenan in Shensi province. By all accounts, during the rest of the 1930s he remained faithful to his all-consuming passion, the liberation and independence of Vietnam, but it is unlikely that much more would have come of Ho had not the Second World War broken out in both Europe and the Far East. Indirectly, the war opened Ho's way to power in Vietnam.

3.

WORLD WAR TWO AND AMERICA'S COLLABORATION WITH HO

THE SINO-JAPANESE WAR, FRANCE'S
DEFEAT IN EUROPE, AND THE FOUNDING
OF THE VICHY FRENCH GOVERNMENT

China's internal divisions and civil war made it a tempting target for Japanese expansion in a time when the government in Tokyo was increasingly dominated by its militarists. In 1931, Japanese forces invaded China's huge northern province of Manchuria, and, after turning Manchuria into the puppet state of Manchukuo, they launched a new aggression against China by capturing Beijing in 1937. Then they commenced moving south across China's great coastal plain.

In northern China, the Chinese communists resisted Japanese encroachments with guerrilla warfare, and further south Chiang Kai-shek's nationalist armies battled the invaders. But Nanking, the nationalist capital, fell before the Japanese onslaught, and Chiang Kai-shek was compelled to shift his capital to Chungking in China's mountainous hinterland. By the spring of 1940, the Japanese had occupied most of China's coastal areas and in places were far inland.

Chiang's armies continued to survive in part on supplies brought in through French Indochina and British Burma, but these sources had been threatened ever since the Second World War broke out in Europe in September 1939. In May to June 1940, the Nazi Blitzkrieg swept over Norway, Denmark, the Netherlands, Belgium, and France. As France was going down in defeat, old Marshal Henri Philippe Pétain assumed leadership of

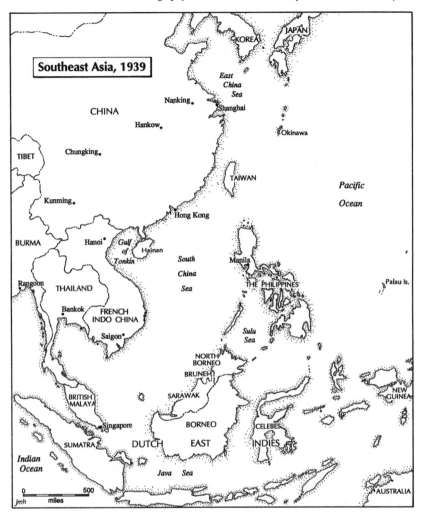

the dying Third Republic. His representatives accepted Adolf Hitler's terms for an armistice that went into effect on 22 June.

Though military victory put Hitler in a position to abolish France's sovereignty entirely, he recognized that to do so would probably result in France's overseas colonies and the French fleet rallying to the side of Britain and continuing in the war against Germany. He therefore agreed that southeastern France would remain unoccupied by the Germans, that Marshal Pétain's government might set up a capital there at the town of Vichy, and that the Vichy government would declare its official neutrality in the war between Germany and Britain.

Most of France's overseas governors, including the governor-general of Indochina, recognized Vichy's authority and were bound by its policies, and only a minority of the overseas governors rallied to the support of General Charles de Gaulle's Free French Movement, founded in Britain shortly after France's defeat.

THE COMING OF THE WAR IN THE PACIFIC

In July 1940, the Japanese demanded that the governor-general of Indochina grant the Japanese the use of air bases, roads, and railroads in Vietnam as far south as the 17th parallel. Provided the French colonial administration cooperated, the Japanese would leave it in place and the French colonial troops would be allowed to retain their arms. The governor-general of Indochina had little choice but to accept the Japanese terms, and retroactively his decision was approved by the Vichy government. But the Japanese advance into Tonkin and northern Annam plunged the deteriorating relations between Tokyo and Washington to a new low.

American foreign policy aimed at assisting Chiang Kai-shek's government and stopping any further expansion of Japanese power in Asia. President Franklin D. Roosevelt chose to bring Japan to heel by ordering a partial freeze of American trade ties with Japan and by stationing the U.S. Pacific fleet, normally located at San Pedro in California, at its advanced base at Pearl Harbor in Hawaii. But the Japanese remained undeterred by Roosevelt's actions. They signed the Tripartite Pact with Germany and Italy in September 1940, one that obligated the European Axis powers to come to Japan's aid if it was attacked by another Pacific power. The Pact was obviously aimed at the United States.

Emboldened by their Axis alliance, in the summer of 1941 the Japanese pressured the French into allowing them to march into southern Vietnam. From there they would be in a position to threaten British Malaya and the Dutch East Indies, both parts of the southern resources area that could meet so many of Japan's needs in raw materials, including oil. President Roosevelt retaliated for the Japanese advance into the rest of Annam and Cochinchina by effectively suspending all U.S. trade with Japan. What hurt Japan most was the American embargo on oil shipments, for Japan imported 90 percent of its fuel requirements from the United States.

The growing crisis between the United States and Japan intensified in the fall of 1941, when the American terms for resuming trade, including the shipment of oil, were made stiffer by demands that the Japanese must withdraw not only from French Indochina, but from all of China as well. Though the Japanese diplomats in Washington continued to negotiate with the U.S. State Department, the die was cast in late November, when the Japanese cabinet under General Heideki Tojo secretly decided on hostilities with the United States. The Japanese launched the Pacific War on 7 December 1941 with a sudden carrier-borne air attack on the U.S. fleet at Pearl Harbor.

THE PACIFIC WAR AND THE WAR FOR EAST ASIA

The surprise attack on Pearl Harbor partially paralyzed the U.S. Pacific fleet and made it impossible to send reinforcements to the American Philippines, Guam, or Wake Island in time to fend off Japanese invasion. Making things worse for America, both Nazi Germany and Fascist Italy declared a state of war with the United States on 11 December. Faced with a war on two fronts, for about six months the United States was largely impotent in the Pacific. During those months, Japanese forces swept over the American Philippines, British Malaya, and the Dutch East Indies (Indonesia) and, after intimidating Thailand into an alliance, invaded British Burma and pushed to the borders of India. By June 1942, the southern resources area was firmly in the Japanese grasp, and, in addition, the Japanese manned an outlying chain of Pacific islands that served as a barrier to any American return to the Far East.

The period of Japanese ascendancy in the Pacific began to fade when the reviving U.S. Pacific fleet turned back a Japanese invasion force off eastern New Guinea in the Coral Sea in May 1942, and in June the U.S. fleet inflicted a severe defeat on the Japanese navy at the Battle of Midway, a thousand miles west of Hawaii. Still, the first American ground offensive in the Pacific War did not commence until August 1942, when U.S. Marines landed on the island of Guadalcanal in the Solomon Islands in the South Pacific; subsequently, another Allied offensive was launched by General Douglas MacArthur in eastern New Guinea.

The "Island War" that followed mainly took the form of Allied advances through the central and south Pacific, and by October 1944 the Allied forces were converging on the Philippines. Once the key islands were secured, one of the Allied aims was to use the Philippines as a base to sever Japan's lines of water communication to its conquests in the southern resources area, an area that included Indochina.

THE FOUNDING OF THE VIET MINH AND
RESISTANCE TO THE JAPANESE

From the time that the Japanese entered Vietnam in 1940, Ho Chi Minh had seen an opportunity to foment resistance to both the French and the Japanese presence there. Returning to his homeland for the first time in thirty years, in February 1941 he trekked across the mountainous border between China and Vietnam to a suitable headquarters set up by his collaborators near Cao Bang. Among his collaborators were Pham Van Dong and Vo Nguyen Giap, both of whom would later play prominent roles in America's war in Vietnam.

At his mountain base in Vietnam, Ho announced to his confederates that the time had come to form a broad front of Vietnamese patriots of all classes to work and fight for Vietnam's freedom and independence. The new organization would be called the Viet Nam Doc Lap Dong Minh (contracted to Viet Minh), or the "League for the Independence of Vietnam." The communist aspect of its leadership was downplayed in the interests of attracting as wide a support from the Vietnamese population as possible. Ho would take aid from any source so long as it was inclined toward his goal of freeing Vietnam from foreign tutelage, and after December 1941 he leaned toward an Allied victory in the Pacific War, in expectation that Japanese defeat would make it easier to throw out the French colonials in turn.

At first the Viet Minh's activities were more political than military, for it was vital for Ho to win the trust of the peasantry in the mountains and then to extend it over time to as much of the rest of the rural population as practicable. The weak Franco-Japanese presence in the remote areas of the north made the conversion of the peasants there the easiest, but the Viet Minh also needed arms and equipment for the armed struggle when the time was right. For that and other reasons, Ho made numerous trips back to China. On one trip he was imprisoned for a time by Chiang Kai-shek's nationalists, but he was released in the interests of a united front against the Japanese.

AMERICAN COLLABORATION WITH HO

Early in the Pacific War, the U.S. Office of Strategic Services (the forerunner of the Central Intelligence Agency, or CIA) established a branch headquarters at Kunming, China. Ho soon sought to win its approval and support, and as the OSS learned of the Viet Minh's activities, gradually it and

Ho moved toward collaboration in the common interest of defeating the Japanese.

When American forces under General MacArthur invaded the Philippines in October 1944, Ho believed that they would soon also land in Indochina. Hence, the time for armed struggle had arrived. Accordingly, in December Ho authorized the creation of the first unit of what was to become the Viet Minh Liberation Army (VMLA) with Vo Nguyen Giap as its commander. It was then a tiny force, only thirty-four men equipped with primitive arms, but from that small beginning the VMLA would eventually grow into a powerful military organization.

But as 1945 began, the expected American landings in Indochina did not occur. Instead, the Americans left forces in the Philippines to root out the last Japanese resistance there, and turned their efforts to invading Iwo Jima in February and then Okinawa in April for air and land bases for an invasion of the Japanese homeland. Still, American aircraft based in the Philippines carried out frequent raids on Japanese targets in Vietnam, and the Viet Minh rescued downed American pilots and smuggled them to the safety of Allied lines in China. The Viet Minh also passed on intelligence to the OSS at Kunming as to Japanese troop movements and dispositions in Vietnam.

Meanwhile, the French administration in Vietnam, also under the impression that an Allied invasion of Indochina was imminent, began secret preparations for a military revolt to overthrow the Japanese occupation. Unfortunately for the French, the Japanese caught wind of the preparations, and on 9 March 1945 the Japanese army arrested the French colonial authorities, wiped out the French garrisons that resisted, and disarmed and interned those that did not. Only some French soldiers on exercises in the field in Tonkin managed to escape over the Chinese border.

As the Japanese wished to make it appear that their coup against the French was taken in Vietnamese interests, they offered the restoration of Vietnam's independence and unity under Japanese "protection" to Emperor Bao Dai, then sitting with his court at Hue. Bao Dai had little choice but to accept the new protectorate, one that the Japanese made more palatable by restoring all three of Vietnam's traditional parts—Cochinchina, Annam, and Tonkin—to a restored Vietnamese state. But by agreeing to the restoration of Vietnam under Japanese protection, Bao Dai laid himself open to charges of being a collaborator, something that might count against him when the Allies finally wrested Indochina from Japanese control.

The future of Vietnam at the end of April 1945 was still in doubt when

Ho first met with Major Archimedes Patti, an OSS agent just arrived at Ho's mountain headquarters. Patti was empowered to aid Ho's effort to defeat the Japanese in Vietnam as far as practicable, and he did not object to Ho's stated opposition to the return of French colonialism once the Japanese were defeated. Official U.S. policy on the question of independence for the states of Indochina was then unclear, for President Roosevelt had promised General de Gaulle that Indochina would be returned to French control after the war, but then later expressed his displeasure with the idea. What Roosevelt's final position on Indochina would have been cannot be known because he died suddenly on 12 April 1945 from a cerebral hemorrhage. Upon Roosevelt's death, the burden of leading the United States fell to Vice President Harry S Truman.

The new president had many more pressing matters on his mind than Indochina's future when he questioned the State Department about its position on the future of the French Indochinese states. It was hardly helpful to him to discover that the European division favored their return to France as a means of bolstering its post-war recovery, while the Far Eastern division, being more aware of the growing sense of nationalism in the area, favored giving them independence or at least some sort of commonwealth status. Such was the unsettled state of American policy when, following the surrender of Nazi Germany on 7 May 1945, the "Big Three" (Truman, Stalin, and Winston Churchill) met in Potsdam in July in order to settle a variety of questions for the post-war world.

At the Potsdam Conference, the Allied leaders reached agreement for a temporary arrangement in regard to Vietnam. At the end of hostilities, Chinese nationalist troops would occupy the country north of the 16th parallel, disarm the Japanese troops found there, and release any Allied prisoners of war. British troops, then in the process of driving the Japanese from Malaya, would follow the same policy in their zone south of the 16th parallel. A final post-war political solution for Vietnam and the rest of the Indochinese states would await decisions to be made after the war.

Meanwhile, the OSS contact with Ho had resulted in the sending of DEER TEAM, a small body of U.S. military advisers under Major Allison Thomas, with a supply of arms for the VMLA. As DEER TEAM began training the VMLA, now grown to several thousand men and women, the Americans found their Vietnamese students were extremely quick in mastering the assembly of small arms (such as rifles, machine guns, and mortars), and the carrying out of small-unit tactics. As increasing numbers of Vietnamese were enlisted in the ranks of the VMLA, guerrilla-style operations were launched against Japanese outposts as the way was laid for the

VMLA to gain control of all of the mountainous area of Tonkin adjacent to China. Though the Viet Minh's presence in central and southern Vietnam was weaker than in the north, even in those areas Ho was able to create a covert Viet Minh political and military force.

But before the Viet Minh could lead a general uprising against the Japanese, the dropping of the atomic bombs on Hiroshima and Nagasaki on 6 and 9 August 1945 brought an unexpected early end to the war. Both DEER TEAM and their Viet Minh allies were caught by surprise by the war's sudden ending, but when a general armistice went into effect on 14 August, the Viet Minh were the most-organized and best-armed Vietnamese in the country.

THE AUGUST REVOLUTION AND THE FOUNDING OF THE DEMOCRATIC REPUBLIC OF VIETNAM

On 16 August 1945, two days after the armistice in the Pacific War went into effect, Ho formed a National Liberation Committee, effectively a provisional government for the establishment of the Democratic Republic of Vietnam (DRV). Though Ho was the self-appointed head of the DRV and fellow communists filled many key positions, the new government also included non-communists. Ho's policy at the time was to give his government as wide a base in the Vietnamese population as possible.

Ho also knew the importance of the concept of the Mandate of Heaven in the eyes of traditional Vietnamese. As he did not want his countrymen to think that the DRV was entirely forged on the anvil of opportunity, on 25 August a Viet Minh–inspired delegation arrived at Hue to urge Emperor Bao Dai to abdicate the imperial throne in favor of the DRV and thereby peacefully transfer the Mandate of Heaven. Believing that Ho had American support and that he himself might be accused of collaboration for accepting the Japanese protectorate established in the previous March, Bao Dai decided to abdicate. In return for Bao Dai's cooperation, Ho appointed him as "supreme adviser" to the new government, an honorary title that would shelter the former emperor from future Allied prosecution. After his abdication, Bao Dai went to Hanoi, where, on Ho's orders, he was treated with great respect but was given few real duties.

After Bao Dai's abdication, Ho wasted little time in preparing a formal declaration of Vietnamese independence. On 2 September 1945, the same day that General Douglas MacArthur formally accepted Japan's surrender on the deck of the battleship *Missouri* in Tokyo Bay, Ho read the document to thousands of his cheering countrymen in downtown Hanoi. Major Patti and other uniformed Americans were in attendance. Perhaps with the American members in his audience in mind, Ho's speech began with the words:

> "All men are created equal. They are endowed by their creator with certain inalienable rights, and among these are life, liberty, and the pursuit of happiness." This immortal statement was made in the Declaration of Independence of the United States of America in 1776. In a broader sense, this [statement] means that all the peoples of the earth have a right to live, to be happy and free.

Nevertheless, Ho went on to say, for more than eighty years the French imperialists had deprived the Vietnamese of every democratic liberty, had artificially divided Vietnam into three parts in order to disguise its nationality, and had drowned Vietnamese uprisings against their rule in rivers of blood. They had built more prisons than schools, and, in order to weaken the native population, they had forced on it the use of opium and alcohol. They had taken control of Vietnam's mines, forests, and raw materials, and they had invented numerous unjustifiable taxes through which they had reduced the peasantry to a state of extreme poverty. They had also hindered the prospering of the middle classes. Ho concluded:

> For these reasons, we, members of the Provisional Government, representing the whole Vietnamese people, declare that from now on we break off all relations of a colonial character with France; we repeal all international obligations that France has so far subscribed to on behalf of Vietnam, and we abolish all special rights the French have unlawfully acquired in our Fatherland. The whole Vietnamese people, animated by a common purpose, are determined to fight to the bitter end against any attempt by the French colonialists to reconquer our country.

At the end of Ho's speech, an American plane flew over the city square where thousands of Vietnamese were listening to Ho's words. When the crowd recognized the American insignia, they broke out in spontaneous cheers. In less than twenty years, the same insignia on an airplane would provoke a storm of fire from Vietnamese weapons. Though Ho could not have known it on 2 September 1945, the happy days of collaborating with the Americans were almost over.

4.

AMERICA AND THE
INDOCHINA WAR, 1946–1954

Ho Chi Minh's declaration of Vietnam's independence on 2 September 1945 made little impression on the Allies. Once Japan had surrendered, they proceeded to put into effect the agreements made at Potsdam in regard to Indochina. During September, British troops under General Sir Douglas Gracey occupied Vietnam south of the 16th parallel (in effect, Cochinchina and part of Annam), while Chinese nationalist troops under General Lu Han occupied the area north of it (the rest of Annam and Tonkin). Trouble soon followed the occupations.

General Gracey was a colonial soldier, and from the outset of his duties he was sympathetic to a French return to power in Vietnam. Though the Viet Minh had set up a Provisional Executive Committee in Saigon to govern southern Vietnam, Gracey refused to recognize its authority. Instead, he made an alliance with Jean Cédile, the French representative, and even used Japanese soldiers to supplement his own troops in enforcing his rule. He made the situation more dangerous by rearming the freed French colonial soldiers, many of whom were spoiling for a fight with the Vietnamese.

While the Japanese soldiers remained well behaved until their services were no longer required and they could be returned to their homeland, the French colonial soldiers acted otherwise. On 22 September, French paratroops and Foreign Legionnaires went on a rampage in Saigon, using force to oust the Viet Minh's Provisional Executive Committee and attacking other Vietnamese all over the city. The Viet Minh retaliated by calling a citywide labor strike and by launching physical attacks on the French. Apprised of the disintegrating situation in southern Vietnam, the new Labor government in London under Prime Minister Clement Attlee set about helping Charles de Gaulle, then heading a provisional government in Paris, to get a French expeditionary force to Indochina as quickly as possible. De Gaulle appointed Admiral Georges Thierry d'Argenlieu as high commissioner for Indochina, and in October the admiral relieved Gracey of responsibility for southern Vietnam. As soon as a French expeditionary force of 35,000 troops could be assembled in southern Vietnam, the British garrison departed.

The French expeditionary force wasted no time in launching operations to clear Saigon and the Mekong delta of formal Viet Minh opposition, and then it pushed into the Central Highlands to occupy its key centers. At length, the Viet Minh in southern Vietnam broke off formal military resistance and retired to their secret bases in the countryside. As Viet Minh resistance seemingly vanished, the French commander declared in February 1946 that Vietnam south of the 16th parallel was once more securely under French control. The reality was that the Viet Minh infrastructure was still largely intact, and its leaders were awaiting further orders from Ho.

But Ho had little time to spend on his country's plight in the south. He was struggling to keep his government in power in Hanoi, to deal with the effects of a widespread famine in the north, and to limit the pillage of Lu Han's 200,000 Chinese troops above the 16th parallel. The Truman administration had withdrawn Ho's American advisers in the fall of 1945, and by December Ho's situation was dire. Perhaps impressed by the stated American intention to give the Philippines independence in 1946, he wrote a letter to President Truman in which he proposed that if Vietnamese independence could not be achieved immediately, then Vietnam would accept transfer to the United States as a trust territory in preparation for independence. Ho did not receive so much as a reply to his offer.

The problem of the Chinese occupation of northern Vietnam was unexpectedly solved for Ho when the French proposed to Chiang Kai-shek that they relinquish the old French concessions in Shanghai and other Chinese ports in exchange for allowing French troops to replace the Chinese forces north of the 16th parallel. After Chiang accepted the offer, Lu Han's army departed early in 1946. Ho was then faced with the prospect of a French return to northern Vietnam, and some of Ho's collaborators urged him to order the VMLA to fight. Instead, he decided to try negotiations first and to resort to war only as a last resort.

Ho offered to accept the French back in the northern part of the country temporarily, provided that they recognized the legitimacy of the DRV and placed a time limit on the presence of French troops everywhere in Vietnam. After prolonged negotiations at Hanoi with Jean Sainteny, the French representative, the chief sticking point turned out to be the future of Cochinchina. Unlike the French protectorates of Tonkin and Annam, Cochinchina was technically a French colony. The French proposed to grant diplomatic recognition to Ho's republic, but only if Cochinchina remained under French control. Ho refused the French offer and declared that he could never submit to a partition of Vietnam.

Just when the negotiations seemed on the point of breaking down, Ho and Sainteny reached a compromise agreement on 6 March 1946. Under its terms, France would recognize the DRV as a free state within the French Indochinese Union, French Union troops would be stationed in the DRV for no longer than five years, and the status of Cochinchina would be worked out by face-to-face negotiations in Paris between representatives of the DRV and the new Fourth French Republic.

THE COMING OF THE INDOCHINA WAR

As French troops began to return to northern Vietnam, on 31 May a DRV delegation led by Ho left for Paris to conduct negotiations. But almost as soon as Ho had departed, Admiral d'Argenlieu proclaimed from Saigon a "Republic of Cochinchina," a move clearly intended to create a French puppet state in the south. Then upon his arrival in France, Ho was further humiliated when his delegation was shunted off to a meeting site in Fontainebleau, sixty miles from Paris. Still worse, the government of the Fourth Republic seemed to be dragging out negotiations through the summer and into the fall of 1946 as d'Argenlieu used the time to prepare for a French reconquest of northern Annam and Tonkin.

As more and more French troops occupied Haiphong and Hanoi, General Vo Nguyen Giap, both commander of the VMLA and leader of the DRV's government in Ho's absence, alerted Ho by coded cables to the fact that French military action was imminent. In October, Ho's tedious and unproductive talks with the French government collapsed and his delegation returned to Hanoi. By November the proximity of Viet Minh and French forces in the Red River delta had raised tensions between them to the breaking point.

The first clash occurred on 23 November after quarrels over whether the French or the Viet Minh had the right to collect customs at the port of Haiphong. That day the French command demanded that all VMLA

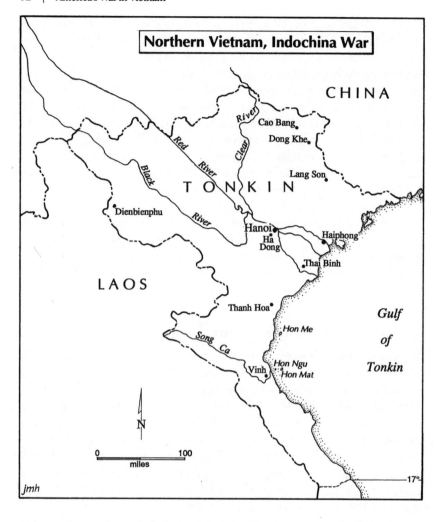

troops evacuate Haiphong within two hours. At the expiration of the ultimatum, the French cruiser *Suffren* in the harbor opened fire on the Vietnamese quarter of the port, and French troops followed up the bombardment by launching an offensive to drive Giap's troops from the city. Within
a few days of the French attack, the Viet Minh forces had been forced to
withdraw up the Red River to new positions near Hanoi.

At Hanoi an uneasy truce stopped the fighting temporarily, but the last
chance for peace was lost when the French demanded that the VMLA
disarm before further negotiations could take place. The situation exploded into irreversible war on the night of 19 December 1946, when troops of

the VMLA blew up the municipal power plant and then attacked the French garrison. The French forces counter-attacked, and Hanoi became a battleground. The fighting in Hanoi lasted through nearly the rest of December, but gradually the French got the upper hand. As the VMLA began withdrawing to the countryside, Ho escaped to Ha Dong, a town a few miles from Hanoi, and from there he broadcast over radio an appeal to his countrymen of all classes to join with the Viet Minh in a "war of national liberation." By the beginning of 1947, the Indochina War, as it would be called, was well underway.

THE COLD WAR AND THE
AMERICAN GLOBAL PERCEPTION

At the beginning of the Indochina War, the U.S. government was largely a spectator, one more sympathetic to the French than to the Viet Minh but favoring a compromise peace between the two. But that view soon changed, and largely because of events outside of Indochina. The cause was the emergence of the so-called Cold War, a term for the bitter rivalry between the Soviet Union and the communist world on the one hand and the United States and the other Western powers on the other.

The Cold War began with disputes over the terms of a peace treaty with Germany, and extended to Western objections to the Soviet-imposed communist governments in eastern European states liberated by the Red Army. As early as 15 March 1946, while giving a speech at Fulton, Missouri, Winston Churchill declared that an "Iron Curtain" had been rung down across Europe from Stettin on the Baltic Sea to Trieste on the Adriatic. Stalin had been slow to withdraw Soviet forces from northern Iran—occupied during the war—and he had put pressure on Turkey for a revision of the Russo-Turkish borders. But most disturbing to the West was a communist-led insurgency in Greece. Despite British support for the restored monarchy, Greek guerrillas based in Yugoslavia and Albania continued to threaten the authority of the government in Athens. By the beginning of 1947, Britain—itself in severe financial straits—could no longer support the Greek government against its internal enemies. When London appealed to the U.S. government to step into the breach, President Truman took swift action.

Before a special session of both houses of Congress on 12 March 1947, Truman described the gravity of the world situation and made particular reference to the situations of Greece and Turkey. The very survival of Greece as a free nation, he said, was menaced by a militant, communist-led minority, which he claimed was exploiting post-war want and misery to create political chaos. And Turkey was threatened by more overt Soviet aggression. In enunciating what became known as the Truman Doctrine, the president declared:

> I believe that it must be the policy of the United States to support free peoples who are resisting attempted subjugation by armed minorities or by outside pressures. I believe that we must assist free peoples to work out their own destinies in their own way. . . . The free peoples of the world look to us for support in maintaining their freedoms. If we falter in our leadership, we may endanger the peace of the world — and we shall surely endanger the welfare of our own nation. Great responsibilities have been placed upon us by the swift movement of events.

Truman called upon Congress to appropriate $400 million for assistance to Greece and Turkey and to grant authority to send civilian and military missions to instruct the Greek and Turkish civil services and armed forces. Congress responded favorably with the Greek-Turkish Aid Act, signed into law by Truman on 22 May 1947. The Truman Doctrine would be later cited as justification for American assistance to the anti-communists in Indochina.

In June 1947, George C. Marshall, then Secretary of State, proposed the European Recovery Program (ERP), or extensive U.S. economic aid to all the war-torn countries in Europe. Stalin forbade any communist government in eastern Europe to accept such aid, but, after coordination with the Western European governments, Congress passed the necessary legislation in April 1948. Among the countries most generously assisted was the French Fourth Republic. It converted some of the Marshall Plan credits to purchases of arms and equipment for the French forces fighting in Indochina.

The Truman Doctrine and aid under the Marshall Plan greatly contributed to the revival of Western Europe and to maintaining Greek and Turkish independence and security, but in February 1948 a communist coup in Prague overthrew the coalition government in Czechoslovakia and the new government aligned itself with the Soviet bloc. Czechoslovakia was the only East European state to avoid a communist-dominated government just after World War II, and the fall of its democratic government reminded Western leaders of the Nazi subjugation of Czechoslovakia in 1938–1939.

The next European crisis occurred when Soviet occupation forces in Eastern Germany commenced a blockade of the Western sectors of Berlin in June 1948. By closing West Berlin's land communications to the West, they hoped to force the Western garrisons to withdraw from their occupied part of the German capital. The United States and Great Britain responded to the Berlin Blockade with the Berlin Airlift, a shuttle of air transports to supply both the garrisons in West Berlin and the two million Germans living there. In addition, sixty U.S. B–29 bombers—capable of carrying atomic weapons—were flown from the United States to airfields in England as a show of force.

After the passage of almost a year, in May 1949 the Soviets grudgingly reopened the Western ground communications to West Berlin. In the same month, the Western occupying powers, who deemed the West Germans ready for democracy and self-government, converted their occupation zones to the Federal Republic of Germany (FRG), with a capital at Bonn. Stalin retaliated for the creation of the FRG by converting the Soviet zone of occupation in Eastern Germany to the German Democratic Republic (GDR) and establishing the communist capital in East Berlin.

Meanwhile, fear that the Soviet Union might launch an attack on Western Europe led the Western powers to create the North Atlantic Treaty Organization (NATO) in April 1949. NATO's purpose was to deter attack on any member in the North Atlantic region, and its initial membership included the United States, Canada, Britain, France, Italy, Belgium, the Netherlands, Luxembourg, Portugal, Denmark, Norway, and Iceland. (NATO membership was extended to Greece and Turkey in 1951, and to the FRG in 1955, when West Germany was allowed to rearm.) A NATO Council set policies for the organization, and a formal military alliance existed among NATO's members. Stalin denounced NATO as a fascist alliance to prepare for Western aggression against the Soviet Union and its allies, and he used it as his justification for keeping large Soviet and Soviet-satellite armies under arms in Eastern Europe. And by testing an atomic bomb in August 1949, Stalin both broke the four-year American monopoly on atomic weapons and further heightened Cold War tensions with the West.

The Cold War extended to the Far East. At the end of the Second World War, Korea, annexed by Japan in 1910, was occupied by Soviet troops north of the 38th parallel and American troops to its south. The line of demarcation at the parallel, originally established to determine to whom the Japanese troops in Korea would surrender, hardened into a permanent political frontier when efforts by the new United Nations Organization to get free elections throughout Korea were rejected by Stalin. In consequence, there emerged in 1948 a Republic of Korea (ROK) under the American-educated Syngman Rhee south of the 38th parallel and a Soviet-sponsored People's Democratic Republic of Korea (PDRK) under Kim Il Sung north of it. Korea, like Germany, seemed to be permanently divided between communist and anti-communist governments.

During the Second World War, the civil war in China between Mao Tse-tung's communists and Chiang Kai-shek's nationalists had been put on hold, but after the war it burst forth anew despite American attempts to mediate a peace. Then the United States identified the nationalist cause with that of containing the spread of communism in Asia, and it assisted Chiang's armies with arms and equipment. Mao Tse-tung's armies contin-ued to achieve victory after victory over the nationalists, and Chiang's inept and corrupt regime finally collapsed in the fall of 1949. After its remnants fled to the island of Taiwan (Formosa), on 1 October 1949 Mao proclaimed the People's Republic of China (PRC) on the mainland. The United States recognized only the Republic of China (Taiwan) and blocked the PRC's admission to the United Nations.

Though the charge was baseless, American conservatives blamed Tru-man's administration for having "lost" China to the Soviets, and the Re-publican Party found that the public's fear of communism, both inter-nal and external, was an especially fertile field for votes at election time. The more unscrupulous Republican politicians alleged treason in Tru-man's Democratic administration, and in February 1950 Senator Joseph McCarthy (R-Wis.) even claimed that fifty-seven "card-carrying members of the Communist Party" were serving in the State Department. Though it was an absurd claim, American fears of subversion reached paranoid pro-portions as real Soviet agents were uncovered in the United States. As a consequence, elected and appointed officials were subject to loyalty oaths and background checks, and some innocent people were driven from the State Department and the Foreign Service merely for being suspected of being disloyal.

By 1950 the American global perspective was that of a bipolar world—communist and anti-communist—and one that did not allow for local complexities and ambiguities such as existed in Vietnam. American policy makers and the majority of the public believed that world communism was monolithic and Soviet-controlled and that it had become all the more dangerous in the Far East once China entered the Soviet camp. They believed that communist expansion could be prevented only by collective measures on a global scale, and that belief extended to the French struggle in Indochina.

THE STRUGGLE IN INDOCHINA, THE FOUNDING OF THE STATE OF VIETNAM (SOV), AND AMERICAN RECOGNITION

During 1947, the French forces drove most of the troops of the VMLA from the Red River delta into their old World War II strongholds in the moun-tains adjacent to China, but there the war stagnated. In the mountains of the far north, the Viet Minh were among a friendly population, and the VMLA could fight in terrain well suited to the kind of guerrilla war that it had earlier waged against the Japanese. Though this kind of warfare could not drive the French from Vietnam, it could weaken their forces, wear out French patience at home, and prepare the way for waging war on a grander scale at a later time. Besides the operations of the VMLA in the far north, Viet Minh agents and armed groups carried on campaigns of ambush, sabotage, and terrorism in the rest of Vietnam.

As the French war effort bogged down, the French realized that they would need more military aid in the form of war materials from the United States. They also grasped that they were more likely to get this aid if they appeared to be the champions of Vietnamese nationalism and anti-communism rather than as the agents of a reimposed colonialism. The French saw the former emperor Bao Dai as the front man for this effort at bogus nationalism.

As early as 1947, Bao Dai had abandoned his post as "supreme adviser" to Ho's government and moved to Hong Kong. There the French approached him about his heading up a French client state consisting of Tonkin and Annam, with the French retaining Cochinchina as a colony. Bao Dai refused to head up a truncated Vietnamese state, and the talks collapsed. But as the war in Indochina continued to drag on, the United States put increasing pressure on the French government to stimulate a non-communist nationalism in Vietnam, and the "Bao Dai solution" became increasingly attractive to the French. Eventually, the political leaders of the Fourth Republic accepted the necessity of a French-sponsored Vietnamese state composed of all of its parts in order to win over the former emperor.

After Bao Dai moved to France, the French resumed negotiations with him, and on 8 March 1949 their representatives reached the Elyseé Agreements at Paris. Under the Agreements, the French recognized an independent and united "State of Vietnam" (SOV) as one of the Associated States of Indochina (i.e., Vietnam, Laos, and Cambodia) within the French Overseas Union. The Agreements designated Bao Dai as the SOV's "Chief of State" and obligated the French to raise a Vietnamese National Army (VNA) and to provide for all of the other trappings of an independent country. The government in Paris claimed that the SOV represented genuine and non-communist Vietnamese nationalism, and it urged the United States to confer on it diplomatic recognition.

But when Bao Dai went to Saigon in June 1949 to take up his new duties as chief of state, he discovered that the "independence" of the SOV was so much window dressing. The French retained effective control over his army, his finances, and his foreign policy, and his position as chief of state in Saigon turned out to be not much different from his old one as a powerless, figurehead emperor in Hue. Disillusioned, Bao Dai returned to France and left the running of the SOV's affairs to prime minister Nguyen Xuan and the French.

Nor was the Truman administration taken in entirely by the French charade, and at first it withheld diplomatic recognition. But T. Jefferson Caffery, the American ambassador in Paris, urged it to recognize the SOV because he believed that Bao Dai was the only alternative to Ho Chi Minh. Moreover, such was the state of politics in Paris that no French government could go further in making concessions to the Vietnamese nationalists. Even so, the Truman administration continued to hesitate until January 1950, the month in which the People's Republic of China and then the Soviet Union recognized Ho's DRV as the legitimate government in Vietnam. Almost immediately, the Cold War mentality took over in American councils, and on 7 February the United States retaliated by recognizing the SOV as the legitimate government of Vietnam. Further, Dean Acheson, by then the U.S. secretary of state, recommended that the United States allocate money for the prosecution of the French war in Indochina and for the support of Bao Dai's government.

THE KOREAN WAR AND ITS IMPACT ON AMERICAN POLICY IN INDOCHINA

As U.S. plans for helping the French and Bao Dai's government in Vietnam were taking shape, on 25 June 1950 the North Korean army invaded South Korea. Washington perceived the invasion as a testing of both the policy of communist containment and the ability of the United Nations to maintain the peace. With the approval of the U.N. Security Council, but without consulting Congress, Truman used his unexpired wartime emergency powers to plunge U.S. forces into the war on the side of South Korea. The American forces there became the major part of the U.N. Command under General Douglas MacArthur. But even while the U.N. forces were straining to contain the advance of the North Korean army, on 26 July Truman signed a far-ranging military assistance order to aid the French in Indochina. And on 17 September, a small U.S. Military Assistance and Advisory Group, Indochina (MAAGI) arrived in Vietnam pledged to aid the French in military-technical matters.

Large-scale American support in arms and equipment for the French and the SOV for the Indochina War continued even after the Chinese communists entered the Korean War late in 1950 and drove the U.N.

forces below the 38th parallel. In the spring of 1951, the U.S. 8th Army and other U.N. forces fought their way back to the vicinity of the old border in Korea, but there the war stalemated. Negotiations followed the military stalemate, but they were still deadlocked in January 1953 when the Republican administration of Dwight D. Eisenhower replaced Truman's. Though an armistice reached on 27 July 1953 left South Korea secure behind U.N. lines, its future safety rested essentially on the presence of American forces stationed there for the indefinite future. Even more important, the experience of the Korean War sealed the U.S. government's attitude that all communist movements were hostile to the interests of the United States and its allies and that the anti-communist effort in Vietnam was part of the struggle of the "Free World" against global communist expansion. That notion would influence its policy for the next two decades.

THE FRENCH ROAD TO DIENBIENPHU, 1950–1954

During the Indochina War, the United States spent three billion dollars on the French war effort and paid for 80 percent of its costs. Yet, despite American aid to the French in arms and equipment, the tide of the war shifted in favor of the Viet Minh. In 1950 the PRC began shipping to the VMLA arms and equipment that had been captured from the Chinese nationalists (and later from American forces in Korea), and Soviet arms and equipment began to arrive via China. By the fall of 1950, the VMLA had developed the capability of taking on the French in formal battles, and its offensive in September and October so severely defeated the French that they were forced to fall back to the Red River delta.

But then a relatively brief period of equilibrium was achieved. General de Lattre de Tassigny, the new commander-in-chief in Indochina, rallied the French Union forces, and strengthened them by adopting a policy of *jaunissement*, or the "yellowing" of their composition. He was successful in mobilizing the Catholic Vietnamese living in the Red River delta to assist the French in its defense, and between January and May 1951 these allies succeeded in throwing back Giap's offensives. In addition to the 76,000 troops raised for Bao Dai's Vietnamese National Army (VNA), eventually some 200,000 Vietnamese and Lao troops were enlisted in the French Union forces, or more than the 150,000 French and French colonial troops drawn from outside Indochina.

The tougher French resistance forced Ho and Giap to change their strategy and to return to protracted war. But de Lattre—easily the most talented French commander during the Indochina War—suffered from cancer, and the disease compelled him to turn over command to General

Raoul Salan before dying in January 1952. Meanwhile, the Viet Minh opened the Ho Chi Minh Trail (actually a complex of trails and roads) through the mountainous border area between Vietnam and Laos, which enabled them to infiltrate troops and supplies into central and southern Vietnam. By the same means, they could render aid to the Pathet Lao, the communist movement in Laos.

In 1952 General Salan tried to prevent the VMLA's infiltration south by launching air attacks on the Ho Chi Minh Trail and by launching motorized columns into the mountains to raid it. But his strategy failed to work. With great persistence, the Viet Minh repaired the bomb damage and kept the flow of men and supplies moving, and they frequently ambushed and destroyed the motorized French columns that entered the back country. By the time Salan handed over command to General Henri Navarre in May 1953, the French situation in northern Vietnam was becoming critical.

In order to reverse the direction of the war, Navarre believed that he had to shut down the Ho Chi Minh Trail, and to that end on 20 November 1953 he launched an airborne operation to capture Dienbienphu, a town 220 miles northwest of Hanoi on the Lao border and a key nodal point on the Trail. But after the French established a large earthen fortress at Dienbienphu, from where its sizable garrison could launch attacks on the Trail, Navarre ignored warnings that Giap was concentrating much of the VMLA's strength around Dienbienphu in order to eliminate the threat. Rather than withdraw the French forces by air from Dienbienphu, Navarre convinced himself to fight a set-piece battle there. In such a battle, he imagined that the French garrison could inflict such losses on the VMLA that the tide of the war would turn in favor of the French.

Navarre ordered the garrison at Dienbienphu heavily reinforced, and by March 1954 Colonel Christian de Castries, its commander, had about 12,000 troops, fifty artillery pieces, and many automatic weapons. But Navarre had underestimated the VMLA's ability to move overwhelming forces from its main bases two hundred miles away, including heavy artillery and anti-aircraft (AA) guns. Giap had seen an opportunity to win a decisive battle over the French, and, with Ho's approval, he had shifted from protracted war to grand war. With thousands of soldiers and civilians dragging guns and supplies over formidable mountains, Giap gradually massed 50,000 combat troops, 55,000 support troops, two hundred artillery pieces (most of them of American manufacture), and many AA guns around Dienbienphu. His forces had hacked out roads as they went, and often worked at night in order to escape bombing by French aircraft.

When the VMLA's preparations were complete, Giap launched the battle for Dienbienphu on 13 March 1954. Within two days, two French hill positions outside of the fortress had fallen and VMLA artillery had achieved fire-supremacy over the outgunned French inside the main base. On 16 March, the last major French reinforcement—a thousand paratroopers—reached the garrison by air. Thereafter the VMLA's AA fire was so intense that further major French troop reinforcement became too risky to attempt. In addition, most French supplies dropped by parachute ended up behind VMLA lines. Running short on food, water, and medical supplies, and under almost constant shelling, the French garrison passed through an ordeal that the French historian Bernard Fall has aptly described as "hell in a very small place." Without outside intervention, the garrison at Dienbienphu was doomed.

THE AMERICAN DECISION NOT TO INTERVENE

As the French faced an impending disaster at Dienbienphu, General Paul Ely, the French chief of staff, flew to Washington on 20 March 1954 and formally asked the Joint Chiefs of Staff (JCS) for help. Admiral Arthur Radford, chairman of the JCS, was sympathetic to the French plea. He proposed Operation VULTURE to his colleagues on the JCS, whereby sixty American B–29 heavy bombers stationed in the Philippines, as well as attack planes from American aircraft carriers to be sent to the Gulf of Tonkin, would be used to bomb the Viet Minh siege lines around Dienbienphu. Radford was even prepared to use tactical atomic weapons, in line with Eisenhower's "New Look" in defense policy.

But General Matthew Ridgway, chief of staff of the U.S. Army, opposed any American military intervention, and Ridgway was experienced in fighting wars in Asia. Besides commanding the U.S. 8th Army in Korea, he had succeeded MacArthur as the commander-in-chief of the U.N. Command. He had no confidence that air strikes alone could save the garrison at Dienbienphu, nor could he recommend an American intervention on the ground. Studies conducted by the Army suggested that Vietnam would be very difficult for the Americans to deal with in operational terms, and an effective ground intervention might require as many as eight U.S. Army and Marine divisions, or a force about as large as the United States had sent to fight in the Korean War. Given the continuing American defense commitments in South Korea, in Europe, and in other parts of the world, maintaining such a force in Vietnam would place a tremendous strain on American resources.

Ridgway's arguments against U.S. intervention finally won over the other members of the JCS except Radford, but President Eisenhower was under pressure to intervene from John Foster Dulles, his secretary of state. Dulles had been as keen a supporter of the French effort in Indochina as he was of all global measures to contain communist expansion. The Republican Party had made great gains with the electorate by its propaganda that the Democrats were responsible for "losing China" in 1949, and its unflinching opposition to communist expansion seemed to appeal strongly to voters. An American failure to prevent a French defeat in Vietnam might be blamed on the administration and dim its luster.

Nevertheless, Eisenhower made it clear to Dulles that he would not sanction a "go-it alone" American intervention. He insisted that any U.S. action must be supported by, and participated in, by America's allies in Europe, especially Great Britain. But when Dulles proceeded to consult with the allied leaders, he found that—France aside—none of them favored intervention in Indochina. Winston Churchill, once again Britain's prime minister, agreed with Sir Anthony Eden, his secretary for foreign affairs, that there was no point in running grave risks while trying to help the French out of the impossible situation in which they had put themselves. Instead, the British government favored a negotiated end to the war through an international conference already meeting on Far Eastern questions in Geneva, Switzerland.

Nor, as it turned out, was the American public keen on intervention to save the French cause in Indochina. Eisenhower discovered this fact when he tried a "trial balloon" in a press conference on 7 April by arguing that the fall of Indochina would set off a chain reaction of falling anti-communist governments and peoples throughout Southeast Asia "like a row of dominoes." Though the Domino Theory would be successfully revived at a later time by other administrations, in 1954 the public response was tepid. The Korean War had been over less than a year, and many Americans were uncomfortable with the idea of another expensive military commitment on the mainland of Asia, especially one that might provoke another war with communist China.

Thus, there was to be no U.S. military intervention to save the French garrison at Dienbienphu, and the VMLA's forces finally overran the last of the French defenses on the night of 6–7 May. Having already lost 7,000 men to death, wounds, and disease, de Castries surrendered what remained of his garrison. Though the siege had cost the VMLA perhaps 20,000 casualties, Giap's persistence in laying it had paid off with a decisive victory.

Despite the fact that the Eisenhower administration had decided against American intervention, Secretary Dulles observed that the situation in Indochina was "a perfect example of the Soviet Communist strategy for colonial and dependent areas which was laid by Lenin and Stalin and which the Communists have practiced to take over much of Asia." Stalin had died in March 1953, but Dulles saw no reason to believe that the new communist leaders in Moscow thought any differently.

THE GENEVA ACCORDS

On 8 May 1954, nine national delegations assembled in the old League of Nations building in Geneva to open discussions on how to end the Indochina War. The conference was co-chaired by Sir Anthony Eden and Vyacheslav Molotov, the Soviet foreign minister. At the outset, Pham Van Dong, chief delegate from the DRV, put forward proposals that the French leave forthwith and allow the Vietnamese and the other Indochinese peoples to resolve their internal differences without foreign interference. French premier Joseph Daniel rejected Pham Van Dong's demands point blank, and the conference quickly reached an impasse. But the French public was tired of the war and began to demand diplomatic action to end it. In the face of public protests, Daniel's government resigned and Pierre Mendès-France, a long-time critic of the war, formed a new cabinet in mid-June. He pledged to end the war within a specified time or he would resign. He also took personal charge of the French negotiations at Geneva. Soon he was working closely with Chou En-lai, the head of the Chinese delegation.

The French premier began to see an opening to break the impasse in negotiations when he discovered that Beijing was far more interested in attaining peace and security on China's southern frontier than in realizing Ho's dream of an independent and unified Vietnam. The Chinese feared that if the Indochina War went on much longer the American "imperialists" might replace the French in Indochina, and their presence would be a far more formidable threat to China than the French could ever be. The Russians too were concerned about the war spreading throughout the Far East.

In order to end the fighting on terms acceptable to the PRC, Chou suggested the possibility of "two Vietnams," the DRV in the north and the SOV in the south, even if on some temporary basis. Except for French withdrawal from Indochina, and the foreclosing of any possibility of American military bases and influence there, he posed no other special conditions for peace. The Soviets also raised no objections to a peace under the Chinese terms. Mendès-France then saw that there were limits to Sino-Russian support of the DRV's position, and he quickly seized on this rift in the communist front.

As there was no dispute that Cambodia and Laos should be given full independence and neutrality, the French premier soon gained Chinese, Soviet, and British support for ending the Indochina War by a temporary division of Vietnam. But when this plan was proposed as the price of peace, the DRV's delegation bitterly opposed it. From the DRV's perspective, the Indochina War had been fought as much over the issue of Vietnam's unity as for its independence, and Ho Chi Minh had never wavered from both goals. But Chinese and Russian support for a temporary division of Vietnam put the DRV's delegation in a difficult position. The DRV could hardly afford to alienate its principal suppliers of arms and equipment as well as its chief sources of diplomatic support, and it was clear that the governments in Moscow and Beijing would put their interests before those of the DRV. With great reluctance, Ho finally instructed the DRV's delegation to give in on the issue of a temporarily divided Vietnam.

The Final Declaration at Geneva, signed by most of the national delegations present, made it clear that the political division of Vietnam under the Geneva Accords was to last only until all-Vietnamese elections could be conducted under international supervision in July 1956. These elections held out the possibility that Vietnam would be reunited peacefully and under a government chosen by the majority of the Vietnamese people. As for the other terms of the Geneva Accords—a series of agreements signed between 21 and 23 July 1954—the SOV and the DRV were to be temporarily separated by a three-mile-wide Demilitarized Zone (DMZ) at the 17th parallel, and the military forces of the opposing sides were to regroup on either side of the DMZ within three hundred days of the cessation of hostilities. During that time civilians were free to choose to live in either the ROV or the DRV. No foreign troops or military bases were to be allowed in either the ROV or the DRV, and neither was to enter into a military alliance with, or accept arms from, any foreign power. An International Commission of Control and Supervision (ICCS)—composed of representatives from Canada, India, and Poland—would oversee the implementation of the terms of the cease-fire and also supervise the all-Vietnamese elections to be held in two years. Meanwhile, the French colonial administration and its military forces would complete their withdrawal from Indochina.

The Eisenhower administration's response to the negotiations at Geneva, and to the subsequent Geneva Accords, was ambiguous. Both Eisenhower and Dulles viewed the French defeat as a disaster for the policy of communist containment in the Far East, and they were so suspicious of the negotiations at Geneva that the American delegation sent there was instructed to observe but not to participate. Dulles made a brief appearance at the beginning of the conference, but he left Geneva after a week. Walter Bedell Smith and U. Alexis Johnson alternated in heading the American delegation.

At the conclusion of the conference, and acting on instructions from Washington, Smith made a public declaration in which his government "took note" of the Accords and promised that the United States would refrain from disturbing them. But he also stated that the United States would view any "renewal of aggression" in Southeast Asia with grave concern and consider it a threat to international peace and security. His statement did not make clear just what the U.S. government would construe as "a renewal of aggression," or by whom, but some delegates suspected that "aggression" would be defined in Washington as any communist attempt to change the divided condition of Vietnam.

The realization of the hope for the peaceful reunification of Vietnam as expressed in the Final Declaration finally depended on the attitudes of the two Vietnamese governments. That of the SOV was not good. By the time the Geneva Conference broke up, it was no secret that Ngo Dinh Diem, Bao Dai's new prime minister in Saigon, looked upon its outcome with distaste, and upon Diem's instructions the SOV's chief delegate refused to sign the Final Declaration. And when Diem found that the U.S. government was in agreement with his views and was determined that South Vietnam would not be united with the communist north in 1956 or at any other time, he had even less reason to respect the agreements made at Geneva. But whether Eisenhower, Dulles, and the other policy makers in Washington understood it at the time, a collusion between the SOV and the United States to undermine the Geneva Accords would make another war in Indochina a near certainty.

5.

EISENHOWER AND THE ROAD TO AMERICA'S WAR IN VIETNAM, 1954–1960

SEATO AND THE AMERICAN ALLIANCE WITH SOUTH VIETNAM

The obsession of the Eisenhower administration with containing the spread of communism in Southeast Asia manifested itself even before the signing of the Geneva Accords. Secretary of State John Foster Dulles lobbied vigorously for a collective security pact in the region, and when that effort met with favorable responses from other countries, he began to envision an alliance that would form a military-political force in Southeast Asia that the communists would not dare to challenge. The American diplomatic efforts culminated in a conference in Manila, the Philippines, early in September 1954 for the signing of a treaty that founded the South East Asian Treaty Organization (SEATO). The signatories to the treaty were the United States, Great Britain, France, Australia, New Zealand, Thailand, the Philippines, and Pakistan. Dulles personally led the American delegation at Manila, and he made his conception of SEATO clear on 6 September when he told reporters:

> We are united by a common danger, the danger that stems from international Communism and its insatiable ambition. We know that wherever it makes gains, as in Indochina, these gains are looked on, not as final solutions, but as bridgeheads for future gains. . . . We can greatly diminish that risk by making clear that an attack upon the treaty area would occasion a reaction so united, so strong and so well-placed, that the aggressor would lose more than he could hope to gain.

The formal signing of the SEATO treaty was accomplished on 8 September. Under its terms the parties recognized that aggression by means of armed attack in the treaty area against any of their number, or against any state or territory that the parties by unanimous agreement thereafter designated, would endanger their collective peace and safety. In such an event, they would meet the common danger after joint consultation and in accordance with each member's constitutional processes. By a protocol to the treaty, the parties designated the states of Cambodia, Laos, and "the free territory under the jurisdiction of the State of Vietnam," to be areas in which aggression would be deemed hostile to their interests.

At the time, commentators compared SEATO to NATO, but SEATO was much more vague in form and function than NATO. Only two members of SEATO — Thailand and the Philippines — had homelands in Southeast Asia, while Pakistan, a Southwest Asian state, apparently joined SEATO in order to woo away American support from its rival India. Australia and New Zealand were members out of a justifiable concern that whatever affected Southeast Asia was likely to affect them. As British forces had been fighting a communist insurgency in Malaya since 1948, Britain also had a motive. (The so-called Malayan Emergency, fought from 1948 to 1962, ended in an independent but non-communist state of Malaysia.) But Anglo-French action in regard to the states of former French Indochina under the SEATO treaty was compromised by the obligations that London and Paris had earlier undertaken under the Geneva Accords. A further weakness of the SEATO treaty was that it did not specify how an act of "armed aggression" in the treaty area was to be defined or how the parties to the treaty were to respond beyond consultation.

In fact, the treaty obligations under SEATO were so replete with loopholes that a genuine joint effort by its members was perhaps never really anticipated by Washington. The primary usefulness of SEATO to the United States was to give the United States a cloak of international authority to take military action on behalf of South Vietnam, Cambodia, or Laos. Whether the United States could really rely on significant armed support from the other SEATO members, especially Britain and France, was doubtful from the outset.

Almost simultaneous with the formation of SEATO was Washington's announcement that Premier Diem of South Vietnam had accepted an American offer to furnish $2 billion for the purposes of rehabilitating the VNA. Diem had not blinked at the fact that his acceptance was a clear violation of the Geneva Accords. Washington proceeded to transform MAAGI into the Military Assistance and Advisory Group, Vietnam (MAAGV), to increase its strength gradually to a thousand officers and men, and to give it a new mission of instructing and training the VNA.

Eisenhower also promised Diem that in the future the United States would render his government every necessary aid—economic as well as military—to develop and maintain "a strong, viable state." His pledge could be construed to be a violation of the American pledge in 1954 not to disturb the arrangements made in Geneva. In addition, the democratic government that the Eisenhower administration claimed that it was fostering in South Vietnam hardly turned out that way.

DIEM: AMERICA'S MAN IN SAIGON

Ngo Dinh Diem, the man with whom American fortunes in South Vietnam were caught up for almost a decade, was born into a Roman Catholic family in Hue on 3 January 1901. He was the third of six sons of Ngo Dinh Kha, who was for a time a mandarin-counselor at the emperor's court. But Kha's resentment of French domination of the emperor led him to resign his post in 1907, and thereafter he avoided contact with the French as much as possible. He passed on to his sons a legacy of ardent Vietnamese nationalism and resentment of the French, but one laced with traditionalism and opposed to social change.

As Diem reached maturity, he followed in the footsteps of his eldest brother Khoi by enrolling in the French school for native bureaucrats. After graduating first in his class in 1925, he was made a provincial governor in 1926. He performed his duties so well in that post that in 1933 Emperor Bao Dai appointed him to the post of minister of the interior. But Diem's attempts at reform while in the imperial cabinet were so rebuffed by the French that he resigned after a few months in office. For a decade thereafter, he vegetated at the family home in Hue.

During the Japanese occupation of Vietnam in the early 1940s, Diem tried to convince the occupying authorities to abolish the French administration, to unite the three parts of Vietnam and restore its name, to declare Vietnam's independence from France, and to make it a Japanese protectorate. As explained above in an earlier chapter, the Japanese finally followed that course in March 1945, but with Japan facing imminent defeat the gesture only compromised Bao Dai and indirectly led to his abdication in favor of the DRV during the "August Revolution."

During the disorders in Indochina accompanying the "August Revolution," the Viet Minh took Diem and other members of his family captive. They accused Diem's brother Khoi and Khoi's son of collaboration with the Japanese, and they executed both of them. But Diem was more fortunate. Ho Chi Minh had learned of Diem's reputation as an able administrator, and he ignored his past behavior in regard to the Japanese. He even offered Diem a ministerial position in the DRV. But Diem was bitter over the deaths of his brother and nephew, and he refused to have anything to do with a communist-dominated government. Despite Diem's refusal to serve the DRV, Ho allowed him to go free in 1946.

When the Indochina War broke out late in 1946, Diem found himself caught between a nationalist movement dominated by the communists and a repressive colonial regime under the French, and neither side could attract his support. He tried to form a political party not associated with either of the warring sides, but he was unsuccessful. Fearing for his life, in 1950 he left Vietnam to go to Japan, then to Rome, and finally to the United States on a visa. He spent most of the next three years at the Maryknoll Seminary in Lakewood, New Jersey, during which time he cultivated relations with senior Catholic clergy. In this regard, he especially impressed Cardinal Francis Spellman. Among the other influential Americans he met and impressed were William O. Douglas, associate justice of the U.S. Supreme Court, and senators Mike Mansfield of Montana and John F. Kennedy of Massachusetts.

In May 1953, Diem left the United States and migrated to a Benedictine monastery in Belgium. From there he traveled frequently to Paris to meet with his brother Luyen, an engineer. Gradually, he acquired a following among the Vietnamese Catholics living in France, and Bao Dai, who was sitting out the war in Indochina at his château near Cannes, became acquainted with Diem's reputation as an ardent nationalist, an anti-communist, and someone well connected to influential Americans.

All the pieces came together for Diem during the Geneva Conference, when Bao Dai realized that the survival of the SOV would not be possible without support from the United States. He hoped that Diem's American connections might be able to provide it. Bao Dai appointed Diem as his new prime minister in June, and on 7 July 1954 Diem returned to Saigon in order to take up the reins of government.

After the signing of the Geneva Accords, Diem wasted no time in courting American military and economic aid for the SOV. And just as he had no qualms about violating the Geneva Accords in respect to seeking a foreign military alliance, neither did he hesitate to refuse cooperation with the DRV and ICCS in arranging all-Vietnamese elections for the summer of 1956. Eisenhower supported his decision by rationalizing that Ho Chi Minh would get all the votes in North Vietnam anyway and therefore Diem would be put at an unfair disadvantage. With American assistance, Diem was determined that South Vietnam would remain an independent, anti-communist state, and one firmly under his personal control.

THE EISENHOWER ADMINISTRATION
AND DIEM, 1954–1960

With approval from Washington, the U.S. Central Intelligence Agency (CIA) sought to bolster Diem's position by exploiting a provision of the Geneva Accords that allowed for the free movement of populations to either of the two Vietnams for a period of three hundred days after the armistice went into effect. (The original time limit was later extended to a year.) The Roman Catholic population in the DRV was already uneasy as to its future under the communists, and in this unease Colonel Edward G. Lansdale, the CIA station-chief in Saigon, saw an opportunity for a propaganda coup and a way to strengthen Diem's political base in the south at the same time.

Lansdale launched a program of "disinformation" against the DRV in order to frighten Vietnamese living there into fleeing to the SOV while the free movement of populations was possible. The CIA's effort had the desired effect from the American point of view. By the summer of 1955, motivated by fear (and in the case of Catholics, also by the urging of their priests), some 880,000 Vietnamese living in the north—660,000 of them Catholics—had moved from the DRV to the SOV. Diem welcomed especially the Catholic refugees, for they were more likely than the Buddhist majority in South Vietnam to be loyal to him. He sealed their loyalty by favoring them in the allocation of land and by giving them offices in his government and in the VNA.

At the time of the population exchanges, the Eisenhower administration made much of the fact that only 150,000 Vietnamese in the SOV chose to move to the DRV. But while this fact made excellent propaganda for the popularity of Diem's regime, the reality was that most Vietnamese in the south saw little purpose in moving north if, as prescribed by the Geneva Accords, general elections were going to occur in July 1956 and one government was going to rule a united Vietnam in their aftermath. Especially for the southern supporters of Ho Chi Minh, it made more sense for them to stay in the south and to play a useful role in the elections. And should those elections not take place, they could form the cadre for a new resistance.

Despite their great public show of confidence in Diem, as early as the fall of 1954 both Eisenhower and Dulles began to have private doubts about his ability to establish a viable state in South Vietnam. In November, Eisenhower dispatched General J. Lawton Collins, one of his former commanders in Europe during World War II, to South Vietnam on a fact-finding mission. In his two-month stay, Collins gained the impression that Diem showed few of the qualities required of an effective national leader, and he became aware that there were many non-communist elements in South Vietnam ready to challenge Diem. When Collins returned to Washington in January 1955, he rated Diem's chances of survival in power at no better than fifty-fifty.

But Diem surprised Eisenhower and Dulles by showing an unsuspected adroitness in dealing with rival elements in South Vietnam. When Diem learned that General Nguyen Van Hinh, the chief of staff of the VNA, was preparing a coup to overthrow him, he managed the general's relief and his exile to France. He then confirmed his grip on the VNA by appointing senior officers who were beholden to him. With the aid of bribes, he won over most of the leaders of the Cao Dai and Hoa Hao religious sects, each of which had a private army and was wavering in its loyalty. (The Cao Dai's form of worship was a mixture of Catholicism, Buddhism, and local animism, while the Hoa Hao practiced a form of Buddhism.) In April 1955, Diem sealed his grip on power by defeating the Binh Xuyen, the criminal syndicate in Saigon that was directed by Bay Vien and controlled the city's organized vice. This final victory involved a virtual civil war in the streets of Saigon, but it turned American doubts about Diem into confidence. On 30 April, Dulles reaffirmed American support for Diem's government.

The French resented Diem's rise to power, for they considered him to be an American protégé, from whom they could expect no special treatment. They had hoped to have some influence in South Vietnam after their forces departed, but their prospects were so dim by the summer of 1955 that they completed their pullout from Indochina ahead of schedule. With the French gone, and with the approval of his American sponsors, Diem was ready to move further to consolidate his grip on power.

In October 1955, Diem held a national plebiscite on the question: "Do the people wish to depose Bao Dai and recognize Ngo Dinh Diem as the Chief of State of Vietnam with the mission to install a democratic regime?" It was, of course, a loaded question. Bao Dai was not a popular figure among South Vietnamese, and Diem's notions of a "democratic regime" would soon make a mockery of the term. But though Bao Dai posed no threat to Diem's winning of the plebiscite, Diem took no chances. He caused the vote to be rigged, and in one area of Saigon there were more ballots cast than there were registered voters. Officially, 98 percent of the electorate favored Diem, a margin of victory so obviously fraudulent that it even shocked Lansdale, Diem's closest American adviser, but in the aftermath Bao Dai faded into obscurity, living out his days in France.

With a supposed mandate from the people, in late 1955 Diem converted the State of Vietnam into the Republic of Vietnam (ROV), with himself as president. The former Vietnamese National Army was renamed the Army of the Republic of Vietnam (ARVN). Diem applied for the ROV's membership in SEATO (another violation of the Geneva Accords), and the application was accepted. Provided that the U.S. government was not too scrupulous about democracy in South Vietnam or about the honoring of international agreements or undertakings, it appeared that the Eisenhower-Dulles gamble on Diem had worked.

DIEM'S REPRESSIVE POLICIES
AND THE RISE OF THE VIET CONG

A managed plebiscite and a self-election were the least objectionable features about Diem's government. Much more objectionable were his further measures to ensure his grip on power. These included a bloody purge of former Viet Minh and non-communist dissidents alike during 1955–1956 as the ARVN, the police, and the internal security apparatus run by Diem's brother Nhu killed or imprisoned thousands of people in the cause of eliminating any possible challenge to Diem's authority. Heretofore, under the emperor and even under the French, the 2,500 villages of South Vietnam had been largely self-governing in their internal affairs, but in the summer of 1956, Diem abolished the elected councils that ruled the villages and replaced them with provincial governors with authority in even the smallest of matters. And wherever the Viet Minh had driven away large landowners and redistributed the land among the peasants, Diem either required the peasants to purchase the land or forced them to pay rent. Except for some "showcase" land redistribution and a pretense at controlling land rents to satisfy American demands for constructive "nation building," Diem restored much of the pre-war social and economic system.

Peasant resentment of Diem's policies helped to create ties between many small farmers and the Viet Cong (VC), the term Diem used for the Vietnamese communists in the south. Under the leadership of Le Duan, the surviving communists began to organize peasant resistance to the Diem regime in 1957. Diem found it convenient to blame this internal opposition to his rule on subversion fostered by the DRV, and Eisenhower and Dulles were all too ready to accept such an explanation for the insurgency. They were not ignorant of Diem's repressive and undemocratic methods, for the CIA reported on them regularly, but they rationalized that only extreme measures would work in defeating the Viet Cong. They comforted themselves with the idea that after the communists were defeated, Diem's regime would moderate its policies. And when Dulles died of cancer in May 1959, Christian Herter, his successor as secretary of state, continued his predecessor's policy of advocating support for Diem and looking the other way from his excesses.

But Diem's policies began to alienate even commanders and troops in the ARVN, and the smoldering resentment among the military burst into the open on 11 November 1960, when three paratroop battalions and a marine unit launched an attempt to overthrow him. The attempt miscarried and its leader fled to Cambodia, but American officials in Vietnam could no longer shut their eyes to the effects of Diem's policies. In December 1960, Ambassador Elbridge Durbrow reported to the State Department that the United States "might be forced in the near future to undertake the task of identifying and supporting an alternative leadership to Diem."

But in December 1960, Eisenhower's administration was about to give over to a Democratic administration under John F. Kennedy, and it was no time to disturb the public's confidence in American policy toward Southeast Asia. Hence, few members of Congress, and even fewer people among the American public, were informed that the ROV was not the model member of the "Free World" that the Eisenhower administration would have them believe it to be. As Kennedy took office, most Americans remained blissfully unaware of the trouble lying ahead in that country.

HO CHI MINH'S PURIFICATION PROGRAM IN THE DRV

President Diem's persecution of former Viet Minh personnel in South Vietnam and his refusal to participate in arranging all-Vietnamese elections in the summer of 1956 as provided by the Geneva Accords would have been provocations enough for Ho Chi Minh to have supported an insurgency against the Republic of Vietnam. That Ho did little in that regard for almost three years was due to his self-imposed problems connected to a "purification" program in the DRV. For a time, they threatened to sow the seeds of insurgency in the north.

With the end of the Indochina War, Ho's republic had less need to coddle its non-communist supporters than before, and the totalitarian inclination of its Politburo—a policy-making body of about twenty individuals who, along with Ho, effectively ruled the DRV—began to assert itself. The Politburo arbitrarily decided that "landlords" and other "feudalists" amounted to 2 percent of the North Vietnamese population living on the land and that these holdovers from capitalism and colonialism must be eliminated. It further decided that the Lao Dong (the communist Workers

Party) would be given the task of carrying out the "purification" program through revolutionary tribunals empowered to charge, try, and punish these "enemies of the people."

The resulting number of executions and imprisonments at the hands of the tribunals conformed more often to the Politburo's estimate of the number of "feudalists" and "landlords" than to the reality of their existence. Anyone suspected of being hostile to the government or its policies was vulnerable to being charged, and to be charged was tantamount to being found guilty. Conviction usually meant either a sentence of death or a long term of imprisonment. Injustice was compounded by the practice on occasion of tribunals meeting their quota of persons deemed to be "enemies of the people" by compelling villagers to draw lots to determine who among them were "feudalists" and "landlords." No figures were ever released as to how many people were finally eliminated in the "purification" campaign, but it must have numbered in the many thousands.

Gradually, peasant resistance to the "purification" program began to materialize, and in one province there was even an armed revolt. General Vo Ngyuen Giap, commander of the People's Army of Vietnam (the former Viet Minh Liberation Army) put it down with force, but unlike Diem in South Vietnam, Ho recognized when his government had gone too far. In August 1956, he publicly confessed that "errors have been committed," apologized to his countrymen, and promised that those peasants incorrectly classified and imprisoned would be released. In the rehabilitation of his image as the kindly "Uncle Ho," he placed blame for the excesses of the "purification" program on Truong Chinh, the secretary-general of the Lao Dong at the time, who was dismissed from office and used as a scapegoat. Ho gradually regained the loyalty of the peasants north of the 17th parallel, but the internal mistakes of his regime weakened the ability of the DRV to assist the insurgency in South Vietnam for some time.

THE DRV'S AID TO THE INSURGENCY IN THE SOUTH

Not until 1959 did the Politburo adopt a program of giving substantial aid to the VC in the south. That it did so was in large part due to the lobbying of Le Duan, who in the same year was made the secretary-general of the Lao Dong, further cementing the ties between communists in the north and south. The DRV reactivated the Ho Chi Minh Trail and infiltrated arms, and some of the southerners who had come north in 1954, into the ROV. The men were cautioned to rely primarily on local help, not on aid from the north. To this end they were not only to oppose Diem's policies and engage in assassinations of unpopular rural governors and officials, but also to ingratiate themselves with the southern peasantry by providing them with medical aid, helping them to sow and harvest the rice crop, and serving them in any other way that would improve the VC image. The VC goal was to create a rural rebellion that would require minimal assistance from the north in order to overthrow the Diem regime.

In December 1960—the last full month of the Eisenhower presidency in the United States—leaders of the various dissident elements in South Vietnam gathered under communist leadership to form the National Liberation Front (NLF). Like the former Viet Minh, the NLF was a popular front organization that included both communists and non-communists. Nguyen Huu Tho, a Saigon lawyer whom Diem had once imprisoned, became its chairman. Its military arm was the Vietnamese People's Liberation Army (VPLA), a guerrilla force modeled after that which had served the Viet Minh against the French in the Indochina War.

THE PROBLEMS OF LAOS AND CUBA

As Eisenhower approached the close of his second term in office, he was uneasy about the developments in Southeast Asia, but he was more disturbed about developments in Laos than in South Vietnam. In Laos, the arrangements set forth under the Geneva Accords had broken down in 1959 when a right-wing army coup had overthrown the neutralist government in Vientiane, the administrative capital, and reignited a civil war with the Pathet Lao, the Laotian communist movement. Aided and supported by the DRV and the Soviet Union, by December 1960 the Pathet Lao appeared to be on the way to winning that war. Before leaving office, Eisenhower expressed his belief to the incoming president that Laos would prove key to the outcome of the struggle between communism and the "Free World" in Southeast Asia, and especially to the fate of South Vietnam. He thought that Kennedy's measures would have to take that reality into account.

And then there was the question of Cuba, only ninety miles from the shores of Florida. In January 1959, after a long guerrilla war, Fidel Castro's forces had been successful in toppling the right-wing government of General Fulgencio Batista. While few Americans mourned the passing of the corrupt Batista dictatorship, matters took on a new complexion when Castro announced his embrace of communist ideology, seized American private property in Cuba, and aligned his government with the Soviet Union. For a super-anti-communist administration like Eisenhower's, the appearance of a communist Cuba almost on America's doorstep was intolerable. The CIA began training a Cuban exile brigade in Guatemala for an eventual landing in Cuba to spark a popular revolt to overthrow Castro, but its plans were not complete when Eisenhower's term in office came to an end. The problem of Cuba, like the problems of Laos and Vietnam, was passed on to the new Kennedy administration to solve.

6.

KENNEDY'S WAR:
COUNTER-INSURGENCY AND
THE FALL OF DIEM, 1961–1963

KENNEDY'S FOREIGN AND DEFENSE POLICIES

The presidential campaign of 1960 was fiercely contested between Democrat John F. Kennedy and Republican Richard M. Nixon. Nixon had served two terms as Eisenhower's vice president, and his anti-communist credentials were beyond question. From the time he had entered Congress shortly after World War II, he had largely made a career of alleging both an internal and an external communist menace. As vice president under Eisenhower, Nixon had visited Vietnam, and he strongly supported the policy of containment of communism there. His performance over the years had brought him national notoriety and made him popular in conservative circles.

In order to defeat such a rival as Nixon at the polls, Kennedy had to offset public doubts about Democratic willingness and ability to take on the communist threat. The albatross of having "lost China" in 1949 was still hanging around the Democratic neck. Hence, at times during the 1960 campaign, both contenders for the presidency had outdone themselves in promising to be "hard" on the global communist threat. And Kennedy's narrow victory at the polls in November — by only about 100,000 votes among the many millions cast — made it clear that he could not afford to be perceived as being "soft" or ineffectual on communism if he hoped to be reelected in 1964.

Accordingly, Kennedy's foreign policy was not markedly different from the policies of the preceding Truman and Eisenhower administrations. He accepted the obligation of helping to protect the Republic of Vietnam (ROV) and, if necessary, the kingdoms of Laos and Cambodia, as pledges carried over from the Eisenhower administration. Dean Rusk, the new secretary of state, had at one time served as an assistant secretary to Dean Acheson. For all of his quiet demeanor, he fully embraced the beliefs that communism was monolithic, that its threat was global in extent, and that it had to be contained in Southeast Asia as well as in other parts of the world.

But if Kennedy's foreign policy showed little variation from that of preceding administrations, there were important differences between the Eisenhower and the Kennedy defense policies. During the 1960 presidential campaign, many Democrats supported Kennedy's view that a nuclear war on any scale would be a catastrophe for America; hence they were critical of Eisenhower's "New Look" that since 1954 had caused the United States to rely heavily on nuclear weapons for thwarting all levels of threat to the national security. The "New Look" suggested to its critics that whenever the "Free World" was faced by a communist military challenge, it was given, in Kennedy's words, "a choice between holocaust or humiliation."

Kennedy maintained that in smaller wars against the communists the United States should rely on conventional (i.e., non-nuclear) and special forces, and especially on the latter in conflicts in which the enemy used guerrilla warfare and other irregular means. Kennedy favored an expanded Army Special Forces (the Green Berets) and their training in the techniques of counter-insurgency (CI). By the spring of 1961 he had dispatched several hundred of these troops to South Vietnam in order to organize militia self-defense forces among the peasants for CI warfare. The idea was to defeat the guerrillas with their own techniques of "little war."

Kennedy was also impressed with retired General Maxwell Taylor's book *The Uncertain Trumpet* (1959), which had criticized the "New Look" and called for American armed forces capable of "a flexible and graduated response" to communist military threats. Taylor had commanded the 8th Army in Korea at the time of the armistice there, and then had served for a time under the Eisenhower administration as the Army's chief of staff. In that post, he had criticized the "New Look" and had supported the Army's development of helicopters, aircraft well suited to a variety of missions, including CI warfare. Kennedy recalled Taylor from retirement to serve as his private military adviser.

For the vital post of secretary of defense, Kennedy chose Robert S. McNamara, former head of the Ford Motor Company. McNamara was also interested in new approaches to defense problems, and it turned out that he worked well with Taylor. A Harvard Business School graduate commissioned as a major in the U.S. Army Air Forces during World War II, McNamara had served as a management expert with various overseas commands. Among his accomplishments had been better bombing techniques for the U.S. 8th Air Force in Europe. After the war he built a reputation in the automobile industry as an advocate of management through cost-effectiveness. From his experiences in World War II and in the automobile industry, McNamara came to believe in civilian, centralized decision making, and he chose as his closest advisers defense intellectuals, systems analysts, research scientists, and economic experts of academic repute.

Those in the higher echelons of the military who were resentful of McNamara's sweeping reorganization of the Pentagon referred sarcastically to the new group in power as the "Whiz Kids" or "McNamara's Band," but Kennedy had no doubts about McNamara's housecleaning. Of the original five members of the Joint Chiefs of Staff (JCS) when Kennedy took office, only the chairman and one chief (the commandant of the Marine Corps) had not been replaced within a year. Before a second year was out, Taylor had succeeded to the post of chairman of the JCS. As McNamara and Taylor acquired dominance over the making of military policy, the JCS retired into the background.

AMERICA'S COVERT WARS
IN LAOS AND SOUTH VIETNAM

While Kennedy shared Eisenhower's concerns for the fate of Laos at the beginning of 1961, he found good reasons to avoid a formal American military involvement there. He heeded the military's warnings that at least 60,000 U.S. troops would be required to assure the rightist forces of victory over the Pathet Lao and that Laos would be an even more difficult place in which to fight than Vietnam. Moreover, given Laos's common border with China, an overt American military intervention there might well trigger a Chinese military intervention. Therefore, while pursuing a diplomatic solution at Geneva (which resulted in new but ineffectual Geneva Accords on Laos in July 1962), Kennedy relied increasingly on a covert operation by the CIA to organize a native resistance to prevent the Pathet Lao from seizing control of the country. The resulting force, whose existence was unknown to the American public and to most members of Congress, was dubbed by administration insiders as the "U.S. Secret Army." The heart of the U.S. Secret Army was the Hmong contingent under Vang Pao, a local warlord, but it also contained other Montagnards and even mercenaries from Thailand. With transport and supply provided by Air America, an airline controlled by the CIA, the Secret Army successfully disputed control of the strategic Plain of Jars for many years, and effectively barred the path of the Pathet Lao through northwestern Laos until the end of America's war in Vietnam.

But the Secret Army was not located where it could do much to prevent the flow of men and supplies from the DRV to the VC insurgency in the ROV via the Laotian "panhandle," and other CI measures had to be adopted to deal with that threat. A partial solution to this problem was found by enlisting Montagnards living on the western border of South Vietnam in a Civilian Irregular Defense Group (CIDG). Units of the CIDG were stationed in the mountainous border area under the direction of the Green Berets. While the Montagnards had little reason to care for any Vietnamese government, some tribes, such as the Nung and the Bru, proved ready to join the CIDG if they were paid and supported by the Americans in return for fighting Vietnamese communists who invaded their territory. The best of these troops were the "strikers" in "Mike Force," or soldiers used on the offensive to ambush, raid, harass, and spy on the enemy, sometimes even going into neighboring Laos in order to carry out their missions. By mid–1963, a thousand or so Green Berets had recruited 10,000 troops for the CIDG, and eventually 20,000 CIDG troops were recruited. The most active of these troops were divided among eighteen Army Special Forces–CIDG surveillance camps along the ROV-Lao border.

THE BAY OF PIGS, THE BERLIN WALL, AND THE RAISING OF THE STAKES IN SOUTH VIETNAM

Events going on in countries outside Southeast Asia greatly influenced Kennedy's attitude toward South Vietnam in his first year in office. Eisenhower had passed on the problem of Castro's Cuba, as well as the CIA's plan for Operation ZAPATA, which called for a brigade of Cuban exiles trained in Guatemala to invade the island at the Bay of Pigs in hopes of sparking a popular uprising against Castro. During the 1960 election campaign Kennedy had made public promises of action against Castro's regime, and after taking office he gave his approval for launching ZAPATA in April 1961.

But nothing went right for ZAPATA. After the landing of the exile brigade in the Bay of Pigs, there was no popular uprising within Cuba in its support, and within three days Castro's troops had defeated the brigade and captured most of the survivors. As Kennedy had refused to commit U.S. forces to save the enterprise during the battle, in its aftermath conservatives raised questions as to whether Kennedy was tough enough to deal with the global communist menace. Kennedy could ill afford another embarrassing defeat at the hands of the communists.

But such was the appearance of affairs when Kennedy met with Soviet premier Nikita Khrushchev at Vienna in May 1961. The premier attempted to browbeat the president into accepting Soviet terms for the long-deferred peace treaty with Germany. Although Kennedy did not give in to Khrushchev's bluster, some Americans had the impression that the Soviet leader had the better of the exchange. Kennedy himself told reporters that the communist world would have to be made more respectful of American power and that Vietnam might be the place to do it.

Khrushchev was not bluffing entirely in his threats about Germany. He took Kennedy and the other Western leaders by surprise when in August 1961 the Soviets and their East German allies threw up the Berlin Wall. For the first time, Berliners were not allowed free movement back and forth between East and West Berlin. Kennedy went to West Berlin and declared publicly that the Western alliance would resist all communist attempts to strangle the city, but he could not conceal that his Democratic administration had suffered another reversal at communist hands.

On the other hand, the Cuban Missile Crisis of October 1962 gave the Kennedy administration an object lesson as to the limits of power in the nuclear era. Potential disaster for both the United States and the Soviet Union was forestalled only by Kennedy's skillful use of the threat of force and his patient firmness and flexibility in negotiating with the Soviets. He ordered a naval "quarantine" of Cuba to prevent the delivery of any more Soviet missiles to the island, from which they could threaten the continental United States, and he insisted on the withdrawal of the Soviet missiles already there. Khrushchev proved unwilling to risk war in order to challenge the quarantine, and he finally agreed to withdraw the missiles already in Cuba on condition that Kennedy withdraw American missiles based in Turkey and pledge that the United States would not threaten Castro's regime in the future. Kennedy agreed to those conditions and the crisis subsided. The Cuban Missile Crisis served to sober American policy makers as to the ease with which the superpowers could slide into a mutually annihilating nuclear war, a concern that extended to the People's Republic of China (PRC) after it became a nuclear power in 1964.

THE CREATION OF MACV AND
THE STRATEGIC HAMLET PROJECT

In 1961, President Diem requested additional American aid so that the ARVN could be increased from a strength of 170,000 troops to 270,000 troops in order to combat the VC more effectively. Such an expansion would also involve increasing the U.S. Military Assistance and Advisory Group, Vietnam (MAAGV). At the outset of his administration, Kennedy had tripled its strength to 3,000 officers and men, but even that expanded force was far too small to support Diem's desired expansion of the ARVN.

Kennedy dispatched General Taylor and Walt W. Rostow, then Kennedy's deputy national security adviser, to South Vietnam in order to investigate the matter. Upon their return to Washington, Taylor and Rostow recommended to Kennedy that he increase ARVN's size to 250,000 troops and subsume MAAGV under an expanded U.S. Army command. In line with these recommendations, Kennedy authorized aid for ARVN's expansion and ordered MAAGV subsumed under a new U.S. Military Assistance Command, Vietnam (MACV). General Paul Harkins assumed the title of Commander, U.S. Military Assistance Command, Vietnam (COMUSMACV) when MACV was activated in February 1962. A slow but steady build-up of American military advisory and technical forces in South Vietnam followed MACV's creation, and by November 1963, the month in which Kennedy was assassinated, its strength had reached 16,300 troops. Except for the Green Berets, however, all MACV troops were officially advisers and technicians, not combat soldiers, though the distinction became ever harder for the Kennedy administration to maintain.

Until 1962, units of the Vietnamese People's Liberation Army (VPLA), the armed forces of the National Liberation Front (NLF), were rarely seen in units larger than platoons and companies (i.e., units of fifty to a hundred men and women apiece). Normally, they engaged in guerrilla hit-and-run attacks or in terrorist actions and sabotage, but in 1962 VPLA units sometimes appeared in battalion strength (units of five hundred men and women apiece), fought the ARVN more stubbornly, and posed a greater threat to the ROV's self-defense militia. Some of the communist soldiers were Vietnamese who had gone north after the Indochina War and had been reinfiltrated into South Vietnam by way of the Ho Chi Minh Trail, but the CIA placed their number at no more than 26,000. By 1963 the majority of the 74,000 VPLA troops had been recruited from the population south of the 17th parallel. That fact should have suggested to Frederick Nolting, Kennedy's ambassador to the Saigon government, that the VC insurgency had strong popular support within the ROV, but Nolting clung to the belief that the insurgency was chiefly the work of the regime in Hanoi and its infiltration of former southerners into the ROV. Moreover, after Vice President Lyndon B. Johnson visited South Vietnam in May 1961, he gave ringing praises for President Diem and blamed North Vietnam for the insurgency.

At the end of 1961, General Taylor urged Kennedy to commit some regular U.S. ground combat units to stiffen the ARVN against the growing strength of the VPLA, but Kennedy decided on other measures instead. He authorized the sending of some three hundred U.S. helicopters to the ROV in order to facilitate ARVN tactical movements, and he increased the numbers of Green Berets aiding the ROV's militia and the CIDG. He removed restrictions that prohibited American military advisers from accompanying ARVN units in the field, and he approved Operation FARM GATE, whereby U.S. Air Force officers not only trained the fledgling South Vietnamese air force but secretly flew some of its aircraft in support of ARVN ground operations. As much as possible, Kennedy downplayed the growing U.S. military involvement in South Vietnam to both Congress and the public, and he avoided any undue criticism of President Diem.

Another American activity in South Vietnam was its support of the Strategic Hamlet program, directed by William Colby of the CIA. This project called for the removal of village communities suspected of aiding and abetting the VC to specially constructed Strategic Hamlets. These hamlets were surrounded by barbed-wire barriers and watery moats studded with sharpened stakes in order to block VC access, and were watched over from guard towers. The Strategic Hamlets supposedly existed to protect the villagers from VC attack, and had evolved from suggestions by Robert G. K. Thompson, the British CI expert. He had used something similar with effect in the Malayan Emergency; as applied to the ROV, the idea was to dry up the sea of friendly peasantry in which the VC fish swam.

But the insurgency in Malaya had been in several respects quite different from the one facing the ROV. Most of the communists in Malaya were drawn from the Chinese minority, and Chinese and Malays had a long tradition of mutual hostility. Hence, the British were able to exploit their ethnic differences, as well as apply CI tactics, in order to defeat the insurgents. Further, the Malayan communists had no ready outside source of either men or arms, such as the VC enjoyed in South Vietnam. And whereas Thompson thought a minimum of five years would be necessary for the Strategic Hamlet program to show positive results if properly carried out, neither Saigon nor Washington thought they could afford that much time to wait for results.

THE DECLINE IN THE ROV'S FORTUNES

For despite the expansion of ARVN, the increased American assistance to the ROV, and the Strategic Hamlet program, by 1963 the Saigon government was losing the war. General Harkin's headquarters was reluctant to admit as much, and pointed to statistics that supposedly showed increasing numbers of villages secured, enemy casualties exceeding those of ARVN, and the building of ever more Strategic Hamlets (later renamed New Life Villages). But Lieutenant Colonel John Paul Vann, one of the American military advisers in South Vietnam, told a different story to the American press. He had been the senior military adviser to an ARVN regiment at the battle of Ap Bac, fought south of Saigon in January 1963, and in that battle, ARVN commanders ignored Vann's advice and made decisions that caused the defeat of 2,000 of their troops at the hands of a fifth as many VPLA troops. Along with heavy ARVN losses, three U.S. military advisers had been killed. According to Vann, the ARVN's performance at Ap Bac was not atypical, and he believed that the difficulty lay in Diem's preference for loyal commanders regardless of their competence. Vann's outspokenness with the press incurred General Harkins's displeasure, and Vann was soon sent "stateside" and retired from the Army. Vann later returned to Vietnam as a civilian adviser, and was killed there during a communist offensive in 1972.

What Vann said to the press early in 1963 was true enough; the optimistic version of what was going on in the ROV amounted to, in Vann's words, "a bright shining lie." Still, when Harkins declared that he was not going to allow his staff to be pessimistic, his subordinates found it expedient to sound as cheerful as their commander. McNamara did not help matters when, it seems, he was taken in by MACV's statistics whenever they pointed to progress in the war against the VC. Like some of the other American policy makers at the time, he was being deluded because he was ready to deceive himself.

THE FALL OF THE HOUSE OF DIEM

Kennedy's doubts about the war in Vietnam grew as he became ever more perplexed by the seemingly contradictory information he was receiving on its progress. Still, events themselves gradually convinced him that much of the internal opposition to the Diem regime was not so much communist-inspired as it was a result of Diem's policies, especially those practiced toward the Buddhists, a majority of his countrymen.

Though 80 percent of the South Vietnamese population belonged to the Buddhist faith, Diem seemed to go out of his way to antagonize them. Besides giving preferential treatment to the Catholic population and promoting his religion at the expense of others (in 1959 Diem had formally dedicated the ROV to the Virgin Mary), he made matters worse by discriminating against the free practice of the Buddhist religion. A crisis came to a head in May 1963 when Diem forbade the pagodas from flying religious flags in honor of the Buddha's birthday.

In an act of martyrdom and protest against Diem's policies, on 11 June Thich Quang Duc, an elderly Buddhist monk, seated himself in the lotus position in a public street in Saigon, allowed himself to be doused with gasoline, and struck a match. While Malcolm Browne of the Associated Press took photographs of the grisly affair, the resulting fire burned the monk to death. Browne's pictures were soon on the front pages of American newspapers and on U.S. television screens. Madame Nhu, Diem's sister-in-law, did not help matters when in a press conference she characterized the suicide as a "Monk Bar-B-Que." Her seeming heartlessness earned her the nickname of "Dragon Lady" with the American press.

And matters only became worse. Between June and August 1963, six Buddhist monks committed public suicide by self-immolation with advertisement beforehand, and all of the episodes were well covered by American television as well as by still photographs. After Ambassador Nolting, who was on an extended vacation in Europe, blamed the Buddhist behavior on communist influences, Kennedy lost confidence in his judgment and named Henry Cabot Lodge, a leader in the Republican Party, to replace him.

Though Nolting returned to Saigon in order to shore up the American diplomatic position before Lodge's arrival, he left Vietnam on 14 August before Lodge took up his new duties. By then much of the population in Saigon was seething with discontent. While the American embassy in Saigon was virtually leaderless, on 21 August Diem imposed martial law throughout South Vietnam. In Saigon, his brother Nhu ordered his security troops to invade the twenty-odd pagodas where most of the activist Buddhist monks were located; in the process of arresting 1,450 monks and nuns, the security troops killed a dozen monks and injured many more. Tri Quang, the leading Buddhist dissident priest, barely managed to escape to the safety of the American embassy, where he was granted political asylum. By the time Lodge reached Saigon late on 22 August, mass protests against the Diem regime had broken out.

Soon after Lodge's arrival, he was approached by Lieutenant Colonel Lucien Conein, a CIA officer in close contact with senior officers of the ARVN. He informed Lodge that certain generals and colonels were considering deposing Diem and setting up a new and more popular government in the ROV. They wanted to know whether a new government in Saigon could count on continued U.S. support. Lodge promptly referred the matter to Washington, and the cablegram arrived on Saturday, 24 August, Washington time.

As Lodge's cable came on a weekend, the president and most of the other senior Washington policy makers were absent from the capital. Accordingly, the deputies of the principals took up the matter. Roger Hilsman, the director of the State Department's Bureau of Intelligence and Research, placed his weight behind sending to Diem an ultimatum that amounted to a withdrawal of U.S. support unless Diem undertook drastic changes in personnel appointments and internal policies. Hilsman's position was supported by W. Averell Harriman, the undersecretary of state for political affairs, and by Michael Forrestal, aide and deputy to McGeorge Bundy, the president's national security adviser. After telephone conversations among the senior American policy makers and their deputies back in Washington, a State Department cable—largely composed by Harriman, Hilsman, and Forrestal—was dispatched to Lodge by George Ball, the acting secretary of state in the absence of Dean Rusk.

The cable declared that Lodge should make clear to Diem that he must release all Buddhist monks and nuns held prisoner, remove his brother Nhu from his position as head of his security apparatus and from any other positions of power, and revoke the state of martial law. If Diem failed to comply with these conditions, Lodge was authorized to convey covertly to the ARVN plotters that the Kennedy administration would recognize and support a new government in South Vietnam. Sometimes referred to by historians as the "Green Light Cable," this in effect sent a message that made the U.S. government complicit in the effort to overthrow the Diem regime.

After receiving his instructions from Washington, Lodge met with Diem on 26 August, but he found him unbending and even unwilling to discuss the points that Lodge was instructed to bring to Diem's attention. Though polite, Diem made clear that the U.S. government should stop interfering in the ROV's internal affairs. After his unsatisfactory conference with Diem, Lodge completed his instructions by transmitting his government's views through Conein to the ARVN plotters. Both Lodge and the policy makers in Washington expected that as a result of pledged American support, the coup to topple Diem would occur within days, if not within hours, of Lodge's go-ahead.

But time passed and no coup took place. The ARVN officers involved in the plotting were uneasy about premature exposure and were biding their time. As matters drifted, it appeared to Washington that Diem might be staying in power after all. In consequence, Kennedy began to lay the groundwork for an American policy of limited liability toward the ROV. He took the opportunity of making his new policy public on 2 September, when he was interviewed for television by Walter Cronkite of CBS in the president's back yard in Hyannisport, Massachusetts.

While stressing in the interview that the United States wished to continue its support of the ROV, the president made clear that it was up to the South Vietnamese to win the war. In Kennedy's opinion, the war could be won only if Saigon's government changed its internal policies and built a better rapport with its citizens. Kennedy clearly left the impression in the interview that he envisaged no larger war involving Americans.

Moreover, Kennedy's new tone seemed supported by McNamara and Taylor after they returned from a fact-finding mission to South Vietnam. They rendered a report that praised the "great progress" of the campaign against the VC, and recommended that a thousand U.S. military advisers be withdrawn from the ROV at the end of the year on grounds that they were no longer needed. After Kennedy removed a part of the report that said that the survival of the ROV was vital to U.S. interests, he approved its publication and added a statement that most American military advisers would be out of the country by the end of 1965. Rather clearly, Kennedy was preparing the way to distance the United States from events in South Vietnam.

But then matters in Saigon took a new turn. On 5 October, Conein met secretly with General Duong Van Minh, or "Big" Minh as Americans called him, and learned that the plans for a coup were not dead. While the plotters did not expect tangible American support for a coup, they did want a pledge in advance of continued U.S. military and economic aid to the new government after Diem's overthrow. When Conein informed Lodge of his conversation with Minh, the ambassador immediately cabled the State Department, strongly recommending that Washington provide the assurances that Minh sought.

Though Kennedy had just embarked on a policy of gradual U.S. disengagement from the fortunes of South Vietnam, he reversed course after the arrival of Lodge's cable. He authorized a reply that confirmed the president's acceptance of Minh's terms—with great consequences for the future. By making a pledge on behalf of the United States that obligated him and his successors in office to defend the post-Diem government, he would make it more difficult for later administrations to find an honorable way out of the Southeast Asian tangle.

The long-expected military coup finally took place on 1–2 November, and Diem's government was duly overthrown. But after Diem and Nhu had surrendered themselves to Minh's troops on 2 November, they were murdered out of hand on Minh's orders. Thus, the Diem regime ended in treachery and unjustified violence, and the first Catholic ever to become head of state in Vietnam was assassinated as an outcome, however unintended, of the policy of the first Catholic ever to become president of the United States.

Kennedy was outraged when he learned of the details of Diem's and Nhu's deaths, but he had no choice but to deal with the new government that his actions had helped so much to bring about. But Kennedy did not have to deal with it for long. On 22 November, he himself fell victim to an assassin's bullets while in Dallas, Texas, and to Vice President Lyndon Johnson fell the legacy of the Eisenhower-Kennedy wars in Vietnam and Laos.

7.

JOHNSON'S WAR, I: TO THE BRINK, 1964

THE MINH PROBLEM

Though a pall hung over General Duong Van Minh for his responsibility in the murders of President Diem and his brother Nhu, he won a large measure of support from President Johnson by canceling martial law in the ROV, releasing the Buddhist monks and nuns who had been incarcerated by the Diem regime (Minh himself had a Buddhist background), and promising equal treatment of Buddhist and Catholic Vietnamese in future. But Johnson's satisfaction with Minh was short-lived.

To Johnson's dismay, Minh planned to dismantle the discredited Strategic Hamlet program and to seek some kind of understanding with the communist-led National Liberation Front (NLF). He seemed to favor the neutralization of the ROV through the mediation of President Charles de Gaulle, who, having returned to power in France in 1958 and established the Fifth Republic, was critical of American policy in Southeast Asia and believed that a return to the 1954 Geneva Accords was the best answer to resolving the conflict in the ROV. Any kind of a coalition government in Saigon that included the communists was anathema to the Johnson administration, lest it be advertised by the Republicans, and perceived by the public, as a "sell-out" to the communist world. The specter of the "betrayal of China" was ever before the eyes of the Democratic policy makers, and they thought that they could not afford a repetition of that event in South

Vietnam without punishment at the next election. Thus Minh turned out to be not a solution, but a new problem.

THE SEASON OF COUPS

Other Vietnamese generals sensed the American lack of confidence in Minh and were emboldened to act against him. On 30 January 1964, a coup in Saigon led by generals Nguyen Khanh and Tran Thien Khiem toppled Minh's government. Minh himself was kept on only in the status of a powerless figurehead of the ROV. Khanh took charge of the military junta in Saigon, the real power in the ROV since Diem's death, and he won Washington's approval by pledging no compromise peace with the NLF or North Vietnam. Yet Khanh had little claim to the Mandate of Heaven (legitimacy) in the eyes of traditional Vietnamese, and Tri Quang, leader of the Buddhist opposition, was hostile to the new government.

While Khanh was struggling to make his government effective, Henry Cabot Lodge resigned his post as ambassador to the ROV in June in order to return home to seek the Republican nomination for president in the fall election. Maxwell Taylor accepted Johnson's offer of Lodge's vacated post as ambassador in Saigon. In turn, he handed over his position as chairman of the JCS to General Earle G. Wheeler of the U.S. Army. In the same month, General William C. Westmoreland, who had served as the deputy commander of MACV since January 1964, succeeded Paul Harkins as COMUSMACV.

But though a new array of talent, both diplomatic and military, began to supervise the American effort in the ROV, the country's chronic political instability and its declining military situation only worsened. After public disorders in August 1964, Khanh declared a state of emergency, reimposed press censorship, and promoted himself to president. When popular opposition to these changes became too great, Khanh abruptly resigned his office, and a triumvirate composed of Generals Khanh, Minh, and Khiem took over the key leadership positions. Under American pressure, the generals restored the façade of a civilian government in October by appointing a civilian head of state and civilian prime minister, but few South Vietnamese were taken in by the changes. And on 20 December, Air Marshal Nguyen Cao Ky and General Nguyen Van Thieu joined with Khanh in a coup to oust Minh and Khiem and to establish a second triumvirate, with Khanh as its head. And still another coup was to come early in 1965. Jack Valenti, an aide to Lyndon Johnson, would remark that the ROV's coat of arms should have been a turnstile.

JOHNSON'S STRATEGY IN VIETNAM TO DECEMBER 1964

Though President Johnson worried about the chronic political instability of the ROV, and even raged against its tendency to military coups, he persisted in treating the war as if it were entirely the fault of North Vietnam. In consequence, early in 1964 he decided to bring direct but covert pressure on Ho Chi Minh's government by approving the Pentagon's Operations Plan 34A (OPLAN 34A). Among other things, OPLAN 34A provided for the dropping of South Vietnamese saboteurs into North Vietnam and the creation in Danang of a Special Operations Group (SOG) to assist South Vietnamese commandos in carrying out raids on North Vietnam's coastline.

Johnson also made William Bundy, the new assistant secretary of state for the Far East, responsible for policy planning regarding the conduct of the war. In turn, Bundy formed a kind of *troika* with his brother McGeorge Bundy, the president's national security adviser, and with Walt Rostow, chairman of the Policy-Making Committee of the State Department, to work out a plan of action. The result of this effort was that on 1 March 1964 William Bundy sent Johnson a set of proposals that amounted to a plan for open warfare against the DRV.

The main features of the plan were a bombing campaign to destroy North Vietnam's railroads, industries, barracks, and training camps and a naval blockade of Haiphong harbor and other ports in the DRV to choke off aid by sea from the communist bloc nations. Bundy's justifications for this open warfare were that it would force North Vietnam to desist from assisting the insurgency in the ROV and that it would show other countries in Southeast Asia that the United States was prepared to take strong action to prevent the spread of communism in the region.

At first Johnson was not enthusiastic about Bundy's plan. In order for him to execute it legally, he would need a declaration of war or other emergency authority from Congress, and he thought that he was unlikely to get either. The authority under which Truman had brought the United States into the Korean War without consulting Congress had long since expired, and, in any case, Johnson thought that Truman had erred by intervening in the Korean War without first getting authority and support from Congress.

Rostow had anticipated Johnson's objections, and he thought he had a solution to the problem. He seized upon the precedent of a joint resolution passed by both houses of Congress in January 1955, which authorized President Eisenhower to use military force to repel any Chinese communist attack on the nationalist-held islands of Quemoy and Matsu in the Formosa Strait. A similar resolution might meet Johnson's need for congressional authority for military action relative to the American defense of South Vietnam and Laos. After Dean Rusk agreed with Rostow's idea, the State Department prepared the draft of an enabling resolution for the president to put before Congress. But Johnson still took no action. He was not convinced that the moment was right for such a resolution, and he put it aside for the time being.

Instead of putting an enabling resolution before Congress, Johnson ventured a diplomatic initiative to secure peace in Vietnam. To that end, he chose J. Blair Seaborn—the Canadian delegate on the International Commission on Control and Supervision (ICCS)—to be his confidential emissary. But when Seaborn presented Johnson's proposals in Hanoi, they turned out to be diplomacy by "the carrot or the stick." The "carrot" was an offer of U.S. diplomatic recognition of the DRV and a grant of generous economic aid if it ceased aiding the VC insurgency in the ROV; the "stick" was the threat of air and sea action against the DRV if the offer was rejected.

In response, Premier Pham Van Dong indignantly refused Johnson's proposals for peace. He declared that the only acceptable alternative to war in South Vietnam lay in American withdrawal from the ROV, the formation of a neutral government in Saigon that included representatives of the NLF, and free elections to decide the future status of South Vietnam. When Seaborn passed on Pham Van Dong's reply, Johnson declared it unsatisfactory and largely abandoned his pursuit of a diplomatic solution for the time being.

THE GULF OF TONKIN INCIDENTS AND THE GULF OF TONKIN RESOLUTION, AUGUST 1964

On 3 July 1964, MACV headquarters in Saigon requested Admiral U. S. Grant Sharp, Commander-in-Chief, Pacific (CINCPAC), to authorize a DESOTO patrol in the Gulf of Tonkin to acquire further information on the DRV's radio and radar electronics for coast defense. The specially equipped destroyer *Maddox*, skippered by Commander Herbert Ogier, was assigned to the task, and Captain John Herrick was ordered to sail aboard the ship and to take charge of the mission.

Despite the fact that the DRV claimed a twelve-mile limit to its territorial waters, Herrick's orders permitted him to bring Ogier's ship as close as eight miles to the DRV's mainland coast and as close as four miles to any of its offshore islands. Moreover, just as the *Maddox* was entering the Gulf of Tonkin, South Vietnamese commandos based at Danang raided the

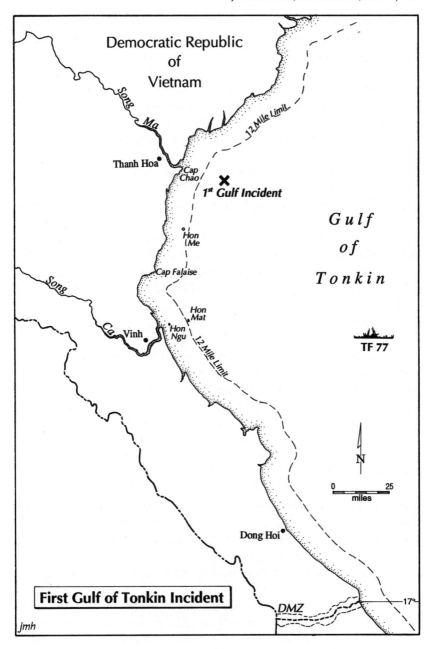

Democratic Republic
of
Vietnam

Song Ma

12 Mile Limit

Thanh Hoa

Cap
Chao

✕
1ˢᵗ Gulf Incident

Hon
Me

Cap Falaise

Hon
Mat

Hon
Ngu

Vinh

Song Ca

12 Mile Limit

Gulf

of

Tonkin

TF 77

N

0   25
miles

Dong Hoi

First Gulf of Tonkin Incident

DMZ

17°

jmh

North Vietnamese islands of Hon Me and Hon Ngu on 31 July. Therefore, tensions were high in the Gulf when on Sunday, 2 August, the *Maddox* came within some miles of the island of Hon Me.

As the destroyer steamed back into international waters, three DRV patrol-torpedo (PT) boats from Hon Me followed it. As time passed and the boats began to overtake the destroyer, Herrick assumed hostile intent. He radioed for help from Task Force 77, some fifty miles away, and the carrier *Ticonderoga* launched a group of jets led by Commander James Stockdale to come to the aid of the destroyer. Meanwhile, at 3:30 P.M., Herrick had ordered the *Maddox* to open fire on the approaching boats.

Before the planes could arrive, the PT boats pressed home their attack on the *Maddox*, launching two torpedoes and opening fire with their small-caliber weapons. The *Maddox* dodged the torpedoes, and the fire from its 5-inch (diameter) guns disabled one PT boat, which lay dead in the water. By the time the American planes from the *Ticonderoga* arrived on the scene, the other two PT boats were fleeing toward the coast of the DRV. The planes pursued them and damaged both boats with gunfire and rockets before breaking off their attacks. During the encounter, one small shell had struck the *Maddox* and inflicted minor damage. There were no American casualties.

From the firing of the first shots by the *Maddox*, the whole action— soon to be known as the First Gulf of Tonkin Incident—had taken about twenty minutes. By clocks in Washington, D.C., the event had taken place before dawn on 2 August. Later that day, Secretary of Defense McNamara held a detailed briefing about the incident before reporters and TV cameras. He claimed that the *Maddox* had been conducting a "routine patrol" in the international waters of the Gulf of Tonkin when it was the victim of an "unprovoked attack." He revealed nothing about the destroyer's electronic-surveillance mission, its earlier presence in waters claimed by the DRV, or the South Vietnamese commando raid conducted against the DRV's coast a short time before the incident. Journalists, Congress, and the public were led to believe that the attack was a wanton assault on a U.S. warship peacefully patrolling in international waters.

Nor did McNamara reveal that he and President Johnson made no effort to avoid a repetition of the encounter. To the contrary, the *Maddox*, reinforced by the destroyer *C. Turner Joy*, was ordered to continue its DESOTO patrol, while the carrier *Constellation* was ordered to join Task Force 77 as part of the covering force. Between 2 and 4 August, Herrick's flotilla made shallow penetrations of the DRV's coastal waters, though no closer than nine miles to its offshore islands. Still, Herrick feared that the penetrations might lead Hanoi to order another attack, and his crews were keyed up accordingly. As Herrick was not looking for a fight, on the night of 4 August he moved his destroyers into international waters well inside the Gulf of Tonkin.

Unfortunately, bad weather and darkness made it impossible for the American crews to see very far, and false radar echoes made electronic coverage of the waters around the two destroyers uncertain. When Herrick was informed that blips on his ships' radar screens suggested that "skunks" —unidentified and possibly hostile vessels—were approaching the American flotilla, Herrick called the crews of both ships to their battle stations. When a sonar operator aboard the *Maddox* reported hearing torpedo-propeller noises in the water, Herrick assumed that North Vietnamese PT boats were attacking his flotilla. He ordered the *Maddox* and *Turner Joy* to open fire, and called for aerial assistance from Task Force 77. For hours, at intervals, the two destroyers blazed away at images reflected on their radar screens, but no one aboard the American ships visually sighted an enemy craft. After the third wave of three alleged attacks had been beaten off early on 5 August, Herrick reported loss of contact, the possible sinking of three PT boats, and no damage or casualties suffered aboard his ships. Upon returning to their carrier, the airmen sent to Herrick's assistance reported that they had made no contact with the enemy.

The events of the Second Gulf of Tonkin Incident were reported to the Pentagon almost as soon as they occurred, and by clocks on the East Coast of the United States they took place on the Sunday morning of 4 August. But the administration released no word of the attack to the press, and that afternoon Johnson closeted himself with his advisers to discuss measures of retaliation. Not until 6:00 P.M. did Arthur Sylvester, assistant secretary of defense for public affairs, announce to journalists that a second unprovoked attack on American warships had occurred in the Gulf of Tonkin. His press handout claimed that prior to the attack the *Maddox* and *Turner Joy* had been peacefully cruising in company about sixty-five miles from the DRV's coast. Taken at face value, the attack on the night of 4–5 August was an unprovoked assault on American warships proceeding lawfully in international waters.

As Johnson doubtless knew it would, news of the second attack outraged Congress and much of the public, and he took full advantage of the nation's rancor. At 6:45 P.M., Johnson convened a special and confidential briefing of congressional leaders at the White House, in which he told them what measures he was about to take by way of retaliation for the most recent attack. Then he brought out the enabling resolution that the State Department had prepared months before, and he asked the congressional leaders to put it before Congress. After they assured him that the resolution, now modified to reflect the attacks in the Gulf, would be speedily debated and passed, he arranged to appear on American TV screens later that evening to give his public version of the Second Gulf of Tonkin Incident and his response.

A little past 11:30 P.M., Johnson commenced his speech to the American public. After repeating the information handed out to the press earlier and praising the performance of the American sailors and airmen in repelling the latest attack, Johnson declared to his TV viewers that "repeated acts of violence against the armed forces of the United States must be met not only with an alert defense but with a positive reply." That reply, he said, was being given even as he spoke, and was directed through air action against the North Vietnamese PT boats at their bases. Then Johnson went on to say that he had asked Congress to "pass a resolution making it clear that our government is united in its determination to take all necessary measures in support of freedom and peace in Southeast Asia," and that he had been given assurance by the congressional leaders that such a resolution would be "promptly introduced, freely and expeditiously debated, and passed with overwhelming support."

Johnson had calculated correctly that after two "unprovoked attacks" on American vessels on the high seas, Congress and the American people would be in a mood to give him wide powers to carry out military action in Southeast Asia. Rarely has Congress approved such important legislation as the Gulf of Tonkin Resolution so swiftly or by such overwhelming majorities. The vote in the House of Representatives on 6 August was unanimous, and on 7 August the Senate passed the resolution by ninety-eight yeas to two nays. In the entire Congress, only senators Wayne Morse (D-Ore.) and Ernest Gruening (D-Alaska) were opposed, and both senators had been against Johnson's Vietnam policy before the Gulf of Tonkin Incidents.

But the resolution might have met with stiffer opposition had Congress and the public known what the Johnson administration had learned since the alleged second attack. Following an investigation of the incident, Herrick came to the conclusion that his flotilla had never been attacked on the night of 4 August. He believed that his crews had become overwrought under the strain of their duties and had overreacted to an imaginary danger. In his opinion, the blips on the radar scopes interpreted as enemy PT boats were due to "freak weather effects," and the sound of torpedo propellers in the water were misinterpretations of other shipboard noises by an "overeager" sonar operator.

Moreover, Commander James Stockdale, USN, who had led the flight of aircraft from the carrier *Ticonderoga* (and who had earlier led the flight that aided the *Maddox* on 2 August), had reported that although he could see the destroyers' wakes and the flashes of their gunfire, his repeated passes over the waters where the PT boats were allegedly maneuvering had revealed nothing. He arrived back at his carrier convinced that the surface navy was shooting at non-existent targets. Stockdale experienced not a little shock when the next morning he was alerted to lead a retaliatory air raid on North Vietnam's PT boat bases for an attack on U.S. ships that had never taken place.

Herrick's report was sent to Admiral Sharp's headquarters in Hawaii, but the CINCPAC insisted that an attack had occurred, and so expressed himself in forwarding the report to Washington. McNamara made efforts to confirm whether or not an attack had taken place, but he seems to have received nothing he thought convincing but Sharp's comments and intercepted but ambiguous North Vietnamese radio messages. (After further analysis, those messages turned out to be describing the action on 2 August.) Also, the American press seems not to have noted the inconsistency that Hanoi, which had quickly claimed a successful defense of its waters in the First Gulf of Tonkin Incident, denied that any of its boats were involved in an engagement with American ships on the night of 4–5 August. Only years later, and through the Pentagon Papers, were the American people to learn on what shaky grounds — essentially in retaliation for a "non-event"—Congress had dealt Johnson what he considered to be a "free hand" for conducting a war in Southeast Asia. Nor were they to learn until a long time later that soon after the "non-event," Johnson had come to a private conclusion that the Second Gulf of Tonkin Incident had never taken place.

Nevertheless, the Gulf of Tonkin Resolution had been passed, and as Johnson was to cite it in future as his authority for waging war in Southeast Asia, it is quoted here in full:

> WHEREAS naval units of the Communist regime in Vietnam, in violation of the Charter of the United Nations and of international law, have deliberately and repeatedly attacked United States naval vessels lawfully present in international waters, and have thereby created a serious threat to international peace; and
>
> WHEREAS these attacks are part of a deliberate and systematic campaign of aggression that the Communist regime in North Vietnam has been waging against its neighbors and the nations joined with them in the collective defense of their freedom; and
>
> WHEREAS the United States is assisting the peoples of Southeast Asia to protect their freedom and has no territorial, military, or political

ambitions in that area, but desires only that these people should be left in peace to work out their own destinies in their own way;

NOW, therefore be it Resolved by the Senate and House of Representatives of the United States of America in Congress assembled,

THAT the Congress approves and supports the determination of the President, as Commander in Chief, to take all necessary measures to repel any armed attack against the forces of the United States and to prevent further aggression.

THAT the United States regards as vital to its national interest and to world peace the maintenance of international peace and security in Southeast Asia. Consonant with the Constitution and the Charter of the United Nations and in accordance with its obligations under the Southeast Asia Collective Defense Treaty, the United States is, therefore, prepared, as the President determines, to take all necessary steps, including the use of armed force, to assist any member or protocol state of the Southeast Asia Collective Defense Treaty requesting assistance in defense of its freedom.

THAT this resolution shall expire when the President shall determine that the peace and security of the area is reasonably assured by international conditions created by action of the United Nations or otherwise, except that it may be terminated earlier by concurrent resolution of the Congress.

JOHNSON'S POLICY, AUGUST–DECEMBER 1964

After passage of the Gulf of Tonkin Resolution, Johnson assumed that he had been given a congressional *carte blanche* to carry on war in Southeast Asia as he saw fit. He ordered the U.S. Air Force to begin moving squadrons into air bases in Thailand (a cooperative SEATO ally) and other squadrons to airfields in South Vietnam, and the U.S. Navy to increase its forces in the Far East.

But Johnson was also cautious before the impending presidential election in November. When another DESOTO patrol in September reported that it had been attacked by Vietnamese PT boats, he wisely withheld action until the event could be confirmed. It turned out to be a false alarm. Likewise, another incident on a DESOTO patrol in October proved to have no foundation in fact. Yet neither Congress nor the public was allowed to know anything of either episode.

Meanwhile, the presidential election of 1964 was underway. Senator Barry Goldwater (R-Ariz.) carried the banner for the Republicans, and he advocated a super hard line against communism and a heavy reliance on nuclear weapons. For all the reigning spirit of anti-communism in America, many people were especially bothered by Goldwater's cavalier attitude toward atomic warfare. In contrast, the Johnson-McNamara policy was to treat American nuclear weapons as primarily useful for deterring an enemy from resorting to such weapons for fear of retaliation. Thanks to Goldwater's bellicose approach, Johnson found himself well positioned to appear to the voters as the candidate of moderation, one with whom the country could safely leave the managing of the war in Southeast Asia and who had a proper understanding of the dangers of nuclear warfare. Johnson's policies of caution and moderation paid off handsomely in the elections on 3 November, when he virtually buried Goldwater's candidacy with 61 percent of the popular vote and a landslide in electoral votes.

Nevertheless, Johnson had to face the fact that the VPLA was stepping up attacks on the American presence in South Vietnam. On 1 November, Viet Cong agents penetrated the ARVN security around the air base at Bien Hoa, twelve miles from Saigon, fired mortar shells at the flight line, and destroyed six B–57 bombers and killed five Americans and four Vietnamese. On Christmas Eve, VC agents exploded a car bomb at the Brinks barracks, a requisitioned hotel in downtown Saigon, an attack that killed two Americans and injured fifty-eight.

In part to retaliate for such attacks, on 1 December Johnson approved Operation BARREL ROLL, a secret bombing campaign against the Ho Chi Minh Trail in southern Laos, the pipeline of supply from the DRV to the VC. But later in December, the CIA reported that troops of the PAVN—commonly referred to by Americans as the North Vietnamese Army or NVA—had arrived from the DRV in the Laotian border areas of the ROV via the Ho Chi Minh Trail. The journey had taken them two months to complete, but the CIA believed that they were the vanguard of a much larger force to come. Once the PAVN troops were in strength in the ROV, they would pose a much greater immediate threat to the Saigon government than the troops of the VPLA, and might require the United States to inject itself more militantly into the conflict. Hence, by the end of 1964 the DRV and the United States had moved to the brink of war with each other, and the prospect of a peaceful resolution of the crisis in South Vietnam was fading rapidly.

8.

Johnson's War, II:
The Year of the Plunge, 1965

The Critical Year

The year 1965 proved critical to the American involvement in Vietnam, for in that twelve-month period the United States took over chief responsibility for waging the counter-insurgency (CI) war, attacked North Vietnam on a sustained basis through the air, and engaged troops of the PAVN, the North Vietnamese army, in the ROV on the ground. In consequence, 1965 proved to be the Year of the Plunge, one that irrevocably committed the United States to victory in South Vietnam or to the worst foreign-policy defeat in its history.

Sigma II–64 and the
Debate over Bombing Strategy

Because President Johnson's advisers advocated an aerial war against the DRV, in the fall of 1964 the JCS and certain civilian members of the Johnson administration took part in a war game known as SIGMA II–64. The game purported to test the efficacy of a sustained bombing campaign against the DRV and specifically sought answers to three questions: Would air attacks alter Hanoi's willingness to support the VC insurgency in South Vietnam? Would they materially aid the South Vietnamese war effort against the VC? And would they significantly affect the operations of the PAVN should its troops join those of the VPLA?

The conclusions drawn from SIGMA II–64 were not encouraging.

The simulated destruction of North Vietnam's heavy industries, such as there were, turned out not to matter much in terms of war production since most of the DRV's war matériel came from China and the USSR. The war game also showed that the selective bombing of the DRV's roads and railways leading to China, and the bombing of ports through which foreign aid came, would hinder but not eliminate North Vietnam's ability to aid the VC in the south. And as most North Vietnamese lived on an agricultural peasant economy that was relatively self-sufficient, the economy was not an easy target for even the indirect effects of bombing, short of bombing the dike system and undermining the rice culture in order to encourage wholesale starvation.

As for bombing to break the will of the DRV's leaders to support the insurgency in the south, General Curtis LeMay, chief of staff of the Air Force, concluded that such a goal could be reached only if the air attacks were intense, were carried out over a relatively short period of time in order to maximize their economic and psychological effects, and were subject to few restrictions on targeting. His staff drew up a list of ninety-four targets against which a relentless attack over sixteen days would, in their judgment, largely paralyze the DRV. The key to success, as they saw it, was the use of maximum force in the shortest possible time.

On the other hand, LeMay strongly opposed an alternative "Tourniquet Strategy." This strategy would allow air attacks only on targets in the DRV in its southern "panhandle" (i.e., the territory between the 20th and 17th parallels), and then gradually extend the "bomb line" northward into the Red River delta if Hanoi did not knuckle under sooner. Unlike the strategy of intense, condensed, and relatively unlimited bombing, the Tourniquet Strategy was not intended to bring about the DRV's collapse, but aimed at causing enough damage to the DRV's limited resources that its leaders would be willing to end aid to the VC in order to get the bombing offensive suspended.

LeMay's doubts about the efficacy of the Tourniquet Strategy were in part based on experience. In historical terms, gradually accelerating bombing campaigns have been less effective, and at greater cost to the attackers, than powerful blows inflicted in compressed periods of time. In World War II, the heaviest losses of the U.S. 8th Air Force in raids over Germany had occurred during its long build-up to maximum strength, while the greatest impact of its strategic bombing had come in the last ten months of the war. The U.S. bombing of Japan had relatively little effect until the mass firebombings of Japanese cities, followed by the atomic bombings of Hiroshima and Nagasaki, had gutted most of Japan's urban areas.

But, issues of humanity aside, it was another matter whether a strategy of mass annihilation made sense against a small communist country with two potential communist allies that were nuclear armed. And even a program of unlimited conventional (i.e., non-atomic) bombing would certainly turn much world opinion against the United States. It might even risk war with the People's Republic of China, if not the Soviet Union. In 1964, Beijing had issued public warnings that it would not be indifferent to the fate of North Vietnam, and a fixed principle of Johnson's policy was to avoid another war with communist China if at all possible.

LeMay retired from active service on 1 February 1965 and was succeeded by General John McConnell as chief of staff of the Air Force. Although McConnell agreed with LeMay's estimate of the effects of limited bombing on the DRV—it would do the enemy harm, but it could not be decisive—President Johnson and Secretary McNamara finally came down on the side of a Tourniquet Strategy for Operation ROLLING THUNDER, as the air offensive against North Vietnam was designated. It was easily the safest in respect to keeping the conflict localized and avoiding provocation of the major communist powers; and by a gradual tightening of the "tourniquet" through expanding the area bombed and the type of target attacked in the DRV, Johnson and McNamara thought the "pain" would become too much for the North Vietnamese leaders to bear. General Earle Wheeler, chairman of the JCS, did not openly dissent from the Johnson-McNamara reasoning over air strategy against North Vietnam, but he was aware that McConnell and the other members of the JCS were uneasy about it.

Once Johnson and McNamara had chosen the form and objectives of Operation ROLLING THUNDER, the air planners decided that the raids would be carried out primarily by fighter-bombers of the U.S. Air Force squadrons based in Thailand and by U.S. naval attack squadrons based on carriers near the Gulf of Tonkin. The huge B–52 bombers of the Strategic Air Command (SAC) based on Guam (and later in Thailand) would be launched from time to time against peripheral areas of North Vietnam—such as the Miu Gia Pass, an entry point to the Ho Chi Minh Trail—but American fear of the Soviet-supplied Surface-to-Air Missile 2 (SAM–2) encouraged a reliance on the more agile fighter-bombers for deep penetrations of North Vietnamese air space.

In addition, the air staff received presidential approval for planning Operation STEEL TIGER, a new and more intense attack on the Ho Chi Minh Trail in the Laotian "panhandle." Operation BARREL ROLL, its predecessor, would be refocused on northern Laos in support of the U.S. Secret Army there and against the Pathet Lao.

THE LAUNCHING OF THE AIR OFFENSIVES
AGAINST NORTH VIETNAM AND LAOS

President Johnson needed a provocation for justifying the unleashing of ROLLING THUNDER against North Vietnam, and his opportunity began to unfold on 7 February 1965 in South Vietnam. That night the VC made an attack at Pleiku in the Central Highlands on Camp Holloway — an American military advisers' compound — and on a nearby U.S. helicopter base. The hit-and-run attacks resulted in the deaths of nine American advisers and technicians, injury to seventy-six more, destruction of several helicopters, and damage to others. It was yet another demonstration that the VC was stepping up attacks on Americans.

The attack at Pleiku coincided with the visit of McGeorge Bundy, Johnson's national security adviser, to Saigon for consultations with General Westmoreland and Ambassador Taylor, and when word of the attack reached the three men they agreed that the DRV should be held responsible. In the spirit of tit-for-tat, they thought that a fitting reprisal would be an American air attack on a target in North Vietnam. Bundy made a trans-Pacific telephone call to Johnson and McNamara in which he recommended this course of action, and the president and the secretary of defense concurred. Within fourteen hours of the attack on Pleiku, the carriers *Coral Sea* and *Hancock* carried out Operation FLAMING DART I by launching forty-four jets in a strike against a North Vietnamese military training camp near Donghoi, located about forty miles north of the DMZ.

But such retaliation did not deter the VC in South Vietnam, and on 10 February their agents blew up the Viet Cuong Hotel, one serving as a barracks for U.S. military advisers, in the city of Qui Nhon. The explosion killed twenty-three Americans and injured twenty-one. This time Johnson required no prodding from Saigon. He retaliated for the attack by ordering Operation FLAMING DART II on 11 February. The target chosen was the PAVN barracks at Chanh Hoa, thirty-five miles north of the DMZ, which was believed to be used for training the VC.

But more important, any reservations Johnson may have harbored about launching Operation ROLLING THUNDER went by the boards. On 13 February, he ordered Admiral Sharp, CINCPAC, to commence ROLLING THUNDER as soon as practicable. But before the air offensive could get underway, another military coup took place in Saigon and Johnson rescinded the order. He decided to withhold action until the new government could be consulted. General Nguyen Van Thieu and Air Marshal Nguyen Cao Ky had ousted General Khanh from their triumvirate, and had taken up practical direction of the Saigon government.

After Thieu and Ky endorsed ROLLING THUNDER, Johnson reissued his order to Admiral Sharp, but the CINCPAC withheld action until a period of extended good weather was predicted. Finally, on 2 March, the first strikes under ROLLING THUNDER were carried out against targets in the DRV's panhandle. Then on 3 April, Operation STEEL TIGER—a stepped-up air offensive against the Ho Chi Minh Trail in southern Laos—commenced as a complement to ROLLING THUNDER. Thus the strategy of a limited but escalating bombing campaign got underway in both North Vietnam and Laos, and in the balance rested the success of the Tourniquet Strategy.

THE DEBATE OVER U.S. GROUND FORCE COMMITMENT, FEBRUARY–JUNE 1965

Events were also moving toward a major American ground-combat commitment in South Vietnam. On 22 February 1965, Westmoreland requested that some of the U.S. Marines based on Okinawa be transferred to MACV for the protection of an American air base being developed at Danang. Johnson approved Westmoreland's request, and on 8 March 3,500 Marines were landed over the beaches and took up defensive positions around the air base. The two Marine battalions were the first U.S. ground-combat units sent to South Vietnam.

After dispatching the Marines, Johnson sent word to Westmoreland that in making future requests he was to assume no limitations on equipment or personnel for the accomplishment of his mission. Westmoreland took the president at his word and promptly requested a U.S. Army division to bolster the ARVN. While Johnson was considering Westmoreland's request, on 20 March the JCS proposed sending an expeditionary force of 40,000 troops to the ROV, the force to consist of one Army and one Marine division, plus support and service troops. Johnson ordered a further study of the proposal, but on 1 April he agreed to send Westmoreland two more Marine combat battalions and 20,000 more Army logistical troops. And on 15 April, he approved the sending of the Army's 173rd Airborne Brigade (3,000–4,000 troops) to protect the U.S. base complex at Bien Hoa, twelve miles north of Saigon.

But Johnson was reluctant to go further with a ground-war commitment in the ROV in the spring of 1965. In part, this was because he was sensitive to the small but growing dissent in Congress and across the country regarding his policies on Vietnam. In the Senate, Wayne Morse and

Ernest Gruening—the original dissenters to the Gulf of Tonkin Resolution—called for a de-escalation of the U.S. war effort and a review of national policy in regard to Southeast Asia. The first student anti-war protest had been staged at the University of California at Berkeley in 1964, and more protests were cropping up on and off college campuses in the spring of 1965. Though the congressional critics and anti-war protesters were still small clouds on Johnson's horizon, he was concerned enough about such opposition that he returned to diplomacy with Hanoi in order to still dissent.

Johnson launched his new diplomatic initiative in a speech he made at Johns Hopkins University on 7 April. First, he blustered that the United States would not be defeated in South Vietnam, nor would it withdraw its forces there under a "meaningless agreement"; but then he proposed "unconditional negotiations" with the DRV and even promised that Ho's government would receive U.S. diplomatic recognition and a share in a proposed project to develop the Mekong River valley if it would call off the VC's insurgency in the ROV. Apparently, Johnson thought that Ho was open to bribery, for after the speech he bragged to his aide Bill Moyers, "Old Ho can't turn that down."

But Johnson's latest peace proposal ignored the history of Vietnam and the determination of Ho Chi Minh and his following to achieve a unified country. In rejecting the proposal, Premier Pham Van Dong set down three conditions for peace: the bombing campaign against the DRV must be discontinued without conditions; American military forces must withdraw from South Vietnam; and a coalition government that included the NLF must be formed in Saigon. Johnson rejected all three conditions, claiming that they amounted to "defeat on the installment plan."

On 20 April, civilian and military representatives of the Johnson administration held a conference in Honolulu on the sending of an American expeditionary force to South Vietnam. Australia (a member of SEATO) and South Korea (a non-member) had offered some troops for a joint expedition, but the real question before the conference was how big a burden the American people could be asked to carry in a war on the mainland of Southeast Asia. In their conclusions, the conferees at Honolulu took the middle ground by recommending to Johnson an Enclave Strategy, one under which an Allied expeditionary force of 80,000 American troops and 20,000 so-called Third Country troops would man the more populated coastal enclaves in the ROV in order to free more ARVN forces to concentrate against the VPLA in the back country.

Johnson concurred with the recommendations of the Honolulu Conference, but while the details of the Enclave Strategy were being worked out in May, VPLA units destroyed an ARVN battalion at the battle of Ba Gia and overran the town of Songbe, the capital of Phuoc Long province. The site of the ARVN defeat, near the Cambodian border, was only about fifty miles north of Saigon. Its impact, along with lesser ARVN setbacks, greatly accelerated the decline of South Vietnam's defense structure. The CIA estimated that the strength of the VPLA had grown to 130,000 troops and that 40,000 PAVN troops were in the ROV or on their way down the Ho Chi Minh Trail. Together, they might be enough to topple the ROV before the end of the year. It became clear to the Washington policy makers that the Enclave Strategy, so recently approved, had been made outdated by the march of events and that more drastic measures were in order.

The gravity of the situation in the ROV was driven home when on 7 June Westmoreland cabled Johnson that the president must consider committing American combat troops in large numbers throughout South Vietnam or be prepared to accept the ROV's fall in the near future. South Vietnamese battalions were being destroyed or were deserting at a rate of about one a week, and the ARVN would be rendered ineffective before the end of the year unless something was done soon to reverse the tide. With only 90,000 U.S. troops in MACV, and most of them advisory or technical personnel, the MACV commander estimated that he must have a minimum of 175,000 troops, of which a substantial portion must be in combat units, before the end of 1965 if he was to save the country from collapse. This initial force should include thirty-four U.S. "maneuver battalions," supported by thousands of troops in the artillery, engineers, and supply and maintenance units. As for Third Country troops, Westmoreland asked for the Australian battalion and the ten battalions offered by South Korea.

JOHNSON'S DECISION TO COMMIT MAJOR GROUND COMBAT FORCES TO SOUTH VIETNAM: JUNE–JULY

Westmoreland's assessment of the situation early in June made it clear that the long and predominantly advisory period of American involvement in the ROV was coming to an end. The war had reached the point where it could be won by the ROV only—if it could be won at all—with the large-scale help of foreign troops on the ground. The Americans were sure to bear the main burden of this phase of the war. Johnson had hoped never to face such a situation, but none of his options seemed very palatable by the summer of 1965.

If the United States failed to commit ground combat forces on the scale that Westmoreland requested, the ROV would surely fall to the communists within a few more months. According to the much-touted Domino

Theory, the fall of the ROV would lead to the fall of other non-communist areas in Southeast Asia and perhaps beyond. In consequence, or so it was widely believed, America's credibility with its allies over the globe would be shaken. And even if only the ROV fell, the Republicans and conservatives generally might heap such blame on Johnson's administration that it might set off a wave of anti-communist hysteria such as had occurred after the "betrayal of China" in 1949. In that event, the last "domino" to fall might well be Johnson's presidency in the 1968 election.

On the other hand, an American-dominated ground war in the ROV had many drawbacks, not the least of which was the danger that it might embroil the United States with China and even with the Soviet Union. If this possibility was to be avoided, America's war in Vietnam would have to be carefully limited, and there was no guarantee that such a limited war would be successful. Also, by taking over the war in the ROV, the Americans would lend credence to communist propaganda that the government in Saigon was a dependency of the United States and that the intervention was a covert form of colonialism. There were also the questions of how long the war would last, how costly it would be in both lives and money, and how well the American people and the economy would bear up under its burdens. No one could confidently give answers to any of these questions.

But as the situation in the ROV continued to deteriorate, Westmoreland and McNamara pressed Johnson ever more strongly for action, and on 21 July the president began a final series of meetings with his advisers as to what course and measures his administration should take. George Ball, the undersecretary of state and chief critic of intervention within Johnson's inner circles, said later that of all the people at the table during these sessions, Johnson was the most cautious. If the president wavered over his decision, it was because he knew it would have tremendous repercussions on America at home and abroad for years to come.

But a decision had to be made, and Johnson announced it on national television at noon on 28 July. In his address, the president reviewed his earlier unsuccessful diplomatic efforts to bring about peace in South Vietnam, discussed the growing military crisis there, and finally told his viewers that he had decided to give Westmoreland whatever he needed to meet the "mounting aggression" of the communists. He concluded by saying, "We cannot be defeated by force of arms. We will stand in Vietnam." By Johnson's action, the United States had taken the plunge.

But what Johnson did not tell his viewers was as important as what he did tell them. He did not tell them that he had rejected the JCS's advice to carry out a general mobilization of the civilian reserves and the National Guard in order to augment the strength of the regular forces. (Johnson preferred to rely on a gradually increasing draft for more men in uniform, a measure that would be less alarming to the public than a general mobilization.) Nor did he really stress that the United States was at war, and possibly a long and costly war at that. Violating his own criticism of Truman's mode of bringing the United States into the Korean War, he did not go back to Congress for further authority. He simply assumed that the Gulf of Tonkin Resolution had already given him enough. He was to find that some in Congress and among the public did not share his view, and the resentment of these groups would come back later to haunt him.

Another matter that would return to haunt Johnson was his decision on the economy. His Council of Economic Advisers warned the president that any war effort in Southeast Asia that would increase the existing budget of $100 billion by 10 percent or more would impose a serious strain. Even Johnson's programs to build a "Great Society" and to wage a "War on Poverty" might suffer in consequence. But Johnson shared McNamara's view that the cost of the first year's involvement would not exceed $6 billion, and in following years the cost would probably be even less. As it turned out, the cost of the war in the fiscal year (FY) from 1 July 1965 to 30 June 1966 was in line with McNamara's prediction, but in FY 1966–67 the war's cost rose to over $10 billion, and in FY 1967–1968 its cost ballooned to over $26 billion. Much too late, Johnson abandoned his policy of "guns and butter" in favor of a surtax to help finance the war, and inflation threatened to wrack the economy. Inflation, additional taxes, and diversion of funds from domestic programs to meet the demands of the war all combined to alienate many of his former supporters over the next three years.

THE WESTMORELAND STRATEGY

By the time President Johnson had decided to commit a large American ground force to the defense of the ROV, Westmoreland had conceived of a three-stage strategy for using it. The first stage conformed to the reality of the enemy's possession of the initiative and his probable desire to crush resistance before large American ground forces could enter the country and affect the war's outcome. As the American troops arrived, Westmoreland planned to deploy them so as to hold the most vital points in the country and especially the American base complex. Because U.S. Marines were already deployed around Danang, Westmoreland decided that their expanding forces would take over chief responsibility for the ARVN 1st Corps Tactical Zone, which encompassed the five most northern provinces of the ROV's "panhandle." From north to south, these provinces were

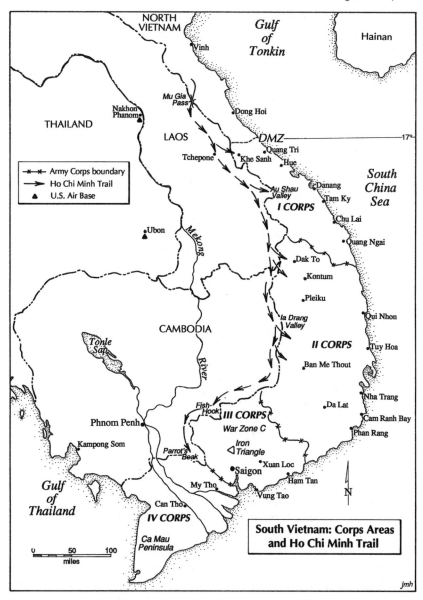

South Vietnam: Corps Areas and Ho Chi Minh Trail

Quang Tri, Thua Thien, Quang Nam, Quang Tin, and Quang Ngai. The Marine responsibility also included defense of the ROV's border with the DRV at the DMZ. The U.S. Army would take responsibility for the ARVN 2nd and 3rd Corps Tactical Zones further south (except Saigon in the 3rd

Corps TZ), while ARVN would assume chief responsibility for the defense of Saigon and for the 4th Corps TZ, which included most of the Mekong delta.

The second stage of Westmoreland's strategy would commence with Allied offensives, utilizing search-and-destroy tactics to seek out and destroy the enemy and his base camps within the country. In this stage, the aim would be to inflict enemy casualties and to destroy his means of sustenance rather than to occupy territory or to control population. If successful, this stage—which might require up to eighteen months to get fully underway—was expected to reduce the enemy to small units capable of only hit-and-run operations. As the chief measure of progress in the second stage, Westmoreland would rely on "body count," or reported enemy dead.

In the third stage of the war, Westmoreland envisaged a rehabilitated ARVN taking over the main burden of field operations, with the gradual withdrawal of other Allied forces as they were no longer needed. As the enemy would be convinced by this stage that he could not overthrow South Vietnam through war, he would be compelled to negotiate peace on the ROV's terms. Westmoreland could not be certain when this stage of the war would be reached, but in any case it would be a number of years away.

THE BATTLE FOR SOUTH VIETNAM, AUGUST–DECEMBER 1965

The 3rd Marine Amphibious Force (3rd MAF), consisting initially of troops drawn from the 3rd Marine Division, was first to engage a major enemy force as new American troops began to surge into South Vietnam. In August, Marine intelligence learned that a VPLA regiment was assembling near the American air base at Chu Lai. In Operation STARLITE (18–21 August), four Marine battalions and a special landing force launched a converging attack on the enemy position by assaulting it over land, by air, and from the sea. The trapped enemy unit—the 1st VPLA Regiment—put up a formidable resistance, but was overwhelmed by the weight of American firepower. When the battle was over, the Marines claimed that 614 VC had been killed and perhaps as many more had been wounded, and 9 prisoners were taken. The Marines suffered 45 men killed and 200 wounded.

Heartened by the Marine success at Chu Lai and the arrival of the U.S. Army's 1st Infantry Division (about 17,000 troops) at Bien Hoa, some ARVN units began to fight with more determination. But General Nguyen

Chi Thanh, the chief military officer at the Central Office, South Vietnam (COSVN) and effectively the VPLA/PAVN commander-in-chief in South Vietnam, was determined to keep the momentum of the communist offensive going. He hoped to exploit the weakened condition of the ARVN forces before the Americans could get many of their combat troops into the ROV, and he even ignored the doubts of General Vo Nguyen Giap, the DRV's defense minister, as to this course of action. Accordingly, Thanh began concentrating PAVN troops along the Cambodian border opposite South Vietnam's Central Highlands in preparation for a drive down Route 19 through Pleiku and An Khe, and finally to the sea at Qui Nhon. Thanh expected that, with South Vietnam cut in half and the ARVN and U.S. forces north and south of the split isolated, a general collapse of South Vietnamese resistance would follow. He reasoned that not even the American forces could long remain in South Vietnam in such circumstances.

Anticipating such a "smash and grab" communist offensive through the Central Highlands, Westmoreland urged the Pentagon to send him an "airmobile division," a type that could move most of its troops and assets by helicopter and was ideal for operations in such rugged terrain. But in the summer of 1965, the Eleventh Air Assault Division (Test) at Ft. Benning, Georgia, was the only large airmobile unit in the U.S. Army, and it was not really a division but only an experimental airmobile brigade. In order to meet Westmoreland's need, the Army hastily added other troops to the airmobile brigade and rechristened the amalgam as the 1st Cavalry Division, Airmobile. (Hereinafter, it is referred to as the 1st Air Cav, its popular *nom de guerre*.) It was then moved by sea from Charleston, South Carolina, across the Pacific to the port of Qui Nhon, arriving during October. A site near An Khe on Route 19 was chosen to be its base camp.

The 1st Air Cav's concentration in the Central Highlands came none too soon, for by late October General Thanh had nearly completed the assembly of his forces for an offensive toward the coast. Two PAVN regiments — effectively the better part of a PAVN army division — were in camps on the Chu Pong massif overlooking the Ia Drang valley southwest of Pleiku, and a third regiment was camped nearby, just inside the Cambodian frontier. As a preliminary to his general offensive, Thanh sent a PAVN raiding party to make a hit-and-run attack on a U.S. Army Special Forces–CIDG camp near Plei Me.

As the raiding party withdrew toward Thanh's camps early in November, it was followed by reconnaissance units from the 1st Air Cav. The Americans pursued the retiring enemy into the Ia Drang valley, where they uncovered the large communist forces being assembled for Thanh's offen-

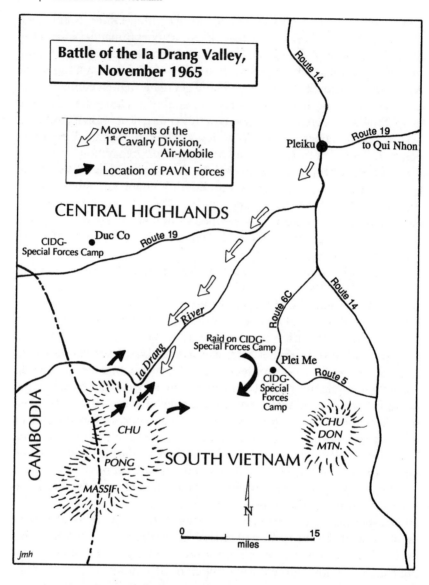

Battle of the Ia Drang Valley,
November 1965

Movements of the
1st Cavalry Division,
Air-Mobile
Location of PAVN Forces

Route 14

Route 19
to Qui Nhon

Pleiku

CENTRAL HIGHLANDS

Duc Co
CIDG-
Special Forces Camp

Route 19

Route 6C

Route 14

Ia Drang River

Raid on CIDG-
Special Forces Camp

Plei Me

CIDG-
Special
Forces
Camp

Route 5

CHU
DON
MTN.

CAMBODIA

CHU

PONG

MASSIF

SOUTH VIETNAM

N

0   15
miles

jmh

sive. General Harry W. O. Kinnard, commander of the 1st Air Cav, reacted
to the discovery of Thanh's forces by launching Operation SILVER BAYO-
NET, an offensive that set off the war's first major action between troops of
the U.S. Army and the PAVN.

The battle of the Ia Drang valley reached its climax over four days in mid-November. On the American side, the fighting was conducted in an innovative fashion and with the latest technology available. The battle saw the large-scale use of the helicopter for moving troops, moving artillery, and serving as weapons platforms for machine guns and rocket launchers. The U.S. infantry used the new and fully automatic M–16 assault rifle for the first time in combat. B–52 bombers flew ARC LIGHT raids in tactical support of the ground forces, each B–52 capable of dropping more than a hundred 500-lb. bombs in thirty seconds, a salvo that created an exploding inferno a mile in length and a quarter of a mile wide.

But even when faced with such firepower and air mobility, the PAVN soldiers proved tough and resourceful. They were masters of camouflage and equally adroit in tactical maneuvering. They were also well armed with the Soviet-designed AK–47 automatic assault rifle, and with effective machine guns, mortars, and rocket-propelled grenades (RPGs). At one point in the fighting, they nearly trapped two companies of the Seventh Cavalry Regiment, these units escaping annihilation only after suffering heavy casualties. Despite their own heavy losses, the PAVN soldiers never lost their will to fight, and in consequence the battle was hardly one-sided.

Still, the outcome was an American victory. The 1st Air Cav had mauled two PAVN regiments, inflicting perhaps two thousand casualties, and had driven the survivors into Cambodia. At the cost of two hundred Americans killed and a thousand wounded, the 1st Air Cav had aborted General Thanh's plan for a quick communist victory by way of the Central Highlands. Moreover, Westmoreland could congratulate himself on a rapid build-up of American troops in South Vietnam. By the end of 1965, instead of 175,000 troops being "in-country" as Westmoreland had requested, President Johnson had dispatched 189,000 and promised that still more troops were on the way. If the object was to "Americanize" the war, that goal was being achieved by leaps and bounds.

Indeed, over the next two years, Johnson dispatched to South Vietnam seven Army divisions, two Marine divisions and part of a third, plus five independent Army brigades and an armored regiment. In addition, he sent a substantial number of Air Force, Navy, and Coast Guard units. He also lobbied members of SEATO for troops, but far and away the best response to his plea was from South Korea, a non-member. Eventually, the Republic of Korea sent two combat divisions, a marine regiment, and support personnel. By the beginning of 1968, MACV's troop strength consisted of 485,000 Americans, 48,869 South Koreans, 11,568 Thais, 7,672 Australians, 1,576 Filipinos, and 552 New Zealanders. On the other hand, neither Britain nor France responded to Johnson's call for "many flags" in

South Vietnam. The government in London was quietly critical, and that in Paris openly critical, of the American plunge into a major war in Southeast Asia.

MCNAMARA'S DOUBTS

The events in Vietnam in the fall of 1965 brought about a transformation in the views of Secretary McNamara. Though publicly he supported Johnson's pledge that the United States would do whatever it took to achieve victory in South Vietnam, he was somewhat shaken by the intensity of the fighting in the fall of 1965 and by Westmoreland's increasing calls for still more troops. But he was made even more depressed by the outcome of SIGMA II–65, a war game carried out on the level of the JCS in September.

The results of the SIGMA II–65 exercise suggested that U.S. forces would find it extremely difficult to find, fix, and destroy enemy units in South Vietnam's terrain whenever the enemy chose to avoid battle, and especially if he could withdraw to safe havens in Cambodia and Laos when hard-pressed. Under those conditions, the communist forces could probably absorb and replace any casualties inflicted by MACV. Further, SIGMA II–65 suggested that operations ROLLING THUNDER and STEEL TIGER—the bombing campaigns against North Vietnam and the "panhandle" of Laos—would have a limited impact on the DRV's ability and will to continue the war. The war game's final implication was that instead of wearing down the communist side, a prolonged war of attrition in Southeast Asia might wear out the Allied side first.

Most strikingly, the conclusions drawn from SIGMA II–65 clashed with Westmoreland's "Concept of Operations in the Republic of Vietnam," a document dated 1 September 1965 and sent to the Department of Defense for approval. Westmoreland's self-designed mission statement defined the American military objective in South Vietnam as ending the war by convincing the enemy that he could not achieve a decisive victory and would therefore have to submit to negotiations favorable to the ROV. McNamara recognized that, stood on its head, Westmoreland's rationale could well be adopted by the enemy. As long as the VPLA/PAVN forces remained in the field and the war seemed to be at a stalemate, war-weariness on the part of the American public and other countries might eventually compel the withdrawal of U.S. and Third Country forces. Such a withdrawal would surely bring about a collapse of the ROV.

THE DEBATE OVER THE BOMBING PAUSE

Therefore, in a memorandum prepared on 7 November, McNamara advised Johnson to order a pause in Operation ROLLING THUNDER in order to give Hanoi a "face-saving opportunity" to come to the negotiating table. The memorandum argued that it was a favorable time to seek negotiations, as an equilibrium had been achieved on South Vietnam's battlefields and the ROV was no longer in imminent danger of collapse. At the same time, and despite General Westmoreland's optimism, the situation might not be so favorable again for a negotiated peace. A suspension of the bombing of the DRV might set events in motion in that direction.

McNamara's proposal deeply divided Johnson's advisers. Ambassador Taylor warned from Saigon that a bombing pause would be injurious to South Vietnamese morale, while Secretary of State Dean Rusk warned that Hanoi could string out a bombing halt indefinitely with meaningless negotiations. Admiral Sharp, Westmoreland, and the JCS opposed a bombing pause on military grounds. McGeorge Bundy and George Ball backed McNamara and supported the idea, as did the majority of the civilian defense intellectuals at the Pentagon.

Johnson wavered between conflicting opinions, but he was alarmed by the escalating domestic opposition to the war, and especially by the grisly self-immolations of two young American war protesters in November. (One man had burned himself to death on the steps of the Pentagon in Washington, the other on the steps of the United Nations building in New York.) Such behavior by Americans would have been unthinkable even a few years before. Johnson knew that the anti-war movement was likely to intensify if his administration did not appear to be seeking peace by every possible avenue, and the longer the war dragged on the less popular it would be with the general public. Also, foreign governments were pressuring Washington to use a suspension of bombing as an opening for a peace offensive.

Finally, after deliberating over the issue at his ranch in Texas in December, Johnson announced just after Christmas Day that the suspension of bombing temporarily in effect over the holidays would be continued indefinitely as an earnest of Washington's desire for peace talks. But the DRV's response to the bombing halt was hardly heartening. Premier Pham Van Dong declared that the bombing would have to cease permanently and without conditions before negotiations could even begin. He repeated his old terms for peace as the withdrawal of U.S. and Third Country forces from South Vietnam, inclusion of the NLF in a neutralist government in Saigon, and elections to determine South Vietnam's future. Hanoi's attitude convinced Johnson that Ho Chi Minh's government had no desire to stop the war on terms that Washington could accept, and after a pause of thirty-seven days, ROLLING THUNDER resumed late in January 1966. As the build-up of Allied and enemy ground forces in the ROV had not slackened over the interval, not an early peace but a long war seemed in prospect.

9.

Johnson's War, III: Moving Toward Defeat, 1966–1967

After the failure of his "smash and grab" strategy in 1965, General Thanh adopted General Giap's preferred strategy of protracted war, the communist version of attrition warfare but one that aimed at wearing away the enemy's will to continue the conflict rather than at winning a straight mathematical competition in inflicting the most casualties. As in the earlier Indochina War, the communists placed their faith in the remarkable Vietnamese ability to endure heavy losses and deprivations until they achieved final victory through wearing down the will of the enemy, or until the communists had the strength to wage grand war, as they had done against the French in the battle for Dienbienphu. And in order to cope with Westmoreland's strategy of attrition and his search-and-destroy tactics, Thanh's weaker forces tried to avoid contact with Allied forces except when their enemies were vulnerable to surprise attack or ambushes or where they could be drawn into storming well-fortified positions at great cost to themselves.

In applying their strategy, the communists enjoyed some special advantages by fighting on home ground. These included: numerous VC sympathizers and agents who could provide the communists with timely intelligence as to Allied intentions and movements; elaborate systems of hidden underground tunnels in rural areas of the ROV that offered shelter and hiding places; safe havens in the border areas of Laos and Cambodia where they might find arms, ammunition, food, and reinforcements; the support of increasing numbers of troops sent from the north; and, finally, the psychological advantage of fighting for a united Vietnam against a government that not only was unpopular but was dependent on foreign military assistance in order to keep Vietnam divided.

THE ALLIED GROUND STRATEGY IN 1966: CONTROVERSY AND RESULTS

Not all of the Allied military leaders agreed with Westmoreland's strategy of attrition and his search-and-destroy tactics in order to defeat the VPLA/PAVN threat. The strategy was being implemented by Allied thrusts into even the most remote areas of South Vietnam, while the search-and-destroy tactics threatened to turn into a "scorched earth" policy. Chief among the dissenters were General Lewis Walt, commander of the 3rd Marine Amphibious Force (3rd MAF), the major U.S. Marine Corps organization in Vietnam, and General Victor Krulak, the commander of the Fleet Marine Force, Pacific.

Both Marine officers believed that a sounder approach than Westmoreland's would be to leave the less populated hinterland in the mountains to the enemy for the time being and, in what they called an "ink-stain strategy," to concentrate Allied resources on securing the areas of greatest rural and urban population. In essence, this was a modified Enclave Strategy. The Marine leaders also proposed that the U.S. Army create imitations of the Marine Combined Action Platoon (CAP) and Combined Action Company (CAC), or small units intended to settle in villages and hamlets in order to win the trust and support of the local population and to undergird the Popular Forces (local militia) in their area. While Walt and Krulak recognized the need on occasion for great firepower against VPLA Main Force and PAVN units, they thought it should be used sparingly in the more populated regions lest it alienate the very people the Saigon government was trying to win over through its pacification efforts.

In his memoirs on the war, Westmoreland recognized the positive accomplishments of the CAPs and CACs in the Marine area of responsibility, but he claimed that he did not have the manpower for such a strategy and tactics in the other areas for which MACV was responsible. The only alternative, he argued, was to make sweeps to uncover enemy troops and bases, and then to engage them in battle in order to destroy them. As for the permanent occupation of territory or population control, Westmoreland relied upon the ARVN, the ROV's Regional and Popular Forces, and the ROV's pacification measures. When it was necessary to deny the support of particular villages to the VC, he favored the forced relocation of their populations to the New Life Villages and the razing of the old sites, thus supposedly denying the VC sustenance and new recruits. He also argued that large-unit operations in remote areas were necessary to prevent the VC Main Force and the PAVN from concentrating enough strength there to break into the heavily populated regions at their pleasure.

Whatever the merits of Westmoreland's arguments, an analysis of reports from the field at the end of 1966 showed that the communists still retained the initiative most of the time in respect to either avoiding or forcing battle. About 88 percent of the combats provoked by the Allied search-and-destroy tactics were initiated by the VPLA/PAVN troops, not by the Allied forces. In two-thirds of the cases, the communists commenced action from prepared bunkers and trenches, which the Allied troops were forced to storm in the face of withering fire. And while the Allied search-and-destroy missions sometimes achieved their purpose of destroying enemy troops and resources, many more enemy troops, bases, and resources remained undiscovered. Countrywide sweeps and forays into the hinterland by Allied troops in helicopters, in other aircraft, in vehicles, or on foot did not fundamentally alter this situation.

Nor did the Saigon government's pacification program go well. Beginning in 1966, Thieu's government attempted to "win the hearts and minds" of the rural population with the Revolutionary Development Program (RDP), under which the Saigon government sent specially trained cadres into villages and hamlets for the purposes of security, public works, hygiene, and education. The cadres lived permanently with the rural population, organized self-defense units, and imitated other previous communist activity at the grass roots. But in a secret memorandum submitted to President Johnson late in 1966, McNamara found no reason for optimism about the progress of Saigon's RDP:

> Pacification has if anything gone backward. As compared with two, or four, years ago, enemy full-time regional forces and part-time guerrilla forces are larger; attacks, terrorism, and sabotage have increased in scope and intensity; more railroads are closed and highways cut; the rice crop . . . is smaller; we control little, if any, more of the population [than before]. . . . In essence, we find ourselves no better [off], and if anything, worse off.

OPERATIONS IN THE U.S. ARMY'S
ZONES OF RESPONSIBILITY IN 1967

With more forces available in 1967, Westmoreland hoped to prove the validity of his strategy and tactics in War Zone C and the Iron Triangle, both located in the ARVN 3rd Corps Tactical Zone. The Iron Triangle, only twenty miles north of Saigon, was so called because it was a VC-fortified area between the forks of two rivers. It was such a hotbed of communist activity that the ARVN had not dared to enter it for years. War Zone C was also believed heavily infested with communist troops and bases. GHQ MACV thought that if the enemy would stand and fight anywhere, it would be in the Iron Triangle and in War Zone C.

In Operation CEDAR FALLS (8–26 January), General Jonathan Seamans's 2nd Army Field Force Vietnam (2nd AFFV) thrust into the Triangle with 30,000 troops in the single largest American ground effort of the war. Yet, the punch largely encountered air. Perhaps forewarned, most of the communist forces in the Triangle retreated to the safety of the border in Cambodia, or else they went into underground hiding places. Whenever the American troops discovered abandoned underground tunnel networks, they removed the local civilian populations to New Life Villages and set about destroying their old homes with demolitions and great earth-moving equipment known as Rome Plows. Aircraft used aerosols containing Agent ORANGE to defoliate whole areas in order to deprive the enemy of both camouflage and food-bearing crops after the departure of the Allied troops. When the 2nd AFFV finished its work, General Seamans confidently told the press that it would be a long time before the Iron Triangle would serve as a useful base to the enemy again.

In reality, the setback to the communists in the Iron Triangle proved to be only temporary. Once their troops returned to the area, they repaired their digs in a remarkably short time and even exploited peasant resentment of American tactics to find new recruits for the VPLA from the native population left in the zone. They also still managed to find enough food to keep themselves alive, and their stores of munitions and equipment were soon refurbished from the reserves in Cambodia.

Things hardly went better for the Allies in War Zone C, where on 22 February the 2nd AFFV launched Operation JUNCTION CITY. As the Allied forces moved forward, a battalion of the 173rd Airborne Brigade parachuted into a landing zone (LZ) about seven miles from the frontier in an effort to cut off the line of retreat of the 9th VLPA division. But the vertical envelopment was not very successful. Some elements of the VPLA division managed to cross safely into Cambodia, while other elements moved into concealed underground positions inside the zone and awaited their chance to seize the offensive.

After the large American units had turned in other directions, on 22 March the concealed enemy near the center of War Zone C came to the surface in order to mount a major attack on American firebase GOLD. (A firebase was a fortified artillery position used to provide support to Allied infantry within a range of several miles.) The battle to prevent GOLD from being overrun was so desperate that the defending artillerymen had to depress the barrels of their 105-mm. guns and fire directly into the ranks of the attacking troops. Such direct fire with heavy weapons against infantry is rarely seen on the modern battlefield. Eventually, a combination of the base's defense and the arrival of Allied infantry reinforcements saved GOLD and its defending garrison, and the enemy faded away as mysteriously as he had come.

The outcome of the fighting in the Central Highlands was also less than decisive in 1967. In the spring and summer, the U.S. Army's 4th Infantry Division repeatedly clashed with PAVN troops in Pleiku province, but the outcome was as indecisive as it was costly in the dense jungle along the Cambodian border. Then, as VPLA/PAVN troops shifted northward to threaten ARVN troops in Kontum province, the 2nd AFFV sent reinforcements to that area.

At the town of Dak To, twelve miles north of the province capital at Kontum City, the 1st Brigade of the 4th Infantry Division, reinforced by the 4th Battalion of the 173rd Airborne Brigade, took up defensive positions that were relatively isolated. The connecting road between Dak To and Kontum City, the latter the site of the nearest garrison to Dak To's, was narrow and winding, and passed through jungle-covered hills and mountains where the enemy could easily conceal himself. The route was so insecure that the Dak To garrison relied on its airstrip for supplies and reinforcements.

In these circumstances, the communists saw an opportunity to cut off and annihilate an American garrison. In early November, VPLA/PAVN troops appeared on the heights above the base at Dak To and began hammering its airfield with barrages of mortar shells. As the airfield began to shut down as a consequence of the shelling, the communists cut the road to Kontum City at several points. When resupply and reinforcement of the Dak To garrison by air began to fail, the Americans were forced to launch an effort to reopen its road communications, and the battle finally climaxed in a fight for Hill 875 (so-called for its height in meters), one that dominated the route and was occupied by two communist regiments.

The fight for Hill 875 went on for days as the communists repeatedly repelled attacks of U.S. and ARVN forces. Finally, after intense U.S. air attacks and artillery bombardments, the Allied forces managed to drive the communists back into Cambodia. But the cost of taking one obscure terrain objective that was soon abandoned amounted to nearly 300 Americans killed, 985 seriously wounded, and 18 missing in action. The number of casualties among the ARVN troops involved was higher still. GHQ MACV pointed out that communist casualties were even higher than the Allied, and claimed that the fight for Dak To had ended in an Allied victory. But critics noted that the two PAVN regiments involved were restructured with reinforcements in Cambodia and soon renewed the fight for the Central Highlands. The outcome at Dak To had not resolved the issue even in one locality.

THE U.S. MARINE CORPS'S WAR, 1966–67

The Marines of the 3rd MAF in the ARVN 1st Corps Tactical Zone had somewhat different problems from those of the U.S. Army during 1966–67. In April 1966, Prime Minister Cao Ky's appointment of a new and less popular ARVN commander of the 1st ARVN Corps TZ set off Buddhist riots and protests in Danang and Hue that lasted into June. General Walt had to walk a fine line in order to prevent a civil war between the Saigon government and the Buddhists while at the same time trying to wage war against the VC. In addition, the Marine efforts to implement their "ink-stain" strategy with CAPs and CACs in the villages and hamlets around both cities were hampered by Westmoreland's insistence on Marine search-and-destroy missions into the mountains to the west. The Marines fought bloody actions with PAVN troops in these remote areas, but, as Walt had predicted, they produced no permanent results.

But the greatest Marine problem had to do with the area just south of the DMZ, the de facto border between North and South Vietnam. In July 1966, the PAVN's 324B Division infiltrated through the three-mile-wide zone into Quang Tri province and established entrenched positions near the coast. Six Marine and five ARVN battalions launched a counter-offensive by sea and air against the coastal group, and still greater forces became involved as the battle extended inland. After bitter fighting that lasted on and off until October, the Allies finally drove the last of the PAVN troops out of Quang Tri province. But as the Marines were forbidden to pursue the retreating enemy into the DMZ and North Vietnam, they knew that the communists might return at any time.

In order to counter future communist invasions via the DMZ, the 3rd Marine Division established a string of combat bases roughly parallel to its southern border. This line extended from Gio Linh near the coast westward to Khe Sanh in the highlands near the Lao border. Because the base at Khe Sanh was in lightly populated mountain country, Walt garrisoned it only at Westmoreland's insistence; he would have preferred to have concentrated his overstretched forces in the low country to the east. But Westmoreland wanted Khe Sanh as a base for supporting the Army Special

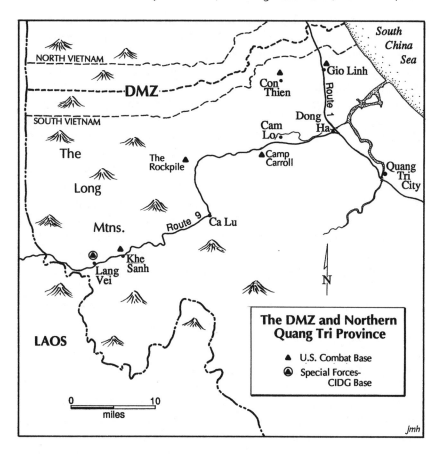

The DMZ and Northern Quang Tri Province

▲ U.S. Combat Base
◉ Special Forces–CIDG Base

Forces–CIDG camp at Lang Vei, still nearer the border with Laos, and possibly as a base of operations to cut the Ho Chi Minh Trail if he could ever get Washington to relax its prohibitions on large-scale American ground operations in Laos. On the other hand, the U.S. Army gave the Marines some relief by assuming responsibility for operations in the South Vietnamese panhandle everywhere but in the two northernmost provinces of Quang Tri and Thua Hoa, both of which remained Marine responsibilities.

The PAVN strategy against the line of Marine bases near the DMZ began to reveal itself on 27 February 1967 when its artillery in the DRV, only a few miles away, commenced a heavy shelling of Con Thien, a Marine base almost on the southern border of the DMZ. The Marines there soon found themselves in a situation not unlike that of troops in World War I. Under frequent bombardments, they were forced to stay underground or behind the protection of sandbags for long periods of time, and except for combat patrols, they had to endure a mostly static warfare that was both wearisome and nerve-wracking. Allied counter-battery fire and air strikes seemed unable to silence the enemy guns in North Vietnam for any great length of time.

Besides bombardments such as at Con Thien, the PAVN strategy encompassed frequent raids and harassments of Marine positions near the DMZ, with special attention given to Khe Sanh, the most vulnerable of the Marine outposts. On 26 April, a general battle erupted there after units of the PAVN 325C Division took possession of hills overlooking the base from the north and threatened its airfield. As Route 9 to the coast was insecure, the airfield was the base's main means of reinforcement and supply. The Marines were obliged to drive the PAVN troops off the hills through laborious and costly attacks that did not accomplish their purpose until 5 May.

The experience of the "Hill Fights" at Khe Sanh, as well as the frequent PAVN raids on the other Marine bases close to the DMZ, led Secretary McNamara to approve Project DYE MARKER, or the building of a continuous line of obstacles, mine fields, and sensors from Gio Linh westward as a shield for the Marine bases. Though DYE MARKER (informally known as the "McNamara Line") was not expected to be a perfect answer to the problem of enemy movements across the DMZ, in theory its components would kill, injure, or detect many of the PAVN infiltrators before they could do harm.

But as the Marines worked on a trial segment of DYE MARKER known as PRACTICE NINE from Gio Linh to Con Thien, the PAVN launched frequent raids to interfere with their work. And on 1 June—the same day that General Robert E. Cushman Jr. relieved General Walt of command of the 3rd MAF—PAVN artillery above the DMZ resumed its systematic hammering of Con Thien. Moreover, as June wore on, the Marine patrols from the base repeatedly encountered PAVN infantry in strength in the area. Finally, on 2 July, an American disaster occurred near Con Thien.

A reinforced Bravo Company, 1st Battalion, 9th Marine Regiment, was on patrol and a short distance from the base when it was ambushed by a PAVN regiment that had infiltrated the area undetected. The PAVN force was greatly superior in numbers to the three hundred Marines, and was able to surround them. By the time a rescue force made its way to the aid of the trapped Marines, one hundred of them had been killed and nearly two hundred of them had been severely wounded. Only twenty-eight men were able to walk back to the base unaided. Relative to the numbers involved, the fight near Con Thien ranks as one of the most costly Marine actions of the war.

Though PRACTICE NINE was finally completed by the end of Au-

gust, the plan to build the rest of DYE MARKER was abandoned as imprac-
tical. As a result, the Marines were left with an indeterminate strategy for
holding the line at the DMZ, one of the most important strategic areas of
the ROV, and one that continued to see heavy fighting during the rest of
1967.

THE SOCIAL DISLOCATIONS OF THE WAR AND THE
FAILURES OF ROV POLITICAL REFORM

While the Allies and the communists engaged each other in great and
small battles throughout the ROV, hundreds of thousands of rural Vietnamese fled to the relative safety of urban areas in order to avoid the
fighting. While they found greater safety in the cities, many were forced to
live in shantytowns on the edge of American bases, performing menial
duties for American soldiers in order to make ends meet. The strong filial
ties characteristic of the Vietnamese frayed under these conditions. Young
women sometimes became prostitutes for American soldiers in order to
survive, and there was an illicit trade with American troops in opium-based
drugs. While some American critics charged that the United States was
destroying South Vietnam while trying to save it, others worried that the
American armed forces were being slowly destroyed morally as well as
physically by the country they were trying to save.

Nor was Washington having much luck in its efforts to make the Thieu-
Ky regime in Saigon more democratic. Thieu composed a new constitution and arranged for elections in which he and Ky offered themselves for
president and vice president respectively, but the subsequent elections
were a charade. Ten candidates ran against the Thieu-Ky ticket, but there
was interference with their freedom to campaign and other electoral ir-
regularities. The Thieu-Ky ticket received 35 percent of the popular vote,
but the plurality was enough for Thieu and Ky to retain their offices.
Though Ky left the government in 1971, Thieu remained the ROV's president almost to its fall in 1975. He stayed in power by playing off the other
generals against one another and by rigging another election in 1971, but
he never really solved South Vietnam's internal problems, much less de-
mocratized his government.

OPERATION ROLLING THUNDER:
THE AIR WAR OVER NORTH VIETNAM

Washington gradually escalated the bombing of North Vietnam in
line with the Tourniquet Strategy adopted at the outset of Operation ROLL-
ING THUNDER in 1965, but for months on end the targets under attack

were all below the 19th parallel. Then, as the DRV showed no sign of ceasing its aid to the resistance in the south, the "bomb line" was extended northward, first to targets below the 20th parallel and then, in mid–1966, to those in the Red River delta, the heart of the DRV. Even then a great many targets were kept off limits. Only beginning in August 1967 were the American fighter-bombers allowed to hit targets nearer the centers of Hanoi and Haiphong. Still, great care was given to avoid hitting targets within twenty miles of the Chinese border, or hitting Soviet and Chinese cargo vessels in Haiphong harbor. The restrictions reflected President Johnson's continuing fear that a bombing incident might provoke a full-scale military intervention by the PRC or create a crisis with the Soviet Union.

The slowness with which the bombing campaign was accelerated allowed the DRV sufficient time to import a formidable air defense system from China and the USSR. As the Americans were relying on fighter-bombers, most of their attacks were launched from below 20,000 feet and at altitudes well within range of the DRV's anti-aircraft (AA) guns. This arm was greatly expanded, growing from 1,500 guns in 1965 to 8,000 guns in 1968. Some AA guns of the larger calibers (such as 100-mm. in bore diameter) were radar controlled and fired shells using the highly effective proximity fuse.

Although the American pilots could usually outfight the enemy's two hundred Soviet-supplied fighter-interceptors (and over the course of the war achieved a kill-ratio of four to one), and the nimble American aircraft could usually outmaneuver the SAM–2 surface-to-air missiles or neutralize them through SAM-suppression measures, they remained vulnerable to the AA guns. In the period from 2 March 1965 to 31 October 1968—the duration of Operation ROLLING THUNDER—a total of 922 U.S. planes were lost over the DRV. Of this total, SAMs accounted for 115 (12.5%), fighters for 55 (6%), but AA guns and ground fire from smaller automatic weapons accounted for 750 (81.5%).

The heavy American air losses over the DRV, as well as the disappointing results of the bombing under ROLLING THUNDER, were reflected in a proposal contained in a speech given by President Johnson at San Antonio, Texas, in late September 1967. Until then Johnson had insisted that the bombing of the DRV would not cease until there had been a complete and permanent suspension of the DRV's aid to the insurgents in the ROV. With his "San Antonio Formula," Johnson retreated from that position. He offered to end the bombing of the DRV indefinitely if the Hanoi government agreed to undertake "productive" peace talks at once and if it did not take advantage to improve the situation of its military forces. But the Hanoi government rejected the "San Antonio Formula," and it clung to its demand that all American bombing, and all other warlike acts against the DRV, must stop unconditionally and permanently before any sort of negotiations could begin. As 1967 drew to an end, the air war seemed as deadlocked as the ground war, and, relative to the numbers involved, about as costly.

THE TALLY SHEET FOR 1966–67

Toward the end of 1967, some critics claimed that the United States had descended into a "Vietnam quagmire," a military deadlock having no foreseeable end and carrying an unacceptable cost. They expressed the belief that despite Westmoreland's strategy of attrition, the enemy in South Vietnam was getting stronger, not weaker, and they claimed that the bombing of the DRV seemed to be having no noticeable effect on either the will or the capability of the Hanoi government to continue its support of the war in the south. Despite the PAVN casualties suffered from the bombing of the Ho Chi Minh Trail, the CIA estimated that over the two previous years a total of 120,000 PAVN troops had reached South Vietnam in a condition to fight. Allowing for casualties suffered after the troops arrived in the ROV, the CIA estimated that 100,000 combat-capable PAVN troops were still there or nearby in the communist sanctuaries in Laos and Cambodia. The CIA projected that many more PAVN troops could be expected to arrive in South Vietnam from the north during 1968.

As for the VPLA, its strength had only grown greater since 1965. Even by the conservative calculations of GHQ MAC, by late in 1967 there were a total of 241,800 such troops, divided among 117,900 in the VPLA Main Force, 86,300 in the guerrilla-militias, and 37,600 in support personnel. But according to Sam Adams, an analyst in the CIA's headquarters in Washington, the VPLA strength was much greater than MACV's figures suggested. Adams believed that Westmoreland's headquarters had erred in grossly underestimated the numbers of the VPLA guerrilla-militias. Under Adams's accounting, their numbers came not to 86,300, but to nearly 600,000 men and women. Moreover, not only were they responsible for inflicting about 20 percent of American casualties through land mines, booby traps, and sniper attacks, they provided the VPLA Main Force its replacements.

Supporting Adams's deductions were the independent estimates of Joseph Hovey, a CIA analyst in Saigon, who concluded by late in November 1967 not only that the VPLA combat effectives were far more numerous than GHQ MACV's figures suggested, but that many of the guerrilla-militias were being organized into additional units of the VPLA Main

Force for some special offensive purpose in 1968. The intelligence section of GHQ MACV disagreed with both Adams's and Hovey's estimates of the enemy's strength and intentions, and the disagreements among the members of the U.S. intelligence community led to rancorous quarrels among the parties concerned.

President Johnson was aware of these intelligence disputes, but, lest Congress and the public draw the conclusion that American strategy in Vietnam was not working, he presented only an optimistic view as to the war's progress. In order to keep Congress and the public behind his war policy, in November 1967 Johnson brought Westmoreland back to the United States so that he could personally reassure the nation. The general played his part, and duly claimed before legislators and on TV talk shows that the enemy was being worn down by irreplaceable casualties and that he could "see the end coming into view." Supporters of the war took heart from his utterances, but his upbeat remarks ill-prepared them for revelations of evidence to the contrary or for any sudden reversal of fortune. Public support was becoming so fragile that unwittingly Westmoreland raised hopes that soon would be dashed, with devastating effects on Johnson's policy.

Just as the administration's spokesmen were not candid in public about the success of the war of attrition, they issued unduly optimistic assurances about the progress of the pacification program in South Vietnam. In May 1967, President Johnson had tried to breathe new life into President Thieu's Revolutionary Development Program (RDP) by appointing Robert W. Komer to head the Civil Operations and Revolutionary Development Support (CORDS). Komer combined under his authority the hitherto scattered U.S. efforts at aiding Saigon's pacification program, and the cutting edge of CORDS was composed of its unified civil-military advisory teams in all of South Vietnam's 250 districts and 44 provinces. Among its other goals, CORDS aimed at protecting the rural population from VC terror and intimidation, and to that end Komer was made responsible for the support and training of the ROV's Popular Forces (village home guards) and the Regional Forces (the provincial militia). In a separate but parallel effort, the CIA's Operation PHOENIX sought to infiltrate local VC networks with its Vietnamese operatives. William Colby, the CIA director of PHOENIX, would later claim that over the course of the war the program "eliminated" some 27,000 covert VC agents.

But unknown to Congress and the public, toward the end of 1967 McNamara reported to the president that only marginal improvements had been made in respect to pacification. In fact, McNamara was so discouraged by all aspects of the war that he urged on Johnson a partial halt to ROLLING THUNDER in hopes of engaging Hanoi in peace talks. He also suggested that the United States should stop the build-up of its ground forces in South Vietnam and concentrate on rehabilitating and expanding the ARVN. And as McNamara himself was becoming increasingly the focus of criticism for the administration's handling of the war, he offered his resignation as secretary of defense. Though Johnson convinced McNamara to remain in his post until he could find a suitable replacement, the president resented the fact that McNamara, once a major supporter of U.S. intervention, had turned "dovish." The relations between the two men remained strained until McNamara left the Department of Defense on 29 February 1968.

THE HOME FRONT WAR AGAINST THE WAR

The early resistance to American policy in Vietnam was centered in groups that had earlier opposed official U.S. policy in other areas and on other issues, such as U.S. development of the hydrogen bomb. First tested in 1952, that weapon was many times more powerful than the bombs dropped on Hiroshima and Nagasaki. But the Soviets had acquired their own so-called H-bomb in 1953, and since then a terrifying race had been going on between the United States and the Soviet Union in developing more powerful thermonuclear weapons and better delivery systems, such as the intercontinental ballistic missile. Though a Limited Nuclear Weapon Test Ban Treaty had been negotiated by President Kennedy during his time in office, the danger of a global nuclear holocaust remained quite real.

The focus of protest groups shifted when the nascent anti-war movement began to condemn the United States for using napalm and chemical warfare agents in South Vietnam, inhibiting Vietnam's search for independence and unity, and shifting resources from social reform at home to the war in Southeast Asia. Sensing that the growing unpopularity of the draft was a point of vulnerability in the Johnson administration, in May 1964, the May 2 Movement (M–2–M) — a recently organized radical youth group — held demonstrations in San Francisco, New York, and other cities. The protesters urged men of draft age (eighteen to twenty-five) to pledge that they would not serve "in a war for the suppression of the Vietnamese struggle for national independence." Later that month, demonstrators in Washington, D.C., urged young people to protest the draft by signing a declaration of conscience.

Meanwhile, a wave of radical politics began to sweep over the nation's university and college campuses. The wave was stimulated by protests against long-standing conditions, such as racial discrimination in America, the arms race with the Soviet Union, and the "red-baiting" tactics of conservative politicians such as the late Senator Joseph McCarthy. Many antiwar dissenters were also in sympathy with a major shift in the attitudes of young people, the so-called youth counter-culture that advocated a greater commitment to open inquiry, the questioning of authority, and explorations of new forms in art, literature, music and politics. Out of idealism or sheer excitement, many young people in college and out joined the counter-culture. Over time, the counter-culture developed its own language and even its own style of music based on rock and roll. Some of the hippies, as the exemplars of this new wave were called, began to follow the advice of Timothy Leary, the dismissed Harvard professor, to drop out of conventional society and to rely on "mind-expanding" drugs for a new lifestyle. They formed their own communities, adopted bizarre styles of hair and clothing, took illegal drugs, and indulged in uninhibited sex.

But a more politically effective breed of rebels against conformity also emerged at this time. Dubbed "the New Left" by sociologist C. Wright Mills, they sought through radical politics to create an America free of poverty, war, and racial prejudice. Their movement was composed mostly of college students who saw themselves as the reforming vanguard of the Baby Boom generation (i.e., those Americans born between 1946 and 1964), and especially the fifty-three million of them who came of age during the war. The Baby Boomers composed the largest young-adult generation in the history of the country.

Among the most important groups of the New Left was the Students for a Democratic Society (SDS), whose 1962 Port Huron Statement—written by Tom Hayden—roundly condemned the policies and attitudes of post–World War II America. In 1964 the emphasis of the SDS shifted to combating America's war in Vietnam on the grounds that domestic reforms were being hindered by the war. By April 1965, the SDS was behind a march and rally against the war, both of which were protests against "the response to poverty and oppression in America with napalm and defoliation in Vietnam." Though the SDS found support from such groups as the American Friends Service Committee, a Quaker organization, and the Committee for a Sane Nuclear Policy (SANE), then the largest peace organization in the country, such anti-war coalitions proved inherently unstable. The other groups differed with the SDS on issues ranging from whether Marxists should be welcomed to the ranks of the anti-war movement to whether a peace in Vietnam was "negotiable."

Among the more conventional critics of the war was Senator J. William Fulbright (D-Ark.), chairman of the Senate's Foreign Relations Committee. In January 1966, his committee held hearings on the American intervention in Vietnam, and Fulbright questioned whether the Gulf of Tonkin Resolution had given President Johnson the authority to escalate the war. Senator Wayne Morse argued before the Committee that the intervention had been a misuse of presidential power and that U.S. forces should be withdrawn forthwith. Whether or not Johnson had acted legally, some senators began to wonder whether the American intervention had been an error. Senator Robert Kennedy (D-N.Y.), brother of the slain president, called openly for a negotiated peace in Vietnam.

Other centers of dissent were found among religious groups. The Clergy and Laymen Concerned About the War in Vietnam included such prominent clerics as the president of the Union Theological Seminary, the president of the Union of American Hebrew Congregations, and the Reverend William Sloane Coffin Jr., chaplain of Yale University. Though such leaders offered reasoned arguments against the war and appealed for support for the anti-war movements on the basis of morality, the Berrigan brothers—both Catholic priests—went much further. On one occasion, they dramatized their opposition to the war by spilling blood over the draft records of a Selective Service office in Maryland.

Still another influential center of resistance to the war was the black Southern Christian Leadership Conference, under the leadership of the Reverend Martin Luther King Jr. In the war's earlier stages, King, acknowledged as the principal leader of the black civil rights movement in America, had been ambivalent about criticizing the Johnson administration's policy toward Southeast Asia because African Americans owed Johnson a debt of gratitude for his championship of the civil rights acts of 1964–1965. Moreover, Johnson's "War on Poverty" program had directly benefited many blacks. But as more and more African Americans died on the battlefields of Vietnam, and as Johnson shifted his domestic priorities away from social reform to meet the costs of the war, King changed his stance. In a speech made on 4 April 1967, exactly a year before he was assassinated, King claimed that the Vietnam War was draining money and resources from Johnson's "War on Poverty" like a "demonic, destructive suction tube." He called for a change in American policy toward Southeast Asia, and urged his following to pressure the political establishment in that direction. King's defection from the ranks of Johnson's supporters was a heavy blow to the administration.

Even among the military professionals, there were dissenters from official policy. General James Gavin, U.S. Army, Ret., had played a leading role in originating the idea of using helicopters as a species of "sky cavalry," but he criticized Westmoreland's strategy and tactics in Vietnam and favored a return to the Enclave Strategy in some form. General David M.

Shoup, a retired commandant of the Marine Corps, had opposed American military intervention in Southeast Asia from its beginning, and he wrote a favorable foreword to Colonel James A. Donovan's scathing *Militarism, U.S.A.* In that book, Donovan, also a retired Marine officer, charged that the Cold War had produced a militarism in America that, as expressed in Vietnam, was destructive of the national interest.

Perhaps the most remarkable anti-war group was formed in 1967 by disillusioned veterans of the war itself. The Vietnam Veterans Against the War (VVAW) saw an early end to the conflict as the only justification for the year or so that each of them had been required to serve in Vietnam. The VVAW's membership numbered hardly more than a hundred individuals when it was first organized, but its numbers grew substantially as the war lengthened. More important, the VVAW's protest against the war was a more convincing argument to many at home than those of protesters who had never been near a Vietnam battlefield.

The anti-war movement was, in fact, a collection of different movements, and the very term "anti-war movement" in the singular may be misleading. Because of the variety of its parts, except for the common goal of somehow ending U.S. involvement in Vietnam, the anti-war movement was divided over so many issues that a highly centralized effort was impossible. The ethics and tactics of the movement also varied from group to group. Some protesters were peaceful and lawful; others practiced "propaganda by the deed," including assaults on police, troops, and property. And while many people in the movement were sincere and unselfish in their motivations for opposing the war, some were simply young men who wanted to avoid the draft and the dangers of military service; there were also mothers, wives, sisters, and sweethearts who did not want their men to have to face the hazards of combat; and some were men and women looking for a reason for defying authority. The influence of the anti-war movement on American public opinion is hard to estimate. Many Americans were put off by the radical tinge of some of its supporters and the extreme behavior of some of its groups. There was also the tendency of older Americans to confuse anti-war protesters with the hippie lifestyle and values, which the older generation generally abhorred. Probably the anti-war movement was less influential in changing minds than were the rising toll of American casualties (16,021 dead and 96,979 wounded by the end of 1967); the inability of the administration to win the war at an acceptable cost of blood, time, and money; and the war's deleterious effects on the nation's economy. As 1967 was ending, public opinion polls indicated that 53 percent of the public no longer approved of Johnson's handling of the war. Even the president recognized that unless this trend could be reversed, his course in Vietnam was surely moving toward defeat.

10.

JOHNSON'S WAR, IV:
THE TURNING YEAR, 1968

THE YEAR OF THE MONKEY

Even though the war would drag on for years after 1968 (or the Year of the Monkey on the Vietnamese lunar calendar), the events of that twelve-month period marked the war's turning point. The siege of Khe Sanh and the Tet Offensive would destroy any lingering confidence the American public might have had that President Johnson had acceptable solutions to the conflict in Vietnam, and public reaction to those events virtually assured that he would have no chance of reelection for another term. President Johnson himself recognized those portents, and on 31 March he announced that he was bowing out of the race for reelection in the fall and would use his remaining time in office to seek a negotiated peace. Though Johnson was unable to bring the war to an end during the remainder of his term, his announcements in March 1968 marked the beginning of a protracted American retreat from Vietnam that would end five years later.

THE COMMUNIST STRATEGY FOR 1968

After General Thanh's "smash and grab" strategy had failed to bring down the ROV in 1965, he had adopted General Giap's strategy of protracted war, that is, one of gradually wearing down American determination to continue its effort in South Vietnam. Giap preferred to follow that strategy indefinitely, for he was confident that communist persistence would outlast American patience and willingness to sacrifice, just as it had worn down the French until the climactic battle of Dienbienphu finally broke their will to continue the Indochina War. With or without a similar climactic battle with the Americans, Giap believed that sooner or later they and their Third Country allies would abandon the ROV, and without their presence the Saigon government would surely fall.

But Thanh died in the summer of 1967 (whether from disease or wounds is not clear), and his death led to a new debate in the Hanoi Politburo over what should be the communist strategy for 1968. Le Duan, a one-time organizer of the resistance in the south and by then secretary-general of the Lao Dong Party, was critical of Giap's strategy of protracted war. He argued that the PAVN/VPLA should undertake greater risks in order to bring the war to an earlier conclusion, and he favored a major offensive in 1968 aimed at the heart of the populated areas of South Vietnam. The goals of such an offensive should be to spark a popular uprising against the Saigon government, to break the will of Saigon's armed forces, to force the Americans to abandon their bombing of the DRV, and to pressure them into embracing peace talks on communist terms.

Giap had opposed Le Duan's proposals, for he thought that a major communist offensive in 1968 would be premature and likely to fail. But after Le Duan finally brought Ho Chi Minh and a majority of the Hanoi politburo over to his way of thinking, Giap turned his hand to drawing up a new plan of operations in line with the strategy dictated by the politburo. The communist offensive would take place in three phases, the first of which would begin early in 1968 with a "general offensive/general uprising." If that did not prove decisive, it would be followed by two more offensive efforts over the course of the year.

The "general offensive/general uprising" phase would begin on 30 January, the beginning of the three-day Vietnamese lunar-new-year holiday known as Tet. In past years both sides had suspended most of their operations during the holiday, and Giap believed that a major offensive at that time would catch the Allies by surprise. Some 80,000 VPLA troops, supported by 27,000 PAVN troops, would carry the main burden of this offensive.

Under Giap's plan, many places in South Vietnam were to be attacked, those in Saigon including GHQ MACV, the headquarters of the ROV joint general staff, the U.S. embassy, radio stations, airfields, and many other sensitive points. Elsewhere, the attacks would include district capitals and towns, the New Life Villages, and the Revolutionary Development Program projects. But the most important place to be attacked, and held if possible, was the old imperial capital at Hue. Because of its great symbolic importance to all Vietnamese, its capture would have a profound psychological effect.

In order to draw Allied forces from those areas in South Vietnam where the Tet Offensive would take place, Giap planned that on 21 January a sustained PAVN siege would commence against the remote Marine base at Khe Sanh near the DMZ. Giap assigned to that task two PAVN divisions (totaling 22,000 troops), one of which—the 304th Division—had led the attack on Dienbienphu in 1954. Giap hoped that its presence at Khe Sanh might help to convince GHQ MACV that Giap intended a repeat of that communist victory, and that the effort at Khe Sanh was the main communist effort for early 1968.

AMERICAN ANTICIPATIONS AND PREPARATIONS

Allied intelligence detected hints that preparations were underway for a communist offensive by both PAVN and VPLA forces early in 1968, but the PAVN's preparations near Khe Sanh drew most of Westmoreland's attention. He formed the impression that Giap hoped to annihilate a major American force at Khe Sanh just as the Viet Minh had destroyed the French garrison at Dienbienphu, and thus to break the American will to continue the war. Though General Philip B. Davidson, chief of MACV intelligence, also reported that the VPLA was planning an offensive operation of some undetermined purpose for early in 1968, Westmoreland concluded that the Viet Cong's effort was probably intended as a diversion to distract GHQ MACV's attention from the main effort at Khe Sanh. In reality, the American commander had reversed the order of importance that the communists attached to the two operations.

If the PAVN wanted to fight it out at Khe Sanh, Westmoreland was more than willing. His staff prepared Operation NIAGARA, a plan that would enlist not only the considerable firepower within the fortress, but also the artillery of other Marine bases within range of Khe Sanh. In addition, the firepower of the formidable American air forces could be placed at Khe Sanh's disposal, including that of the B–52 bombers. Finally, GHQ MACV prepared Operation CHECKERS, the provisional transfer of up to half of the one hundred or so U.S. combat battalions in South Vietnam to the far north if needed. Westmoreland believed that if the communist defeat at Khe Sanh was large enough, it might well force the enemy to the peace table for meaningful negotiations.

THE SIEGE OF KHE SANH

The Allied garrison at Khe Sanh was chiefly composed of Colonel David E. Lownds's 26th Marine Infantry Regiment, plus some minor elements from the other U.S. armed services, ARVN troops, and CIDG soldiers—

altogether about 5,000 men. The American fortress covered an area of about two square miles and included a 4,000-foot-long airstrip. The airfield was the base's main means of resupply and reinforcement, as enemy hit-and-run raids on Route 9 to the coast had made ground transportation east of Khe Sanh insecure. The outlying hills around the base were vital to its defense, and the Marines manned and fortified the most important.

Just past midnight on 21 January 1968, the battle for Khe Sanh commenced as hundreds of PAVN rockets, mortar shells, and rocket-propelled grenades rained down on the Marine position on Hill 861 South, the post especially critical to the defense of the combat base because it overlooked its airfield. A fierce battle raged for control of the hill until dawn, when the Marines there finally repelled the PAVN effort. But then a tremendous salvo of PAVN rockets struck the main base, setting off an explosion in a Marine bunker containing 1,500 tons of stored munitions. The blast swept away tents, small buildings, and even the landing lights and radio antennae around the airstrip. Following the explosion, hundreds of PAVN troops advanced from the south to drive the Marine Combined Action Company and a Popular Force unit from Khe Sanh village and to cut Route 9 further east. An ARVN company, rushed as a reinforcement from Quang Tri City in helicopters, was all but wiped out in a PAVN ambush when it landed just south of the base. Over the next few days, other helicopters brought into the base a battalion of the 9th Marines and an ARVN Ranger battalion, raising the strength of its garrison to 6,500 troops, but these were to be the last major reinforcements to reach Khe Sanh until the siege was formally raised on 8 April.

As the battle for Khe Sanh raged on, it was avidly covered by American print journalists and television commentators. They often compared the American fortress to that of the French at Dienbienphu in 1954. When in late January President Johnson began to show strain concerning the garrison's fate, Walt Rostow, Johnson's national security adviser since February 1966, suggested to General Wheeler that a positive memorandum from the Joint Chiefs of Staff might relieve his anxiety. On 29 January, Wheeler provided Johnson with a written statement that affirmed the JCS's confidence that the fortress would be held.

THE TET OFFENSIVE

The JCS's assurance regarding Khe Sanh was, however, soon offset by the beginning of the Tet Offensive. Giap had decided to delay its the beginning until 31 January, but some VPLA units did not get word of the postponement and launched their attacks prematurely on 30 January. These early attacks were fragmented and uncoordinated, but they served the communists well by confirming in Westmoreland's mind his earlier analysis that VPLA activity would be only diversionary to the main PAVN effort at Khe Sanh.

That comforting notion evaporated on 31 January when the VPLA/PAVN launched the Tet Offensive with full force. Within the first forty-eight hours, communist forces attacked thirty-six of forty-four provincial capitals, mortared or rocketed every major Allied airfield, and battled Allied soldiers in five of the country's six autonomous cities, in sixty-four district capitals, and in scores of lesser towns.

Just as American TV coverage and news commentators helped to dramatize the fighting around Khe Sanh, so they dramatized the Tet Offensive. The brief penetration of the American embassy in Saigon in the pre-dawn hours of 31 January by VC agents shocked many Americans at home, even though the dozen or so Viet Cong bent on invading the embassy were killed before they could do much harm. Then, through February and into March, the American public watched the fighting on the evening TV news night after night as the dramatic events associated with the Tet Offensive unfolded before their eyes. Coming on the heels of the as-yet-unresolved siege of Khe Sanh—and where the nearby Special Forces–CIDG base at Lang Vei was overrun by PAVN troops early in February—the recorded televised images stunned many Americans. Some people formed the impression that the whole Allied position in South Vietnam was dissolving.

In reality, the Marines at Khe Sanh were holding their ground, and while the Tet Offensive inflicted a real setback to the pacification program in rural areas, most of the attacks on large centers, such as Saigon, were soon repelled. There was no general uprising of the population to support the communists, and only at Hue did the enemy seize part of a major city and hold it for an extended period of time. But, besides the ongoing siege at Khe Sanh, it was the fighting at Hue—a city of 140,000 people and the third largest in South Vietnam—that most held the American public's attention.

Prior to 30 January, perhaps 5,000 disguised VPLA/PAVN troops in small groups had infiltrated through the ARVN 1st Division's defenses around the city, using as their cover the annual migration into Hue for the celebration of Tet. Their first goal was to seize the lightly defended Citadel, the enormous masonry fortress built by Emperor Gia Long early in the nineteenth century, by a coordinated *coup de main* on the night of 30–31 January. The Citadel's thick walls enclosed an area of two square miles, and once the mixture of VPLA and PAVN troops were ensconced there they would be difficult to root out.

Exploiting the element of surprise, the VPLA/PAVN troops managed to occupy most of the Citadel's grounds on the night of 30–31 January. They set up their command center in the Imperial Palace at the southern end of the fortress, and by dawn on 31 January the banner of the National Liberation Front was flying from the King's Knight, a massive tower 123 feet tall, the Citadel's dominating feature. The Allies just managed to retain a foothold within the Citadel at the northeast corner of the grounds, where were located the headquarters of the ARVN 1st Division and the U.S. Advisers Compound.

The surprise occupation of most of the Citadel's grounds led to a disorganized Allied response both at the Citadel and throughout Hue, and in consequence the communists were able to seize large sections of the city. They rounded up Vietnamese classified as "enemies of the people" (i.e., in some way associated with the Saigon regime) and even some American civilians, and, before the city was surrounded by Allied troops, they marched their prisoners into the back country and there murdered approximately 2,800 of them. The one American victim was an officer of the U.S. Information Service.

Then when the Allied troops attempted to repossess the occupied parts of Hue, they met with such intense resistance that some districts had to be retaken block by block, building by building, and even room by room. The task was made harder by the fact that the original enemy force had been reinforced by some 7,000 troops coming through the Au Shau valley to the southwest of Hue and by infiltration from the north. The recapture of the communist-occupied parts of Hue required nearly a month of fighting and involved three battalions of the U.S. 1st Marine Division, plus eleven ARVN and South Vietnamese marine battalions.

Supported by heavy artillery, tactical air strikes, and naval gunfire, the Allied forces finally closed in on the Citadel, the enemy's chosen place for a last stand. After hard fighting on 25 February, the Palace of Perfect Peace was retaken. The next day the commander of the 1st ARVN Corps Tactical Zone declared that Hue was officially secured. Among the city's ruins lay some 8,000 VPLA/PAVN dead, but Allied military and civilian casualties also numbered in the many thousands.

By early in March, the worst of the fighting in the Tet Offensive and at Khe Sanh was over. Westmoreland claimed that the Allies had inflicted 15,000 casualties (perhaps 5,000 dead) on the PAVN at Khe Sanh and that a further 37,000 enemy troops had been killed and many more wounded in the Tet Offensive. But 4,778 Americans and some 5,000 ARVN and other Allied troops had died since 1 January, and for every fatality there were two or more wounded soldiers.

But even more damaging to the Johnson administration than the Allied casualties was the fact that the siege of Khe Sanh and the Tet Offensive had blasted the last public confidence in America that the serious fighting in Vietnam was almost over. Though Westmoreland claimed that the communist efforts represented the "last gasp" of a losing cause, few Americans believed him, and along with the loss of Westmoreland's credibility went that of President Johnson. The events in the first months of 1968 confirmed the growing public hostility to the war, or at least to the way the war was being waged.

THE CRISIS OVER THE 206,000-TROOP REQUEST

Matters were made worse for President Johnson as a result of a debate over, and a public misunderstanding of, Westmoreland's request for reinforcements during the Tet Offensive. The MACV commander was still unsure of the outcome as late as 11 February, when he requested that 10,500 troops of the 82nd Airborne Division, the last complete division still held in strategic reserve in the United States, be rushed to the ROV. But as February continued to unfold and the tide of the battle turned in favor of the Allies, Westmoreland believed that if he were given still further reinforcements, he could exploit the enemy's heavy losses in order to mount an effective counter-offensive. He also wanted permission for MACV to attempt to drive the enemy from their border sanctuaries in Cambodia and to cut the Ho Chi Minh Trail by a thrust into Laos.

After Westmoreland's proposals were received in Washington, they excited an intense debate in President Johnson's councils. Johnson would not agree to an expansion of the war by invasions of Laos or Cambodia, but he was undecided about a large troop reinforcement for further operations in Vietnam. General Earle Wheeler, chairman of the JCS, flew to Saigon on 23 February for a two-day conference with Westmoreland, and by the end of the conference he had reached agreement with the MACV commander that he would recommend to Johnson a mobilization of 206,000 reserve and National Guard troops. Of these troops, 108,000 would be sent to South Vietnam, and the rest would be used to fill the almost depleted strategic reserve in the United States.

Upon returning to Washington on 28 February, Wheeler held a briefing for the president and his advisers regarding his conference with Westmoreland. However, he presented the 206,000-troop request in different terms than those discussed with the MACV commander. Wheeler emphasized not the opportunity that Westmoreland saw for exploiting the enemy's heavy casualties suffered at Khe Sanh and during the Tet Offensive, but the danger to the Allied position posed by further communist offensives if MACV was not heavily reinforced. Wheeler declared that the Tet Offensive had been a very near thing, the enemy had the will and capability to continue his attacks throughout the ROV, and even the outcome at Khe Sanh was still in doubt. Hence, many more American troops were urgently needed both to fight in Vietnam and to refurbish the strategic reserve.

Among the people at Wheeler's briefing was Clark Clifford, McNamara's designated successor as secretary of defense. He would not formally take up his new post until 1 March, when McNamara would become head of the World Bank, but he had been sitting in on all important meetings at the Pentagon since December. Johnson had been delighted when Clifford had agreed to succeed McNamara, for he was a long-time Johnson associate and a power in the Democratic Party, and he had played a part in the conversion of the old War and Navy Departments to a unified Department of Defense in the late 1940s. He seemed well qualified to deal with defense matters.

Clifford was puzzled by Wheeler's report on 28 February. Its tenor clashed with that of Westmoreland's cables, which indicated that the worst of the Tet Offensive was over and that the Marine grip on Khe Sanh was secure. Clifford also knew that anti-war sentiment was climbing to new highs at home and that the public would not welcome a general mobilization and a large troop increase in Vietnam. Even the president had been shaken on the evening of 27 February when Walter Cronkite—the influential CBS correspondent who had just returned from South Vietnam—told his TV viewers that the war was at a hopeless stalemate and a negotiated peace was the only way out. Until then Johnson had counted Cronkite as one of his supporters on Vietnam.

After Wheeler's briefing, Johnson appointed Clifford to head an interdepartmental task force to study the Wheeler-Westmoreland proposals for mobilizing more troops for Vietnam. As the work proceeded, Clifford became increasingly skeptical of the proposals. The mobilization of 206,000 more troops would cost the government $10 billion at a time when the budget was already severely strained. In order to get Congress to go along with the added expense, President Johnson would have to cut funds for domestic programs by 25 percent and perhaps reduce funding for other military programs and foreign aid as well.

Moreover, Clifford was distressed by the fact that the JCS could think of no plan to win the war—save continuing the strategy of attrition—unless the administration was willing to relax the geographical restrictions on MACV in regard to Laos, allow intensification of the bombing of North Vietnam, and permit a tight naval blockade of its coasts. Clifford thought that these possibilities were foreclosed by rising public negativism toward the war and the president's ever-present fear of provoking massive Chinese intervention with Soviet support.

By the time Clifford delivered his recommendations to the president on 4 March, he was convinced that the pursuit of victory in South Vietnam as envisaged since 1965 was no longer practical. At the same time, however, he was also convinced that there was no danger of an imminent Allied collapse in South Vietnam. He therefore proposed a modest further deployment to the ROV of only 22,000 troops in addition to those already promised Westmoreland for 1968. And instead of a further major escalation of American force-levels in the ROV, he urged on the president an expansion of ARVN forces with American war matériel, a change in U.S. bombing strategy, and a very limited mobilization of the reserves and the National Guard.

Johnson made no public announcement of his intentions as he pondered the conflicting sets of recommendations, but meanwhile events went beyond his control. After a garbled account of the Wheeler-Westmoreland plan was "leaked" from the Pentagon to the *New York Times*, the newspaper published a story on 9 March that stated that Westmoreland had requested 206,000 more American troops be sent to Vietnam and that the administration was considering a general mobilization of the reserves and National Guard in order to meet his request. Further, the article claimed that a stepped-up draft, a tax increase, and a further imbalance in foreign trade would be some of the consequences.

Once the story in the *Times* was picked up by the rest of the news media, a storm of criticism fell on the administration. Critics demanded to know why Westmoreland needed an additional 206,000 American troops in South Vietnam if his victory over the enemy in the Tet Offensive was as great as he claimed. And as for a mobilization for a wider war, many people had decided that America had already done enough for South Vietnam. The proposed measures, and their ramifications, went beyond anything they could support.

JOHNSON ABANDONS THE PURSUIT OF VICTORY AND REELECTION

The massive criticism of the Johnson administration over the 206,000-troop issue came just two days before the Democratic primary election in New Hampshire on 12 March, the first in the presidential election year of 1968. Johnson was shocked when Senator Eugene McCarthy (D-Minn.), relatively unknown outside his state and running on an anti-war platform, came within a few hundred votes of defeating the president for the renomination of his party in New Hampshire. Some political experts interpreted the New Hampshire vote as one for abandoning the war, while others interpreted it as a vote of protest against Johnson's purported "no-win, no-end strategy." But no matter how the vote was interpreted, the experts agreed that Johnson was in deep political trouble.

Four days after the New Hampshire primary, Robert Kennedy announced his candidacy for the Democratic nomination on a peace platform, and later in the month a resolution in the House of Representatives, sponsored by nearly a third of its membership, called for a congressional investigation of the administration's conduct of the war. Meanwhile, President Johnson's standings in the public opinion polls plummeted. From being the popular reelected president of 1964, by 1968 Johnson had moved on to become one of the most criticized American presidents in history.

A beleaguered Johnson invited a meeting of the so-called Wise Men on 25–26 March, and asked for their recommendations for carrying on the war. The Wise Men were an unofficial group of fourteen presidential advisers drawn from former senior officials who had served in administrations as far back as Truman's. Their group included Dean Acheson, former secretary of state; General of the Army Omar Bradley, a World War II hero and a former chairman of the Joint Chiefs; General Matthew Ridgway, former U.S.-U.N. commander in Korea and former chief of staff of the Army; and Arthur Dean, chief American negotiator for the Korean armistice.

As recently as the previous November, the majority of the Wise Men had supported Johnson's policy in Vietnam, but by late in March 1968 a majority of the group had turned against it. In their representation to Johnson, they supported Dean Acheson's view that the time, resources, and domestic political support necessary to accomplish the original American military objectives in South Vietnam were no longer available. For his part, General Ridgway urged rearming and expanding the ARVN, but getting American combat forces out of South Vietnam within two years. Collectively, the Wise Men recommended changing the ground strategy, reducing or stopping the bombing of the DRV, and, if possible, bringing about an end to the war through negotiation.

The recommendations of the Wise Men brought no pleasure to Johnson, for they amounted to a repudiation of his war policy, but they influenced him in making two momentous decisions. For some time Johnson's advisers had been preparing an address to be delivered over national television, and, as related by Harry McPherson, Johnson's official speechwriter, the speech had started out calling for the nation to "rally round the flag" and to forge on with the war in Vietnam with a still greater effort. After the meeting of the Wise Men, the tone and substance of the speech changed. The outcome was revealed on the evening of 31 March as Johnson addressed the nation over TV.

In his speech, Johnson admitted that the American house had become bitterly divided over the war, and for that reason he had decided to seek a negotiated peace with North Vietnam. In order to induce Hanoi to negotiate, he was ordering U.S. aircraft and naval vessels to make no further attacks on the DRV, except in the area north of the DMZ, where the continuing enemy build-up directly threatened Allied forward positions. The area in which bombing would be suspended encompassed almost 90 percent of North Vietnam's population and most of its territory. Johnson then called upon President Ho Chi Minh to respond to the partial bombing halt by agreeing to negotiations to end the conflict. Finally, and in a trailer to his speech that not even his closest advisers had known about, Johnson announced, "I shall not seek, and I will not accept, the nomination of my Party for another term as your President."

While many Americans were made jubilant by Johnson's speech, and his supporters were stunned that he would not seek another term, most of the country awaited the reply from the DRV with bated breath. On 3 April, Hanoi announced that it was approaching American representatives with the object of obtaining the unconditional cessation of all U.S. bombing raids and other acts of war against North Vietnam, effectively an indirect response in favor of negotiations. A few days later, Johnson announced that the first meeting of U.S. and DRV delegations would take place at Paris early in May, and that W. Averell Harriman would lead the American delegation. At that point many people thought that America's war in Vietnam was about to come to an end.

NEGOTIATING AND FIGHTING, MAY–DECEMBER 1968

The peace delegations arrived at Paris on 10 May, but it took weeks to get them into the same room or even into agreement on the shape of the negotiating table. The Americans would not accept the presence of a separate delegation from the NLF (which restyled itself as the Provisional Revolutionary Government, or PRG), and the North Vietnamese delegation would not sit at the same table with any delegation representing the Thieu government in Saigon. Eventually, the parties settled on a round table, but only late in the year did the United States and the DRV finally agree that the Saigon government and the PRG would be formally represented from

25 January 1969 on. By then Johnson had been out of office for five days, and months had passed without substantive issues being addressed.

Meanwhile, the war went on in South Vietnam. The communists launched the second phase of Giap's offensives on 5 May, one that the Americans labeled as "Little Tet." There were numerous attacks across the country, but the ARVN and the U.S. 9th Infantry Division broke up the attack on Saigon, the one considered to be the most serious. Still the fighting was as intense in some places as it had been during the height of the Tet Offensive, and television coverage reinforced the impression among the American people that the enemy was again knocking at the gates of the most heavily defended centers in the ROV.

Most shocking to the American people was the Pentagon's announcement that over the week of 4–11 May a total of 562 Americans had been killed in action. As it turned out, the number was the highest weekly total for the war. And with about 2,000 American dead for the month, May 1968 turned out to be the bloodiest month of the war for the United States. Then, after a relative lull, a third VPLA/PAVN offensive commenced in August. Still more Americans died until the offensive was finally beaten off in October, and only then did a relative lull descend on Vietnam's battlefields.

By the end of 1968, the number of American fatalities for the year had risen to 14,650, which was nearly half of the 30,610 Americans who had died in the war since 1 January 1961. In point of fatalities, 1968 was to be the most costly year of the war for the United States. The Allies had inflicted staggering losses on the enemy (estimated at 60,000 dead and twice that many wounded), but the communist sacrifices in manpower proved to be not in vain. Well before the end of the year, increasing numbers of Americans at home were beginning to look for a way out of a conflict that they perceived to be both bloody and hopelessly mired.

ELECTION YEAR 1968: A TIME OF TROUBLES

As if the news from Vietnam were not bad enough, the United States was torn by internal conflicts in 1968. While the Reverend Martin Luther King Jr. was in Memphis, Tennessee, he fell victim to an assassin's rifle shot on 4 April. In the aftermath of King's assassination, the nation experienced the worst outbreak of arson, looting, and criminal behavior in its history. Parts of 168 cities and towns were torn asunder or burned as African Americans acted out of anger and frustration. Washington, D.C., the worst hit in the rioting, suffered over seven hundred fires. Nationwide, dozens of people were killed and 21,270 people were injured. In order to restore order, some 55,000 federal and state troops had to be sent into the streets.

And the widening racial divide was only one of the many internal troubles belaboring America in 1968. President Johnson's renunciation of a second term freed other party leaders to join Eugene McCarthy and Robert Kennedy in pursuit of the Democratic nomination, a free-for-all that threatened to divide the party. Hubert Humphrey was Johnson's vice president and heir apparent, but it was awkward for him to denounce a war that he had publicly supported before Tet. Humphrey did not declare his candidacy until 27 April, and for some time thereafter he did not make clear what changes in policy he intended to put into effect if elected. After winning primary after primary on an anti-war platform, Robert Kennedy seemed most likely to get the Democratic nomination, but just after he won the California primary, a bullet from an assassin's pistol fatally wounded him. His death on 5 June threw the Democratic Party into new confusion.

Almost from the beginning of the 1968 campaign, Richard M. Nixon was the front-runner for the Republican nomination for President. He easily won the early Republican primaries, and he would eventually select Spiro Agnew, governor of Maryland, as his running mate. Though Nixon was traditionally associated with right-wing movements, he repackaged himself for the campaign as a moderate who could bring the country together at a time of great crisis.

Moreover, the Republican Party's convention, held in July in Miami Beach, Florida, was a model of decorum. Its delegates seemed to represent the traditional, solid middle-class values held by people whom Nixon would one day describe as the "great, silent majority." The convention's televised image made a positive impression on the many older Americans tired of upheaval, unruly youth, black rioting, and the war in Vietnam. As for the war, Nixon claimed to have a secret plan that would bring about "Peace with Honor." The Republicans went away from their convention united and enthusiastic.

In contrast, the Democratic convention in August at the amphitheater in Chicago became a three-ring circus. Before the convention, the Committee to End the War, an umbrella anti-war organization led by pacifist David Dellinger and including eighty different anti-war groups, announced that 100,000 people would converge on the Chicago convention to impose an anti-war platform. Dellinger's loose organization included traditional pacifists, people who objected specifically to the war in Vietnam, the young and clean-cut supporters of Senator Eugene McCarthy, and hippies and Yippies.

The Yippies were members of the Youth International Party, and it was rumored that some of these youths were going to put the hallucinogenic drug LSD (lysergic acid diethylamide) into the Chicago water supply.

Mayor Richard J. Daley of Chicago, an old-line machine politician, took the threat to the water supply seriously and had it closely guarded. And with the assistance of the governor of Illinois and President Johnson, he also assembled 11,500 police, 5,500 National Guardsmen, and 7,500 federal troops in Chicago to maintain order and to crush any effort by extremists to storm the convention center.

Despite all the ferment, only 12,000 anti-war protesters showed up for the Democratic convention, and most of them did not belong to the extreme element. Still, that element took the limelight on the Wednesday night that Hubert Humphrey was nominated on the first ballot. When a march of 5,000 anti-war protesters to the amphitheater was blocked by two lines of police, a wild melee broke out that was televised across the nation. Americans watched truncheon-swinging police batter not only protesters but some innocent bystanders and people in a nearby hotel where all the leading candidates happened to be staying. While the riot was in progress, Senator Abraham Ribicoff (D-N.Y.) rose in the convention to denounce Chicago police brutality, and Mayor Daley's supporters replied to Ribicoff in less than respectful terms. By the time the convention broke up, many Democrats were angrier with each other than with the Republicans.

During the late summer and fall of 1968, Humphrey worked tirelessly to overcome Nixon's lead in the polls, and as the memories of the Chicago convention faded he began to close the gap by October. He improved his chances by promising to stop all bombing of North Vietnam if elected, and indirectly Johnson gave him a further boost by ordering a complete halt to Operation ROLLING THUNDER after the raids on 31 October. Humphrey was also successful in characterizing the arch-segregationist and pro-war George Wallace and his third-party running mate Curtis LeMay as the "bombsy twins." He also tried to convince the voters that they could not sensibly vote for Nixon, the vice president when America had accelerated its slide down the slippery slope of Vietnam during the Eisenhower administration.

Insofar as the Nixon-Humphrey contest was concerned, the election in early November turned out to be a "cliff-hanger." The final tally was 31,770,222 (43.4%) popular votes for Nixon, 31,267,744 votes (42.7%) for Humphrey, and 9,897,141 votes (13.5%) for Wallace. Nixon was the winner in the presidential contest, but the Democrats retained control of Congress. When Nixon took office in January 1969, his challenge was to end America's war in Vietnam without further dividing a fractured nation. If he wished to be elected to a second term, he would have to do so before the presidential election of 1972.

11.

NIXON'S WAR, I: THE STRATEGY OF WITHDRAWAL, 1969–1970

THE NIXON STRATEGY

The secret strategy that Nixon had talked about during the 1968 campaign for ending America's war in Vietnam had three facets. The first facet embodied what Nixon called his "madman pose," or the threat that he would take drastic action against North Vietnam, and against countries that supported North Vietnam, if the DRV did not become more reasonable about peace terms. Nixon was banking on his reputation as an aggressive anticommunist who might take almost any action to gain his ends.

The second facet was "linkage," or linking progress in improving relations with the Soviet Union to the latter's success in influencing North Vietnam to take more moderate positions in peace talks. Under Chairman Leonid Brezhnev, the Soviet Union had been anxious to cap the expensive strategic arms race with a strategic arms limitation treaty (SALT), and Nixon believed that the Soviets would put their interests ahead of those of North Vietnam.

The final facet was not very different from Robert McNamara's proposal, repeated by Clark Clifford, to President Johnson that the main burden of the war should be shifted to an expanded and more capable ARVN while the American and Third Country combat forces in South Vietnam were gradually withdrawn. Melvin Laird, a former Republican congressman and the new secretary of defense, called this facet "Vietnamization," and it underscored the importance that the administration attached to reducing American exposure to casualties in order to keep the public behind Nixon's policy in Vietnam.

THE BOMBING OF CAMBODIA, HAMBURGER HILL,
AND THE BEGINNING OF WITHDRAWAL

In order to prevent a catastrophe overtaking the Allied forces during the process of Vietnamization, Nixon took military risks, both legal and illegal. Legally, he continued Operation COMMANDO HUNT, the intensified air attack on the Ho Chi Minh Trail in Laos that President Johnson had begun on 15 November 1968 after he halted Operation ROLLING THUNDER. And though Johnson had suspended ROLLING THUNDER, he had authorized so-called protective reaction strikes on North Vietnamese air defenses whenever they posed a threat to American armed reconnaissance flights over the DRV. Nixon kept this policy in effect as well.

But, although he had no legal authority to do so, in March 1969 Nixon ordered Operation MENU to commence. MENU was a program of secret B–52 raids against the VPLA/PAVN sanctuaries in Cambodia, carried out in part as a retaliation for the policy of Prince Norodom Sihanouk's government. The prince's government looked the other way as at the port of Sihanoukville (Sompong Som) Soviet freighters unloaded war matériel destined for the Cambodian sanctuaries of the VPLA/PAVN. But Sihanouk was caught in an impossible situation. He feared that if he did not cooperate with the communists, the North Vietnamese might support the Khmer Rouge against his government and thus draw Cambodia either directly into the war in South Vietnam or into a civil war.

The secret bombing campaign against Cambodia became exposed in May 1970, when a former Air Force major alerted a U.S. senator to the fact that false targeting reports were being filed to make it appear that all ARC LIGHT bombing (B–52 tactical raids) was being conducted inside the borders of South Vietnam. When the *New York Times* got wind of Operation MENU, it revealed the B–52 attacks on Cambodia to the public. Expecting an outcry, Nixon suspended the raids on 26 May. But when the article failed to arouse a protest and Congress took no action, Nixon not only ordered the B–52 raids to resume, he permitted some of them to go even deeper into Cambodia than its border areas.

THE REVISED GROUND STRATEGY

General Creighton Abrams had taken over from Westmoreland as COMUSMACV in June 1968 after the latter had been appointed to succeed retiring General Harold K. Johnson as the Army's chief of staff. In line with Nixon's need to reduce American casualties, Abrams slowly merged the search-and-destroy tactics of the past with new programs of pacification and territorial security in South Vietnam. Under this strategy, GHQ MACV gradually shifted the emphasis from attrition warfare to the accelerated improvement and expansion of ARVN and to the defense of the ROV's more populated areas.

Yet search-and-destroy operations in the back country could not be wholly phased out lest the enemy mass enough men and supplies there to threaten more vital areas of South Vietnam, and early in his tenure Abrams still had enough forces to launch spoiling attacks into the hinterlands. (The number of U.S. troops in South Vietnam at any one time reached its peak of 543,000 while under Abram's command in April 1969— more troops than Westmoreland had at any time during his tenure as MACV's commander.) But however necessary the continuation of the search-and-destroy policy might be, it posed domestic problems for the Nixon administration. A case in point was Operation APACHE SNOW, carried out in the spring of 1969.

For a long time, the Au Shau valley, near the Lao border, had been a favorite staging area and base of supply for VPLA/PAVN troops operating in South Vietnam near Hue. Launched on 10 May, APACHE SNOW was intended to eliminate enemy forces and bases in the valley, and the Allied task force—composed of a brigade of the 101st Airborne Division, the 9th Marine Regiment, and an ARVN regiment—commenced the operation with a helicopter assault into the thick jungle on the valley's western side. While some troops of the 101st Airborne Division were probing the slopes of Ap Bia Mountain (or Hill 937 on American military maps) on 11 May, they encountered fierce resistance by two battalions of the PAVN's 29th Infantry Regiment in a well-fortified position.

After the initial American attack was repelled, further U.S. efforts to capture the position were deferred while artillery and airplanes hammered the PAVN defenses almost continuously for two days straight in hopes of "softening up" enemy resistance. But when on 13 May the 1st Battalion of the 187th Infantry Regiment tried to seize the northwest ridges of Ap Bia, the PAVN troops beat back its assault and inflicted heavy American casualties in the process. U.S. artillery and air forces then battered the enemy defenses for thirty-six hours straight before another attack was attempted by two battalions of the 501st and 506th Airborne infantries on 18 May. Though some of the American troops managed to reach the summit of Ap Bia, a PAVN counter-attack soon drove them down again. After still more preliminary artillery and aerial bombardments, on 20 May three American battalions and an ARVN battalion attacked the Ap Bia position. This time the Allies broke enemy resistance and drove the remnants of the 29th PAVN regiment across the border into Laos. But the slopes of the conquered mountain were littered with Allied as well as PAVN dead.

GHQ MACV declared Ap Bia an Allied victory because twice as many enemy casualties (2,000) had been inflicted as the Allies suffered, but some U.S. soldiers nicknamed the mountain "Hamburger Hill" because they thought they had been sent through a meat-grinder there. The press criticized Abrams for expending lives for a terrain objective that the Allied forces soon abandoned and for resorting to the same search-and-destroy tactics that critics had found so objectionable when carried out under General Westmoreland. At least in terms of domestic support, the Nixon administration could not afford many such "victories" as at Ap Bia.

Nixon diverted the public's attention from the Hamburger Hill episode on 8 June by announcing that the withdrawal of American troops from South Vietnam would commence in July with an installment of 25,000 men. The first U.S. Army combat unit chosen to be ordered home was the 3rd Battalion, 60th Infantry Regiment, 9th Infantry Division. On 8 July, the battalion was flown to McChord Air Force Base outside Seattle, Washington, paraded through the city, and then sent to Ft. Lewis for demobilization. Over the course of 1969, the 3rd Marine Division was relocated to Okinawa, and still more American and Third Country troops prepared to leave the ROV.

At the beginning of 1970, 475,200 American troops remained in South Vietnam, of whom 331,000 were Army and 55,100 were Marines, and the balance belonged to the Air Force, Navy, and Coast Guard. Some 70,300 Third Country troops, most of them South Koreans, were still in South Vietnam, but a phased withdrawal of their troops had begun as well. The number of Americans killed in action in 1969 came to 9,414, or 65 percent of the number of fatalities suffered in 1968. The cumulative total of American dead since January 1961 rose to 40,024. The Nixon administration could point to a drop in the tempo of VC activity in many provinces in South Vietnam during 1969–1970, but the communists showed no inclination to change their positions at the Paris Peace Talks, and the PAVN threat to the ROV was as great as ever.

THE MASSACRE AT MY LAI 4 AND AFTERMATH

In April 1969, a returned veteran of the war wrote to the Department of Defense and members of Congress disturbing letters, in which he claimed that fellow soldiers had told him of a major war crime perpetrated in March 1968 by troops of the 11th Brigade, 23rd Infantry Division (American) in a hamlet nicknamed "Pinkville," Quang Nai province, ARVN 1st Corps Tactical Zone. After the Pentagon identified "Pinkville" as a hamlet officially designated as My Lai 4, one close to the South China Sea, the Department of the Army launched an investigation of the allegations.

The investigation uncovered ample evidence that on 16 March 1968 an atrocity had taken place at My Lai 4 and that the crimes had been chiefly committed by soldiers of the 1st Platoon, Company C, 1st Battalion, 20th Infantry, 11th Infantry Brigade. As Army investigators reconstructed the event, during a sweep of My Lai 4, and without provocation, certain members of the 1st Platoon, Company C, had deliberately shot, bludgeoned, bayoneted, and by other means put to death between one hundred and two hundred Vietnamese men, women, and children. (The ROV province chief put the total of the murdered at 450–500 people and possibly as high as 576.) Further, the investigators alleged that the senior officers of the Americal Division knew of the crime at the time of the incident or shortly thereafter, but by failing to take action they were parties to a cover-up and guilty of dereliction of duty.

As chief of staff of the Army, Westmoreland appointed a special board of officers headed by General William R. Peers, former commander of the 4th Infantry Division, to investigate the matter of an alleged cover-up. After its investigation, the Peers Board issued such a blistering report on the behavior of the commander and his staff in the Americal Division regarding the incident that the Department of the Army subsequently imposed administrative punishments on General Samuel W. Koster, commander of the Americal Division at the time of the massacre and superintendent at West Point at the time of his relief, and on a number of other officers who were on his staff in March 1968. The Army also brought the commander of the 11th Brigade before a court-martial on the charge of dereliction of duty, but the evidence showed that he had no knowledge of the incident, and he was acquitted. As the commander of the 1st Battalion of the 11th Brigade had been killed in a helicopter crash three months after the massacre, he could not be brought to trial.

As for the actual crimes committed at My Lai 4, the Army brought charges against Captain Ernest Medina, commander of Company C; First Lieutenant William L. Calley Jr., the commander of the 1st Platoon, who was deemed most involved in the massacre; and the nine enlisted men of Calley's platoon who were still in the Army. (Twenty-five other soldiers in Calley's platoon at the time of the massacre—including Private Paul Meadlo, allegedly Calley's principal trigger-man—had been discharged from the Army and were beyond its jurisdiction.) In particular, the Army prosecutors claimed that Calley had personally killed, or caused other soldiers to kill, 102 Vietnamese men, women, and children by means of rifle fire at a drainage ditch. If true, it was the most serious U.S. atrocity exposed in the war.

At Medina's court-martial, conflicting testimony as to his whereabouts during the massacre weakened the prosecution's case and contributed to a verdict of not guilty in his case. The enlisted men of Calley's platoon put on trial were also found not guilty. But on 29 March 1971, a court-martial found Calley guilty of committing, or causing others to commit, the murder of twenty-two people at My Lai 4, and sentenced him to dismissal from the service and confinement at hard labor for life. Reviews of his case eventually caused his sentence to be reduced to a dishonorable discharge and time served under confinement. Calley was released on parole from the penitentiary at Ft. Leavenworth in November 1974.

The effects of the exposure of the atrocity at My Lai 4 were unmistakable, for its notoriety tarnished the American cause in Vietnam at home and abroad as no other event of the war had done. It also raised questions as to whether other unreported atrocities had been committed by American troops at other times and places in Vietnam. On this point, the evidence of the Vietnam Veterans Against the War (VVAW) was especially troubling.

While Calley's court-martial was taking place, the VVAW conducted its own "Winter Soldier Investigation" of atrocities in Vietnam, and over a hundred veterans voluntarily described either their own atrocious acts or those of other soldiers in Vietnam. According to Al Hubbard, the executive secretary of the VVAW, their testimony proved that the massacre at My Lai 4 was but "a minor step beyond the standard official United States policy in Indochina." The "Winter Soldier Investigation" took its name from Tom Paine's 1776 pamphlet "Common Sense," and gave an ironic twist to his contempt for the "summer soldier and the sunshine patriot."

THE DEATH OF HO CHI MINH, ANTI-WAR ACTIVITIES, AND THE DIPLOMACY OF LINKAGE

On 2 September 1969, twenty-four years to the day after his reading of Vietnam's declaration of independence in Hanoi, Ho Chi Minh died of heart disease at age seventy-nine. His mantle of leadership fell chiefly on Le Duan, Pham Van Dong, and Vo Nguyen Giap. For most of their adult lives, these men had served with Ho in the struggle to bring about a united Vietnam under a communist government, and their goals did not change with Ho's death. Moreover, as the armistice talks at Paris remained deadlocked, anti-war demonstrations in the United States began to heat up again.

The largest anti-war demonstration in 1969 was the National Moratorium on the War (NMW), conducted in a number of major cities on 15 October. The demonstration in Washington was estimated to have involved a quarter of a million people, and although some protesters destroyed property and provoked clashes with the police, for the most part the participants, which included people of all ages, acted with quiet dignity. Hence, the administration could not shrug off the NMW entirely as another tirade of irresponsible youth.

President Nixon was so alarmed by the drift in public opinion, as demonstrated by the NMW, that he tried to offset its effects in a nationally televised speech early in November. He appealed to "the great, silent majority" of Americans to support his policies in Vietnam as likely to bring about a "Peace with Honor," his 1968 campaign pledge. The tactic was apparently successful, for 71 percent of those polled after the speech took a favorable view of Nixon's policies in Vietnam, and especially that of Vietnamization. But clearly those policies had to show positive results soon if a majority of the public was to be kept in their support.

Meanwhile, William Rogers, secretary of state, and Henry Kissinger, national security adviser, were trying Nixon's diplomatic strategy of "linkage" in order to shorten the war. The essence of linkage was to connect progress in other matters of U.S.–Soviet mutual interest—such as nuclear-arms control—with progress in achieving American goals in South Vietnam. Nixon harbored the view that the Soviets could pressure the North Vietnamese into a more accommodating attitude if they saw it was in their interest to do so.

But the strategy of linkage failed in 1969, and at the beginning of 1970 Hanoi showed no signs of changing its positions at the Paris Peace Talks. Neither had Nixon's "madman pose" made much impression on either the Soviet Union or the People's Republic of China. Nixon's success in ending the war began to hinge increasingly on other diplomatic measures and the success of Vietnamization.

REFORM OF THE DRAFT

The Nixon administration could point to one aspect of the war in which there was genuine progress in 1969–1970, namely the reform of the Selective Service System. Under the Selective Service Act, a draft law enacted in 1948 and amended several times since, all able-bodied and mentally fit American males between the ages of eighteen and twenty-five were subject to two years of compulsory military service. The system had worked reasonably well during the Korean War, but the law's post-war provisions allowed General Lewis Hershey, the long-time director of the Selective Service

System, wide discretion in setting guidelines for local draft boards as to which men to call up and which to defer or exempt.

Until 1967, Hershey's guidelines followed a policy called "channeling," and permitted draft boards to defer men who were college-bound, or who had been admitted to post-graduate study at universities, on the theory they could be drafted when they graduated. But the reality was that as the war in Vietnam became increasingly unpopular, many college students found ways to delay their graduation, or else applied for admission to post-graduate schools in universities where they could expect deferments until they reached their twenty-sixth birthday and were beyond draft age. As a result of the class-bias inherent in Hershey's "channeling" policy, disproportionately more men in the lower socioeconomic orders were being summoned for military service in Vietnam, compared to those in the better-off classes.

As complaints about the unfairness of the draft increased, Hershey changed his policy to allow college deferments until age twenty-four or four years of study, whichever came first. Then the deferred men were subject to the draft unless they either had joined the Reserve Officers Training Corps (ROTC) in college or university and accepted a commission in the armed forces upon graduation or joined the Enlisted Reserve or National Guard. Deferments for post-graduate schooling were reduced to medicine and a few allied fields. Some young men gambled that their units of the Reserve or Guard would not be mobilized and found safe havens for the rest of the war—among them was a future vice president of the United States—but many more attempted to escape all military service.

Given the war's unpopularity by 1967, Hershey's changes in the guidelines in the interest of fairness only exacerbated draft evasion and defiance among the college-age population. There were student demonstrations against the ROTC and against the draft, and there were public burnings of draft-registration cards. (Under the law, all males had to register for the draft at age seventeen and a half.) Thousands of draft-eligible men fled to other countries, particularly to Canada, and increased numbers of men went "underground" in order to avoid induction. Still others used fraudulent medical grounds for exemption. Post-graduate university students were among the most determined to resist compulsory military service, and they often organized and led anti-draft demonstrations among the undergraduates. The draft was so detested that by the time Nixon took office in January 1969, more than half a million men were draft evaders.

Yet if the old system was proving to be so divisive as to be unworkable, some system of compulsory service had to be put in its place until the war in Vietnam was at an end. Otherwise, especially the Army and the Marine

Corps would not have enough men to meet their responsibilities in Southeast Asia, let alone those around the rest of the globe. Nixon and his congressional supporters decided that the best solution to the draft problem was a lottery system, and one was put into effect in January 1970.

The revised draft system involved using the birth dates of men turning eighteen that year, their birthdays drawn at random in order to establish a priority of call early in the year. Those with birthdays well down the list were less likely to be summoned at all, and a particular male's exposure in the draft pool lasted only one year. The luck of the draw (or the lack of it) more than anything else determined who would be drafted. But though the new system was fair and impartial, even it might not have been tolerated had America's war in Vietnam not been winding down. Thanks to Vietnamization, the chances of a draftee being sent to Vietnam dwindled after 1969. Nixon also took some of the onus of "militarism" off the Selective Service System by appointing Dr. Curtis Tarr, an educator, to replace General Hershey as director.

The Selective Service Act was due to expire in mid–1971, but Congress extended it for two years. As the draft was not calling up many men by then, there were few protests. In mid–1973, a few months after U.S. troops had been withdrawn from Vietnam, the Selective Service Act expired, and it was not renewed by Congress. The last American conscript completed his two years of military service in 1974, and since that time all service in the armed forces of the United States has been voluntary.

THE CAMBODIAN INCURSION, THE KENT STATE MASSACRE, AND THE COOPER-CHURCH AMENDMENT

Early in 1970, GHQ MACV began to uncover evidence that PAVN forces were massing in Cambodian sanctuaries such as the "Parrot's Beak" and the "Fishhook" on the borders of South Vietnam. Neither sanctuary was any great distance from Saigon. GHQ MACV also thought that the communist Central Office, South Vietnam (COSVN) was in or near the "Parrot's Beak," and for years it had wanted permission to send troops into this area in hopes of destroying COSVN itself. Though helpful, the B–52 bombing of the Cambodian border areas had not proved a substitute for a ground invasion.

Besides the urgings of the military, Nixon was also influenced by the fact that on 18 March 1970 a military coup in Phnom Penh had overthrown Sihanouk's government while the prince was visiting Russia and China in an effort to restore the neutral status of his country. The coup brought to power General Lon Nol, formerly Sihanouk's prime minister, and with him the Cambodian military in a right-leaning government. In return for the new government's active hostility to the VCLA/PAVN forces on its soil, the United States granted it diplomatic recognition and sent military supplies to the Forces Armées Nationales Khmer (FANK), the Cambodian armed forces.

In the new developments in Cambodia, Nixon, who was trying to find some way both to save South Vietnam and to de-fang the anti-war movement, thought he saw an opportunity to reverse the direction of the war in favor of the Allies. Accordingly, on 29 April, and without prior warning, 20,000 American and ARVN troops invaded the border areas of Cambodia, the limit of penetration being set at nineteen miles. On 30 April, Nixon appeared on television to explain his reasons for the Allied advance into Cambodia, and he described it as an "incursion" rather than an invasion. He justified it on the grounds of maintaining the security of American forces in South Vietnam as well as of improving the chances of the ROV's survival. He also claimed that without such demonstrations of American strength, the United States would be perceived throughout the world as a "pitiful, helpless giant."

But Nixon's old-style rhetoric had little appeal to many younger Americans, and it was especially enraging to those who had expected Nixon to get U.S. forces out of Indochina, not to get them in deeper. Opposition to the Cambodian Incursion jelled on the campuses of 2,000 American colleges and universities across the country. The most violent protest occurred at Kent State University in Ohio, where anti-war protesters burned the ROTC buildings. When local police did not seem able to restore order, Governor James Rhodes ordered troops of the Ohio National Guard to the Kent State campus. But the appearance of troops only further infuriated the protesters, and a crisis was reached on 4 May. A squad of National Guard troops fired a volley at a hostile crowd, the shots killing four youths and wounding more. Critics immediately branded the firing as the "Kent State Massacre," and it did not help matters that some of the slain and injured had been innocent students trying to make their way to classes behind the demonstrators.

The Kent State killings provoked a general public protest against Nixon's policy in Cambodia. The switchboard of the White House was besieged with calls from constituents who believed that any foreign policy that could lead to Americans shooting each other was insane. An estimated 100,000 people converged on the White House to protest Nixon's policy. Ron Ziegler, Nixon's press secretary, vainly argued before the White House press corps that when dissent turns into violence, it invites tragedy, but some professors joined ranks with the dissenting students and parents in expressing outrage that young people could be endangered by "irresponsible" soldiers and officials.

In order to allay the rising dissent, Nixon announced on 8 May that all American troops sent into Cambodia would be withdrawn no later than 30 June. But his measure of "damage control" did not satisfy Congress. During May it repealed the Gulf of Tonkin Resolution, and on 14 June senators John Cooper (R-Ky.) and Frank Church (D-Idaho) proposed an amendment to a Defense Department appropriations bill that forbade U.S. ground forces from being reintroduced to Cambodia, U.S. soldiers from advising Cambodian troops, and U.S. air forces from supporting FANK. The Cooper-Church Amendment marked the first effort by Congress to gain control over the conduct of the war through legislation. A fierce fight in Congress over the amendment followed, but it finally passed in December in modified form, and Nixon grudgingly signed it into law. The final version denied funds to the president for the purpose of sending U.S. ground forces into either Cambodia or Laos, but it omitted the limitation on the exercise of U.S. air power over either country.

As for the military effects of the Cambodian Incursion, they did not turn out to be very productive. COSVN was not located, and relatively few enemy troops were killed or captured. Some arms caches were uncovered, but clearly the majority of enemy forces had withdrawn with their arms and supplies deeper inside Cambodia until the American, and later the ARVN, troops withdrew. Still worse, the Khmer Rouge had received a tremendous boost from Lon Nol's ill-advised attempt to take on the VPLA/PAVN forces, and in their own interests, the PAVN armed as many of the Khmer Rouge as could be enlisted under the leadership of Pol Pot (real name, Solath Sar), the principal Khmer Rouge leader. And, as future events would reveal, he would seek not only to overthrow Lon Nol's government but to reshape Cambodian society through horrific measures. As for Sihanouk, he found sanctuary in the PRC, but there he had little choice but to ally his influence with the Khmer Rouge, whom the Chinese communists favored, and he became the nominal head of the Cambodian resistance movement.

THE MIXED RESULTS OF 1970

Despite the furor caused by the Cambodian Incursion and its aftermath, Nixon's plan of withdrawal from South Vietnam was proceeding on schedule. By the end of 1970, U.S. military strength in South Vietnam had been reduced to 334,600 troops, 200,000 of them in the American ground forces. Third Country forces were withdrawing as well. Although 4,221 Americans had been killed in Vietnam during the year, these fatalities were fewer than half those suffered in 1969. (The cumulative total of American fatalities in Vietnam since 1961 had risen to 44,245.) As for Vietnamization, it seemed a qualified success, but it remained to be seen if the policy could save the ROV as promised. Nixon could ill afford to disappoint the nation in this regard, yet Congress was clearly bent on limiting his freedom of action through budget measures. As a result, some of the most difficult days of America's war in Vietnam lay ahead in Nixon's presidency.

12.

NIXON'S WAR, II: THE
FINAL ROUND, 1971–1972

OPERATION LAM SON 719

At the beginning of 1971, critics of the Nixon administration clamored for a demonstration that Vietnamization was actually working and that as a result the ARVN was a match for the VPLA/PAVN forces without direct American intervention. Nixon urged President Thieu to order the ARVN to undertake an independent operation as a demonstration of its newfound self-sufficiency. The two presidents agreed that the demonstration would consist of a thrust by 17,000 ARVN troops into Laos in order to sever the Ho Chi Minh Trail at the town of Tchepone, twenty-five miles from the ROV-Lao frontier. The ROV's joint general staff named the operation LAM SON 719, after a long-ago Viet victory over the Chinese.

The ARVN expedition used the site of the old U.S. Marine base at Khe Sanh as a starting point, and commenced its advance down Route 9 into Laos on 8 February 1971. But matters went badly for the ARVN force almost from the outset. Three days into the operation and twelve miles from Tchepone, it found its way blocked by PAVN forces. Repeated ARVN efforts to break through their resistance were unsuccessful, and much to President Thieu's embarrassment, the task force remained stalled into March.

Thieu then ordered two ARVN battalions ferried by helicopters to occupy Tchepone from the air, and on 6 March an ARVN airmobile force descended on the town. But within three days PAVN troops threatened to trap it there, and, just in time on 9 March, the ARVN force was airlifted to safety. Thieu then claimed that the brief occupation of Tchepone had accomplished LAM SON 719's mission, and he ordered the stalled ARVN column on Route 9 to commence a retreat to the safety offered by the U.S. forces at the border.

But as the ARVN column withdrew, an estimated 36,000 PAVN troops attacked it in earnest. They cut off and annihilated some ARVN units, and they sent other ARVN soldiers into such a frenzy to escape that they mobbed the helicopters aiding the evacuation. Some overloaded craft left the ground with soldiers hanging from their skids. By the time the surviving elements of the task force had returned to the protection of the American forces at the border, only 9,000 out of 17,000 ARVN soldiers had escaped death or capture. But the worst of the outcome was not the failure of the expedition and the loss of nearly half its force; it was the discrediting of Vietnamization as a whole.

DANIEL ELLSBERG AND THE
PENTAGON PAPERS EPISODE

The shock of the failure of Operation LAM SON 719 had not worn off when another struck the Nixon administration. In part prompted by the disaster in South Vietnam, Daniel Ellsberg, a former official with the Department of Defense, turned over to Neil Sheehan, a reporter for the *New York Times*, photocopies of a classified document entitled "History of U.S. Decision-making Process on Vietnam, 1945–1967." The "History," soon to be better known as the "Pentagon Papers," had been authorized by Secretary of Defense Robert S. McNamara in 1967, and was intended as a classified historical study that would serve as a guide to how decisions were made regarding Vietnam and Indochina, for the information of future secretaries of defense and their advisers. Ellsberg had participated in the research and writing of the study, and in the process he had become disillusioned with the war.

On 13 June 1971, the *New York Times* began publishing excerpts from the Pentagon Papers with commentary, and the *Washington Post* soon followed suit. As Ellsberg had hoped it would, the publication had a highly negative effect on the public's perceptions of the war. Nixon was so alarmed by the public's reaction to early installments of the Pentagon Papers that he sought a permanent injunction from the courts against further publication, on grounds that their public exposure would be injurious to the national interest. In turn, the newspapers appealed the matter all the way to the U.S. Supreme Court. The Court agreed to make a speedy disposition of the case, and on 30 June it rendered its judgment. By a vote of six to three, it denied the injunction. In his concurring opinion with the majority, Associate Justice Hugo L. Black wrote that "only a free and unrestrained press can effectively expose deception in government" and that "the newspapers had nobly done that which the founders of the Republic hoped and trusted they would do."

From the information in the Pentagon Papers, critics of the war concluded that four administrations—Truman's, Eisenhower's, Kennedy's, and Johnson's—had exaggerated the American political, military, and psychological stakes in Indochina in order to get congressional and public concurrence with their policies. The critics blamed the Johnson administration for deceiving Congress in getting the Gulf of Tonkin Resolution through Congress by manipulation of the Gulf of Tonkin Incidents, and then for misleading Congress and the country as to progress of the war in Vietnam. More broadly, the critics held that since 1945 the habit of executive secrecy and manipulation of public and congressional opinion in regard to Southeast Asia on grounds of national security had become a dangerous influence on the democratic traditions of the United States and that not national security but the arrogance of those in power was at the root of the problem. They claimed that the consequence of such malfeasance was a misguided foreign policy that had cost thousands of American lives for the defense of doubtful assumptions regarding communist expansion, as well as the prolongation of an "unwinnable war" in Southeast Asia.

THE WATERGATE SCANDAL

Although the Pentagon Papers did not extend to the time frame of the Nixon administration, their publication went far to discredit the entire American intervention in Vietnam and to jeopardize Nixon's policy in the ROV. The episode also created anxiety for Nixon and his closest advisers that future disgruntled government employees might "leak" to the press information about covert and perhaps illegal operations under Nixon's administration. Such exposure might jeopardize Nixon's chances for re-election. In order to combat the danger of such "leaking," late in June 1971 Nixon created the White House Special Investigations Unit (WHSIU), or the "Plumbers," as White House insiders nicknamed its personnel.

The scope of the Plumbers' operations was soon widened from wiretapping to prevent "leaks" to include a variety of illegal activities against Nixon's enemies. They extended to such enterprises as the September 1971 break-in of the Los Angeles office of Ellsberg's psychiatrist in an attempt to find information that might discredit Ellsberg and thereby reduce the impact of the Pentagon Papers on public perceptions of the war.

But none of the Plumbers' activities was suspected of being the product of a criminal political conspiracy until after police arrested a group that had broken into the Democratic National Committee headquarters in the Watergate hotel-office complex in Washington, D.C., on the night of 17 June 1972. In the aftermath, James McCord, a Plumber and former agent of the CIA, revealed to Judge John Sirica something of the political conspiracy involved. He hinted that its origins extended to persons high in the Nixon administration. Eventually, a congressional investigation into the Watergate matter got underway, and it finally brought about impeachment proceedings that led to Nixon's resignation in August 1974. But, in the meantime, Nixon had been reelected to another four-year term, and the withdrawal of U.S. forces from Vietnam had been completed. Still, the exposure of the Watergate Scandal affected the ROV's survival by further souring the American public on the U.S. enterprise in Southeast Asia and by disillusioning people regarding the honesty of their government.

THE SINO-AMERICAN DÉTENTE AND ITS CONSEQUENCES, 1971–1972

By 1971 both Nixon and Kissinger were aware that the seeming implacable hostility of the People's Republic of China to the United States seemed to be weakening. For much of the war, Beijing had viewed the American intervention in Vietnam as both an act of Western imperialism and a potential threat to China's southern flank. But the grip of both perceptions had begun to diminish with the steady withdrawal of American troops from Southeast Asia after 1969. Moreover, and despite the myth of "monolithic communism" so uppermost in American minds, throughout the decade of the 1960s the PRC and the Soviet Union had quarreled over ideological matters and over the location of the Sino-Soviet frontier. On occasion, their differences had even led to border clashes between their armed forces.

As a consequence of the deteriorating relations between the Soviet Union and China, the government in Beijing increasingly sought better relations with the United States in order to balance off Russian power in the Far East. Chinese aid to North Vietnam in war supplies and training facilities continued as a matter of policy, but an end to the Vietnam War could be seen to be in China's interests if it was connected to a new and positive relationship with the United States. In order to exploit the new Chinese attitude, Henry Kissinger made several secret flights to Beijing for talks with Chairman Mao Tse-tung and Premier Chou En-lai. As a result of those talks, Nixon began to envision a diplomatic coup that would reflect positively on his administration, increase his chances of reelection in 1972, and perhaps positively affect the course of the war in Vietnam.

The first indication that a diplomatic revolution in the Far East was in the offing came with the end of American opposition to the PRC's membership in the United Nations and its replacement of the Republic of China (Taiwan) on the U.N. Security Council. Then, amid much fanfare, in February 1972 Richard and Pat Nixon visited China as Mao's honored guests. After Mao and Nixon conducted private conversations at Beijing, Nixon and his wife went on a triumphal tour of China. When the tour came to an end at Shanghai, a joint Sino-American communiqué was issued that pledged Washington and Beijing to cooperate in resisting "Soviet hegemony" in the Far East. The Shanghai Communiqué forged a new relationship between the United States and the PRC and robbed the original American rationalization for intervening in South Vietnam of much of its meaning.

THE EASTER OFFENSIVE AND
OPERATION LINEBACKER I, 1972

The détente between the USA and the PRC greatly alarmed the leaders in Hanoi, who feared that Beijing might sell out their interest in uniting Vietnam in order to cultivate better relations with the United States. While the Chinese made no threat of withdrawal of support following Nixon's visit, the Hanoi politburo realized that China's supply of arms and other assistance might be threatened in future. In addition, the United States and the Soviet Union were making rapid progress toward a strategic arms limitation treaty (SALT), and Hanoi's leaders could not tell what such collaboration might presage in regard to the Soviet attitude toward providing arms and diplomatic support to the DRV. The DRV's leaders remembered all too well that the Chinese and Soviets had put their interests before those of the DRV at Geneva in 1954, and they concluded that a rapid, as well as a victorious, conclusion to the war with the ROV was more pressing than heretofore.

The Hanoi government placed hope for an early, final victory over South Vietnam in the outcome of Operation NGUYEN-HUE, a PAVN offensive that General Giap had been preparing for some time. It was scheduled to begin on 30 March 1972, and was to be a much more powerful military effort than the Tet Offensive in 1968. By 1972 the PAVN was lavishly equipped with armored forces—including Chinese-supplied T–54 and T–55 tanks and Soviet-supplied PT–76 tanks—and Giap was willing to use those resources in a conventional strategy of conquest. Even though the strength of the ARVN had increased to 750,000 troops under

Vietnamization, Giap based his plan on the belief that without the support of numerous American ground forces the ARVN would collapse under the relentless pressure of conventional battle. American ground strength in South Vietnam had fallen to 90,000 troops, and most of them were support personnel, not combat troops. The circumstances augured well for a North Vietnamese victory.

On 30 March 1972, the Thursday before Easter Sunday, the PAVN offensive began with heavy artillery barrages at the DMZ. These were followed by armored and infantry attacks on the ARVN positions, the weight of the PAVN attack falling chiefly on the front from Gio Linh to Con Thien. ARVN resistance in many of the fortified posts that U.S. Marines had defended so tenaciously a few years before rapidly collapsed, and by 2 April (Easter Sunday), the PAVN advance threatened Dong Ha, the location of the old U.S. 3rd Marine Division headquarters. The communists finally captured Dong Ha and spent the rest of the month completing their conquest of Quang Tri province except Quang Tri City. Allied hopes that the communist advance would be arrested at the provincial capital evaporated on 1 May when its garrison made an ignominious retreat down Route 1 nearly to Hue in Thua Thien province. A further threat developed in the Central Highlands as the PAVN forces there launched attacks on Kontum and An Loc.

Under Operation ENHANCE, President Nixon tried to counter the communist offensive by ordering massive shipments of arms and equipment to the South Vietnamese forces, but after the fall of Quang Tri City it was clear that American aid in war matériel would not be enough to stop what the Americans now called the "Easter Offensive." Therefore, on 7 May, Nixon ordered implementation of Operation LINEBACKER, an American contingency war plan that called for U.S. naval and land-based air forces to bomb vigorously the PAVN's lines of supply running through North Vietnam's "panhandle" and to attack the port of Haiphong in order to stop the flow of supplies by ship from the Soviet Union. In addition, the U.S. Navy commenced a blockade of Haiphong with extensive mine fields. The bombing and mining of a port through which Soviet aid passed to the DRV were especially daring actions on Nixon's part because his critics claimed that they jeopardized the U.S.-Soviet SALT, scheduled for signing in Moscow later in the month. But Nixon reasoned that the treaty, much desired by Chairman Leonid Brezhnev's government, was of greater importance to the Soviet Union than getting aid through to North Vietnam, and his calculation proved correct. The Soviets did not challenge the American naval blockade, and only filed a diplomatic protest when a Soviet freighter in Haiphong harbor was accidentally damaged by an American bomb. And, on schedule, Nixon and Brezhnev signed the SALT in Moscow at the end of May.

The bombing and blockade not only greatly damaged the DRV's ability to carry on with its offensive, it heartened the South Vietnamese troops. Through May and June, they fought with greater resolution than before, and they beat off the last of the PAVN thrusts at Kontum and An Loc in July. With additional arms from the USA, an ARVN counteroffensive was mounted in August and September that recaptured Quang Tri City and Dong Ha. By then both sides were exhausted. Parts of Quang Tri province remained in PAVN hands as the fighting lulled, but as a knockout punch Giap's Operation NGUYEN-HUE had clearly miscarried. The ROV had survived his greatest effort to date.

THE PARIS NEGOTIATIONS AND OPERATION LINEBACKER II, OCTOBER–DECEMBER 1972

The failure of General Giap's Operation NGUYEN-HUE led to a main shift in communist negotiating tactics at the Paris Peace Conference. On 8 October, Le Duc Tho, chief negotiator for the communist side, proposed that the war be ended by an armistice under which the opposing Vietnamese parties would retain the territories they currently held in South Vietnam. The remaining American and Third Country forces would leave the country, all prisoners of war would be exchanged, and South Vietnam's political fate would be left to a National Council of Reconciliation and Concord (NCRC).

As the American presidential election was only a month away, the Le Duc Tho peace plan was artfully timed. Though the remaining American and Third Country troops in South Vietnam were relatively few, the war was still unfinished business for an American president who had pledged "Peace with Honor" four years earlier. Still, if the peace plan was accepted as proposed, South Vietnam would be formally partitioned between Saigon-controlled and communist-controlled areas, and some 140,000 PAVN troops would be left in the ROV. Moreover, the proposed NCRC was an undefined organization, whose actual composition could not be determined until after the armistice. If it failed to find a peaceful solution acceptable to all Vietnamese parties after American departure, the war might resume without any U.S. obligation to intervene. President Thieu was well aware of the dangers the peace plan posed to his government.

Behind the scenes, Thieu argued strongly against negotiating on the basis of the peace plan, but publicly the Nixon White House played down the differences between Saigon and Washington. Unknown to Thieu,

Kissinger and Le Duc Tho met secretly to agree on the essentials of an armistice, based on the plan, that would be signed in Paris on 31 October. On 26 October, Kissinger gave Nixon's reelection chances a major boost when he announced to the press that "peace is at hand." As it turned out, the Nixon administration hedged on signing the pact with Hanoi, but the public impression still held until election day on 7 November that an honorable peace in Vietnam had been accomplished, the ROV had been salvaged, and only minor details were still to be ironed out. Largely for those accomplishments, the American people awarded Nixon a huge victory over George McGovern, his Democratic opponent, with nearly 61 percent of the popular vote and a landslide in electoral votes.

But hardly had Nixon been reelected than the differences between Saigon and Washington became public knowledge. Thieu pressured Nixon to make major changes in the peace plan, and among his demands were that any armistice terms should include formal recognition of the legitimacy of the ROV as a separate state, formal recognition of the 17th parallel as the border between the two Vietnams, and the removal of all PAVN troops from the territory of the ROV. Though Nixon realized that such goals were unobtainable, Kissinger presented Thieu's demands at the Paris peace talks in November.

The Americans were not surprised when the DRV's and PRG's delegations at Paris reacted to Kissinger's proposed changes with indignation. The communists accused the American negotiators of bad faith in going back on terms accepted as the basis of the agreement intended for signing on 31 October, and they denounced the Saigon regime for its stance. Thieu completed the wrecking of the talks when on 12 December he publicly denounced the Le Duc Tho peace plan as a "false peace" to which he would not be a party. The next day the communist delegations walked out on the talks, claiming that they would not return as long as Thieu remained as president of the ROV.

Nixon had foreseen the possibility of a complete breakdown of negotiations, and he had prepared for that contingency with a military measure that he hoped might drive the communists back to the peace table. On 18 December, he unleashed Operation LINEBACKER II, popularly known as the "Christmas Bombing Offensive." On its first day, wave after wave of B–52 bombers—121 aircraft in all—hammered Hanoi and the port of Haiphong, marking the first time that B–52s had been sent against the heartland of the DRV. Other U.S. Air Force and naval aircraft also attacked targets in North Vietnam. Except for Christmas Day, the air effort continued without let-up, the intensity of the attacks even exceeding anything unleashed under LINEBACKER I. Though the authorized targets were military, industrial, and transportation-related in nature—and most of the population in Hanoi and Haiphong had been evacuated in anticipation of the attacks—there were inevitable civilian casualties. The DRV admitted to 1,600 killed and about 5,000 injured over eleven days of bombing, but some authorities believe the real figure was substantially higher.

The North Vietnamese struck back at their aerial attackers with an array of anti-aircraft weapons. SAM–2 missiles brought down or fatally damaged a number of the giant B–52s, and by the end of the campaign the DRV's air defenses had inflicted the loss of twenty-nine American aircraft of all types. Thirty-three American airmen were either dead or MIA, and another thirty-three had been made prisoners after being shot down. But the huge tonnage of bombs being dropped did extensive damage to the DRV, and motion pictures taken by French television crews of the North Vietnamese suffering aroused a sense of revulsion in many countries. Pope Paul VI claimed that the air offensive was inhumane and called for its end, and the bombardment re-aroused the anti-war faction in the United States.

Nevertheless, Nixon kept the pressure on, and after the raids on 29 December, Hanoi signaled that if the bombing was suspended, the communists were ready to resume talks at Paris. The return of the supposedly chastened communists to the peace table on 4 January 1973 was seen by many Americans as a triumph of U.S. air and naval power, but it remained to be seen whether the communists would make meaningful concessions in renewed negotiations. In any case, Congress was about to further limit Nixon's freedom of action in the war, and the president knew that time had about run out for America's war in Vietnam.

13.

THE PARIS PEACE ACCORDS AND THE FALL OF INDOCHINA, 1973-1975

THE PARIS PEACE ACCORDS

The American bombing of North Vietnam under Operation LINEBACK-ER II had brought the communists back to the negotiating table at Paris, but except for giving up their demand that President Thieu resign as head of the Saigon government they did not move far from their previous positions in negotiations. They were especially inflexible on the issue of partitioning South Vietnam into communist-controlled and Saigon-controlled areas, and they insisted on the continued presence of PAVN troops in the so-called liberated zones.

President Nixon's delegation was in no position to haggle over these issues. On 3–4 January 1973, the Democratic caucuses in the U.S. Senate and House of Representatives had voted by large majorities in favor of cutting off all funding for the war as soon as the U.S. troop withdrawal from South Vietnam was complete and all American prisoners of war were repatriated. If America's war in Vietnam was not ended soon, Congress threatened to take even more drastic action. Even so, President Thieu still vigorously objected to the peace plan. In order to get Thieu's acceptance of it, Nixon gave his personal promise of American air and naval support if the communists violated the armistice terms and resumed hostilities. In addition, Nixon threatened to cut off all further military and economic aid to South Vietnam if Thieu continued to block the peace process. A still reluctant South Vietnamese government finally withdrew its objections to the peace plan on 21 January.

With the ROV's objections withdrawn, agreements at Paris were rapidly reached. With the concurrence of the Saigon government and the PRG, Henry Kissinger for the United States and Le Duc Tho for the DRV initialed the twenty-three articles of the Paris Peace Accords on 23 January. Then on 27 January, the Accords were formally signed by William Rogers, the U.S. secretary of state, and by the foreign ministers of the DRV, the PRG, and the ROV. A general cease-fire went into effect throughout Vietnam on the morning of 28 January.

The major provisions of the Paris Peace Accords may be summarized as follows:

(1) The United States pledged to cease all warlike acts against the DRV, not to intervene again in the internal affairs of the ROV, and to respect the independence, sovereignty, and unity of Vietnam as recognized by the 1954 Geneva Accords. It also accepted the temporary partition of South Vietnam into zones controlled by the Saigon government and the "liberated zones" controlled by the PRG. It recognized the legality of the DRV's stationing of up to 145,000 PAVN troops in the PRG zones. The communist side pledged that so long as the Saigon regime observed the terms of the Accords, it would not attempt to unify Vietnam by force.

(2) With the exceptions of a fifty-man mission of the Office of the U.S. Defense Attaché in Saigon and 169 Marine guards stationed at the U.S. embassy there, all American and other foreign forces in South Vietnam were to be withdrawn within sixty days of the signing of the Accords. The remaining armed forces in South Vietnam—the ARVN, PAVN, and VPLA—were not to increase their troop strengths, to move from their zones, or to accept the services of foreign military advisers or military technical personnel. They were also denied additional war matériel except for the replacement of existing armaments damaged, worn out, or used up.

(3) The return of POWs and captured foreign civilians was to be carried out simultaneously with, and completed not later than, the completion of the withdrawal of foreign troops from South Vietnam. The parties to the Accords also pledged cooperation in exchanging information about those military personnel listed as MIA. When such persons were found to be deceased, the parties were to facilitate the location, exhumation, and repatriation of their remains whenever possible. The question of the return of Vietnamese civilian personnel captured and detained in South Vietnam (i.e., agents or suspected agents of the Viet Cong, and agents of the Saigon government held by the commu-

nists) was to be resolved within ninety days of the implementation of the Accords.

(4) A Council of National Reconciliation and Concord — representing the Saigon government, the PRG, and other South Vietnamese parties — was to be established within ninety days of the armistice. The CNRC was to reach agreement on free and democratic elections to determine the future of South Vietnam. The ICCS, created at Geneva in 1954, was to be responsible for supervising the elections and investigating alleged violations of the cease-fire. The reorganized membership of the ICCS would consist of Canada, Indonesia, Poland, and Hungary.

(5) All parties to the Paris Peace Accords pledged to respect the 1954 Geneva Accords on Cambodia and the 1962 Geneva Agreement on Laos and to refrain from using the territory of either country to encroach on the security of adjacent countries. Foreign powers were to end all military activities in Cambodia and Laos and to withdraw any troops, advisers, and war matériel.

(6) The United States pledged to contribute unstated sums toward defraying the costs of repairing war damage in Indochina, but the U.S. Congress would have the final say in this matter.

THE COMPLETION OF WITHDRAWAL, RETURN OF AMERICAN POWS, AND ACCOUNTING FOR MIAS

Upon the implementation of the formal cease-fire, the United States began a orderly and phased withdrawal of its remaining 23,516 troops in South Vietnam during February and March. This process was linked to the staged return of American POWs held by the communist side in Southeast Asia, all of whom supposedly had been turned over to the government in Hanoi for disposition. As the U.S. troops departed in groups from Danang and Saigon, each installment was verified by a Four Party Joint Military Commission established for the purpose. Simultaneously, the DRV's government handed over a group of American POWs to an American delegation sent to Hanoi. The former POWs were then flown out of North Vietnam on American aircraft to receiving centers in the Philippines and thence to the USA. By the time the last group of POWs had been handed over on 29 March, the total came to 591 returned prisoners, of whom 29 were civilians. In addition, the communists provided the American delegation with a list of 55 servicemen and 7 civilians who had died in captivity. When the process of withdrawal and return of American POWs was declared completed, General Frederick Weyand, who had replaced Abrams as the MACV commander in 1972, ordered the formal casing of

MACV's colors. The last American troops in Vietnam left Saigon the same day.

But though the American forces were gone from South Vietnam, there remained the question of the Americans who were listed by the Pentagon as missing in action (MIA) but who did not turn up on communist lists as alive or dead. In January 1973, the Department of Defense (DOD) listed 1,335 Americans as MIA, their fates unknown, but by the time the list was supplied to the communist side the number on it had been nearly doubled to 2,494. The DOD had increased the number of men declared as MIA by adding to the list the names of men in a category known as the KIA/BNR (Killed in Action—Body Not Recovered). It was this expanded and rather misleading list that became the basis of a popular myth in the USA that about 2,500 MIAs were possibly alive and were being held prisoner in Southeast Asia after the war.

In 1974, North Vietnam located and returned the remains of twenty-three American servicemen listed as MIA, and in the same year Corporal Robert Garwood, USMC, listed by the DOD as MIA, turned up alive. Garwood had been a POW who collaborated with his captors and feared retribution from the U.S. government if he returned to the USA in the POW exchange in 1973. He had sought, and obtained, an anonymous asylum in the DRV. He changed his mind in 1974 and voluntarily returned to the United States to face a court-martial and a dishonorable discharge from the Marine Corps. Garwood was to be the only American listed as MIA who was to be found alive after the war. Over the years the remains of other Americans who died in Vietnam have been recovered and identified, and, accordingly, the MIA list has gradually shortened. As of this writing, 1,584 names remain on the MIA list; all of them are presumed dead by the DOD.

THE AMERICAN TOLL IN VIETNAM

From January 1961 to January 1973, 3,403,100 American men and women in the military services of the United States served in Southeast Asia at one time or another. Of these, 2,594,000 actually served in South Vietnam. In January 1973, the official toll in U.S. lives lost in the line of duty in Vietnam and Southeast Asia since January 1961 was declared to be 56,962, but the number has changed repeatedly as the DOD has corrected service records and moved names from the MIA list to the list of known fatalities. Thus when the Vietnam War Memorial was dedicated on 13 November 1982 in Washington, D.C., the names of 58,132 men and 8 women were inscribed on the "Vietnam Wall." (The 8 women were among the 7,500 women in the U.S. armed forces, many of them nurses, who served in Vietnam. The total number of American women who served in Vietnam rises to about 9,500 when the personnel of organizations such as the Red Cross and the Agency for International Development are included.) Still more names have been added to the Vietnam Wall since its dedication in 1982, and as of May 1997 it bore 58,209 names. Of these, 47,343 died as the result of enemy action, and 10,797 lost their lives to such things as accidents and disease. Not listed on the Vietnam Wall are the names of 313,616 veterans who survived wounds or illness in Southeast Asia.

As of May 1997, the American casualty list for the Vietnam War reached a total of 371,825, making the conflict the nation's third most costly. It ranks after the American Civil War in both total casualties and fatalities (1861–1865: 950,000 casualties, 620,000 dead) and World War II (1941–1945: 850,000 casualties, 400,000 dead). In terms of total American casualties, more were suffered in the Vietnam War than were suffered in World War I, but far fewer of them proved fatal (1917–1918: 330,000 casualties, 115,000 fatalities). The Vietnam War ranks ahead of the Korean War in both total American casualties and fatalities (1950–1953: 254,000 casualties, 54,000 fatalities), but behind that war in MIAs (over 8,000 in Korea). There were 4,500 American MIAs in World War I and 78,000 American MIAs in World War II. Assuming that the number of MIAs in the Civil War ran into the many thousands (though the evidence is incomplete on this point), the Vietnam War ranks fifth among American wars in the MIA category. While America's war in Vietnam was a terrible conflict, by no means is it the nation's most costly to date.

THE BREAKDOWN OF THE ACCORDS AND THE RESUMPTION OF WAR IN SOUTH VIETNAM

When the armistice went into effect on 28 January 1973, the chances for a permanent peace in Vietnam were weak at best. The communists saw the Accords as a way of getting the last of the American and other foreign forces out of South Vietnam and, if the post-armistice arrangements broke down, of recommencing the war with a greater advantage over the ROV. For its part, President Thieu's government had no faith in the Paris Peace Accords as a permanent solution to the war, and it had agreed to them only under great pressure from the United States. Therefore, it surprised few people that the Vietnamese parties concerned could reach no agreement on forming a Council of National Reconciliation, or on hardly any other matters except a limited exchange of prisoners.

In consequence, fighting soon broke out among the patchwork of government- and PRG-controlled areas across South Vietnam. The ICCS peacekeepers were increasingly unable to suppress these armistice violations, and after a number of the peacekeepers were killed in a helicopter crash in 1974, the ICCS declared that South Vietnam had become too dangerous a place for its remaining 1,160 observers to carry out their duties. Without even the pretense of peacekeepers' being on the scene, full-scale war between the Saigon government and the communists ensued, and the fate of South Vietnam was to be determined on the battlefield.

Superficially, the ARVN was well prepared for a resumption of hostilities. Under Operation ENHANCE PLUS, which was completed before the armistice terms went into effect, the Nixon administration had rushed to the ROV a billion dollars worth of arms and equipment. In addition, some 7,000 American "civilian" technicians—actually U.S. military personnel temporarily separated from their armed services—were placed under contract by the Pentagon to maintain and repair the more complex of South Vietnam's military equipment, and ARVN's numerical strength had expanded to over a million men by early in 1973. But, as events were to demonstrate, more was needed than arms, equipment, and numbers in order to defeat the communist forces.

CONGRESSIONAL DOMINANCE
AND PRESIDENTIAL WEAKNESS

After the final withdrawal of U.S. forces from South Vietnam, Congress made it increasingly difficult for the administration to play much of a role in Southeast Asia. On 14 June 1973, senators Clifford Case and Frank Church offered an amendment to a State Department funding bill that banned U.S. air combat activities over any part of Indochina after 30 June. The effect of the measure would have been to end Nixon's continuing use of U.S. air power against the communist forces in Laos and Cambodia, a bombing campaign that had been going on since January regardless of the armistice in Vietnam. Nixon strongly opposed the Case-Church Amendment, but in consequence of its passage in modified form, the last U.S. air raid anywhere in Indochina was executed by B–52s against a target in Cambodia on 15 August 1973.

Then on 6 November 1973, and over Nixon's veto, Congress passed the War Powers Act, the most permanent legal consequence of the war. Under the terms of the act, an American president could commit U.S. armed forces to combat for no more than thirty days without justifying his action to Congress in writing. Unless Congress approved further action, the president was allowed to keep forces in combat for only another thirty days. On 17 December 1973, still another blow to presidential independence was inflicted when an authorization bill for foreign aid contained a ban on the use of any funds appropriated by Congress for the conduct of U.S. military operations in or over Vietnam, Laos, and Cambodia. Effectively, by the end of 1973 congressional action had vitiated any executive promises that Nixon had made to the Thieu government.

When Nixon resigned his office on 9 August 1974 in the face of probable impeachment over the Watergate Scandal, he was succeeded in office by Gerald Ford. A former Republican leader in the House of Representatives, Ford had in October 1973 succeeded Spiro Agnew as vice president after the latter had resigned in the face of charges of bribery and income-tax evasion. Ford's position as president was unusually weak, for not only had he succeeded two disgraced leaders from his own party, he had never been popularly elected to either of the two highest posts in the administration. His standing with Congress and the American people was further weakened by his grant of a full pardon to Nixon for any crimes or misdemeanors Nixon might have committed while president. Any plea that Ford might make on the behalf of South Vietnam would carry little weight with Congress.

THE FALL OF SOUTH VIETNAM, 1975

In December 1974, General Giap and the other members of Hanoi's politburo met to plan operations in the south for 1975. General Van Tien Dung, Giap's deputy and commander-in-chief of the PAVN/VPLA forces in South Vietnam, reported that an offensive then underway would soon overrun the province of Phuoc Long in Military Region III (MR-III). As the communists had long since ceased to abide by the armistice's prohibition on increased numbers of troops and armaments in the ROV, Dung expected that his forces in the south would be strong enough to launch an offensive to seize the five northern provinces of South Vietnam in 1975.

But though neither Dung nor Giap anticipated a final victory over the ROV in 1975, the trends of the war were increasingly positive for the communist side. Since the resumption of full-fledged hostilities, the ARVN had been drained of its strength by casualties and desertions, and its numerical strength had declined by 40 percent. Further, the corruption so endemic to South Vietnam had caused much of the war matériel that the Americans had lavished on the ROV to be drained away to improper uses. And when the Ford administration made no threat of armed intervention after PAVN troops overran Phuoc Binh (capital of Phuoc Long province) on 7 January 1975, its inaction removed any lingering doubts in

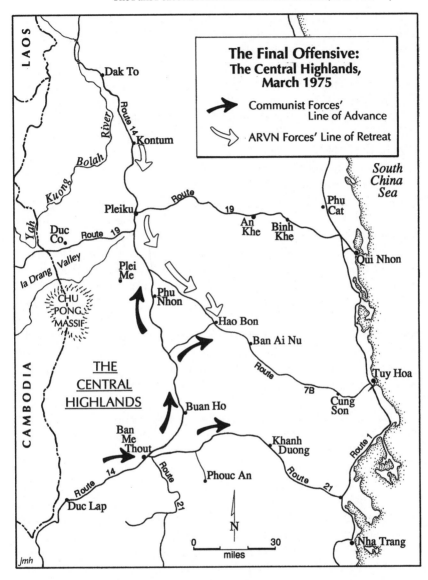

The Final Offensive:
The Central Highlands,
March 1975

Communist Forces'
Line of Advance

ARVN Forces' Line of Retreat

Hanoi as to whether the Americans would intervene militarily on the ROV's behalf.

Early in March 1975, General Dung concentrated three PAVN divisions near the town of Ban Me Thout, just south of the Darlac Plateau at the junction of Route 14 leading north to Pleiku and Route 21 leading to coastal Route 1. On 10 March, the communists launched their attack on

Ban Me Thout, and by the following morning the resistance had collapsed. The PAVN divisions then commenced a move toward Pleiku and Kontum, key centers in the Central Highlands.

Fearing that his garrisons in Pleiku and Kontum would be cut off and annihilated by the PAVN advance, President Thieu ordered his commander in the Central Highlands to withdraw them by Route 7-B to Tuy Hoa on the coast. Once there, the ARVN force could be reinforced for a counter-offensive to retake the lost territory. The ARVN column set out on 15 March, but it never arrived at Tuy Hoa. Swarms of frightened refugees accompanied it and hampered its movements, while its progress was further impeded by many downed bridges. The delays gave the PAVN's 320th Division time in which to intercept its line of march and to annihilate it in a series of battles. In the wake of the disaster on Route 7-B, the ROV's defenses in the Central Highlands collapsed altogether.

Meanwhile, six PAVN divisions in the far north of South Vietnam had commenced their attacks on the ARVN forces there. The South Vietnamese troops were soon disconcerted by the news of the collapse in the Central Highlands, and their resistance in the north gave way to a disorganized flight southward. They abandoned Quang Tri City on 19 March and then Hue on 26 March, and by the time they had fallen back to Danang the communists had blocked the way further south by capturing Tam Ky and Quang Ngai. The subsequent ARVN evacuation of Danang by aircraft and by ship became manic as thousands of civilians tried to flee as well. All order was soon lost, and many ARVN units simply dissolved in the chaos. Such soldiers as could not find air transport or space on ships simply took off their uniforms and disappeared. When PAVN troops occupied Danang on 30 March, they encountered virtually no resistance. By the end of March, most of military regions I and II had fallen into communist hands.

The victory in northern Vietnam and in the Central Highlands had been so quick and sweeping that even General Deng was surprised by the domino effect caused by his initial victory at Ban Me Thout. But Deng knew an opportunity when he saw one, and he asked Giap's permission to widen the scope of his efforts to aim at winning the war before the onset of the rainy season at the beginning of May. The rainy season might bog down his forces. After consulting with the Hanoi politburo, Giap sent his approval.

Early in April, PAVN armor, infantry, and artillery moved southward, often operating on supplies left behind by the fleeing ARVN. The ROV's cities and ports fell one after another to the communist advance, among them Dalat, Qui Nhon, Tuy Hoa, and Cam Ranh Bay (3 April). President Thieu claimed that his forces were retreating in order to regroup for a successful stand to defend Saigon and the Mekong Delta, but most observers grasped that the ROV's days were numbered. In fact, the last sustained ARVN resistance outside the capital was offered by a division at Xuan Loc, some thirty miles east of Saigon, and by the time its resistance was broken, only five of the original eighteen ARVN divisions that had existed on 10 March were still intact. In contrast, sixteen PAVN divisions, aided by numerous VPLA divisions, were swarming over the country.

With final defeat staring the ROV in the face, President Thieu abruptly resigned his post on 21 April and soon after fled to Taiwan. (Eventually, he moved his exile to France.) Thieu was succeeded in office by his aging, half-blind, and ineffectual vice president, Tran Van Huong, but after a week in office Huong also resigned. On 28 April, General Duong Van Minh—the "Big" Minh who had led the coup against Ngo Dien Diem in November 1963—took up the duties of president, but by then Saigon was surrounded by enemy forces—VPLA as well as PAVN—and the further survival of the ROV could be measured in hours.

In the days and weeks before affairs reached such a pass, Graham Martin, the American ambassador, put an optimistic face on the situation in reports he sent to Washington. He claimed repeatedly that the ARVN would rally and contain the communist advance at some point, or, at worst, the communists would end the war by negotiation and leave some remnant of the ROV intact. For fear of spreading panic, Martin refused requests that the embassy's staff and its South Vietnamese employees be evacuated, but other American agencies proceeded on their own to arrange flights out for both Americans and Vietnamese employees and their families. During the first twenty-eight days of April, 43,479 people—5,000 of them Americans—were flown out of Saigon on U.S. Air Force transports or chartered civilian airliners. After a final flight out of Ton Son Nhut airport on 29 April, however, PAVN shell fire caused the airfield to shut down, and further evacuations from the capital had to be carried out by U.S. Marine helicopters operating from an evacuation fleet that President Ford had meanwhile ordered assembled in the South China Sea.

But Operation FREQUENT WIND, the evacuation by the American fleet, commenced with just eighteen hours left in which to try to remove many thousands of people from Saigon to safety, far too little time in which to save all who wished to go. As the evacuation proceeded, U.S. Marines held off mobs before the American embassy as helicopters constantly came and went from a landing pad on the embassy roof. From there and three other places in Saigon, the helicopters managed to fly out 1,373 American evacuees, 6,422 non-Americans, and, finally, the 989 Marines sent to maintain order at the points of embarkation. Two Marines killed by PAVN shell fire are officially the last uniformed Americans to lose their lives in Vietnam.

Although half the flights between Saigon and the evacuation fleet were made in darkness, not a single passenger was lost in the aerial evacuation, and most refugees ended up on the decks of American aircraft carriers. A flotilla of thirty-two South Vietnamese navy ships also carried to sea nearly 20,000 sailors, their families, and other refugees. Thousands more South Vietnamese used every means of available transportation to escape the fall of their country. Altogether, some 130,000 South Vietnamese fled their homeland before the fall of Saigon, and about 90,000 of them eventually found a haven in the USA.

About dawn on 30 April, Ambassador Martin left the U.S. embassy by Marine helicopter for the evacuation fleet. Shortly before 8:00 A.M., the Marines on the embassy roof (officially the last Americans in Vietnam) boarded their helicopter and followed suit. By then mobs had broken into the lower stories of the embassy, and VPLA/PAVN troops were moving rapidly through the suburbs of Saigon towards its center. At mid-morning, Colonel Bui Tin led PAVN troops into Independence Palace, and there he accepted the surrender of President Minh and his cabinet. The communists put Minh on the radio to broadcast a cease-fire to any remaining South Vietnamese defenders, and by noon the "ten-thousand-day war" in Vietnam, one whose roots went as far back as 1945, was at an end.

THE FALL OF CAMBODIA AND LAOS, 1975

After the Paris Peace Accords went into effect, President Lon Nol unilaterally announced a cease-fire in the civil war in Cambodia on 29 January 1973, but the Khmer Rouge ignored it and continued their operations. Supplied and armed by the North Vietnamese, they already controlled much of the countryside. President Nixon continued to assist Lon Nol's government by sanctioning the resupply of Phnom Penh via the Mekong River—convoys of ships making regular trips bearing arms, munitions, and food—and a covert group of American advisers and technicians was sent into the country to aid in its defense. The CIA's Air America also aided FANK, Lon Nol's army, by bringing in supplies from Thailand by way of airfields still in government hands. After he took office in August 1974, President Ford continued Nixon's policy.

But matters reached a crisis point in Cambodia in January 1975. That month the Khmer Rouge succeeded in blocking the Mekong river route, leaving only Pochentong airfield as the last lifeline to Phnom Penh. From January through March, Ford's administration used civilian crews based in

Thailand to make emergency flights to the beleaguered capital, but the outcome was inevitable. Lon Nol, crippled by a stroke, resigned as president in late March, and on 1 April he fled by air to exile in Hawaii. As Saukam Khoy became acting president of the Cambodian republic, Ford ordered an evacuation fleet positioned in the Gulf of Thailand.

On 12 April 1975, the fleet launched Operation EAGLE PULL. U.S. Marine helicopters began removing 276 people from Phnom Penh, including the American embassy staff, Saukam Khoy, and other Cambodians connected to the Americans. Ambassador John G. Dean was made famous when a photograph caught him boarding his helicopter with the embassy flag under his arm. Five days later the Khmer Rouge army entered Phnom Penh and the war was over, but for most Cambodians much worse than the war lay ahead.

The royal Lao government was also on the losing end of the civil war in Laos as the Americans virtually abandoned their Secret Army in that country after the armistice in Vietnam. For many years, only the Secret Army had really stood between the communists and final victory in Laos. Negotiations between the royal Lao government and the Pathet Lao led to a peace agreement announced on 20 February 1973, but then followed intervals of renewed civil war, temporary truces, and more government retreats. This state of affairs went on through 1974. By 1975 the Pathet Lao was in position to make a bid for final victory. In June, Pathet Lao forces seized Vientiane, the administrative capital, and on 23 August they claimed control over the entire country. With the fall of Laos, the last "domino" in former French Indochina came under communist control, and with that victory the final nail was driven into the coffin of the U.S. containment policy in the region.

14.

AFTERMATH AND SUMMING UP

AFTERMATH

Vietnam

The communist victory over the Republic of Vietnam at the end of April 1975 propelled the communist Provisional Revolutionary Government into power. The PRG proceeded to blot out all reminders of the defunct ROV, even to changing the name of Saigon to Ho Chi Minh City. But while the communists executed perhaps 5,000 former South Vietnamese military and civil officials for alleged "crimes against the people," in general they avoided the "blood bath" that some Americans had feared would take place following a communist takeover. Instead, the communists packed off some 200,000 former officials and soldiers of the ROV to "reeducation centers" (forced-labor camps with communist indoctrination). Some of the prisoners in these camps died there, but 90 percent of the inmates had been freed by March 1978. A few of the senior-ranking prisoners were even treated leniently. "Big" Minh, the last president of the ROV, spent only a few weeks in a "reeducation center," and was given a minor post in the new government upon release. Of course, few other people connected to the former Saigon regime were as fortunate as Minh.

The formal union of North and South Vietnam took place in July 1976, when an all-Vietnamese national assembly adopted a constitution prepared by the Hanoi politburo. The constitution established the Socialist Republic of Vietnam (SRV), made Hanoi its capital, and recognized the communist party as the only legal political party in the country. And though the members of the PRG were given posts in the new government, the

North Vietnamese who ruled the old Democratic Republic of Vietnam held most of the power in the SRV.

The tasks facing the SRV in helping a decimated population to recover and to rebuild a war-ravaged land were formidable. Perhaps two million Vietnamese had died in consequence of the war, and another two million had suffered wounds and sickness. Yet Vietnam's population rebounded surprisingly rapidly from its wartime losses. Twenty years after the war, the SRV claimed a population in excess of sixty million people, or about double that of the two Vietnams in 1975. In contrast, Vietnam's economic recovery from the war was much slower, a condition mainly due to immense war damage, the lack of extensive foreign aid, excessive ideological management of the economy, and the U.S. government's refusal to help pay for post-war repairs. Though the Soviet Union provided the SRV with credits worth $3 billion, that sum could not pay for the repair of all war damage, let alone provide for future economic development, and for a decade after 1979 Hanoi further strained the SRV's economy by involving it in a draining war against Cambodia.

Still, as the years passed and a new generation of leaders came to power in the SRV, some of its ideologically based policies on economics, if not on politics, were loosened. A more liberal economic policy adopted in 1986 permitted a greater measure of free enterprise within the country, and changes in trade policy helped to encourage foreign companies to launch profit-making ventures in the SRV. The SRV also tried to normalize relations with the United States, its late enemy, though its efforts in that regard were rebuffed for many years.

Despite changing relations between the United States and other communist governments, the United States came only slowly to accept the outcome of the war and the SRV. In December 1978, President Jimmy Carter's Democratic administration obtained congressional assent to establishing formal diplomatic and trade relations with the People's Republic of China, but conservative circles in Congress continued to block the establishment of the same relations with the SRV. They cited as justifications the unresolved MIA issue, the SRV's arrogance in demanding war reparations, and, beginning in 1979, the SRV's aggression in Cambodia. Many Americans supported a boycott of relations with the SRV because they were not yet adjusted psychologically to the defeat in Vietnam.

But gradually the memories of the war faded and the positions of the governments in both Hanoi and Washington softened. The SRV dropped its demand for war reparations and allowed more recovery teams to enter the SRV to look for the remains of Americans, and in 1989 it withdrew its troops from Cambodia. In 1994, the Democratic administration of President William J. Clinton was able to secure congressional approval for the raising of the embargo on American trade with the SRV. Finally, in May 1997, the United States established full diplomatic relations with the Hanoi government. The first U.S. ambassador to the SRV was a former POW.

The SRV also won acceptance by the non-communist governments in Southeast Asia. In July 1997, the Association of Southeast Asian Nations (ASEAN)—originally founded in the 1960s by Indonesia, Malaysia, the Philippines, Singapore, and Thailand in order to promote peace and economic ties in the region—accepted the SRV as a member. In 1998 Hanoi was a conference center for the ASEAN. Though at this writing the SRV has one of the lowest per capita incomes of any state in Asia, given the country's energy and resources and the high degree of literacy among the Vietnamese under the SRV, the Vietnam of the future may eventually prosper in economic terms. If the political authoritarianism of the SRV gives way to greater political democracy, then the Vietnam of the future may turn out to be a far happier place than the Vietnam of the nineteenth and twentieth centuries.

Cambodia

Nothing negative in the post-war Vietnamese experience equals the disaster that befell Cambodia in the aftermath of the 1975 Khmer Rouge victory in that country. Pol Pot's government—which called itself Democratic Kampuchea (DK)—virtually emptied Cambodia's cities in an ill-conceived attempt to create a countrywide rural commune through forced labor and terror. The horrendous conditions under which people were forced to work, combined with the calculated killing off of whole classes of Cambodians and unwanted minorities (especially Vietnamese and Chams), reduced the Cambodian population of seven million people by perhaps two million between April 1975 and December 1978. Human-rights groups in the West referred to Cambodia as an "Asian Auschwitz," a reference to the infamous Nazi death camp in Poland during World War II.

Relations between DK and the SRV became increasingly strained over DK's persecution of Vietnamese in Cambodia and over border disputes. As a result, Hanoi became receptive to the idea of using Khmer Rouge defectors to help overthrow Pol Pot's regime and to set up a new Cambodian government friendlier to Vietnamese interests. On 3 December 1978, the SRV announced the creation of the Kampuchea United Front for National Salvation, and on 3 January 1979 the PAVN launched an invasion of Cambodia aimed at the overthrow of the Pol Pot regime. Pol Pot and his government fled Phnom Penh to find refuge in the Cambodian hinterland, and the PAVN occupied the Cambodian capital four days after the invasion began. Soon after, the Vietnamese installed Hung Samrin as prime minister of the People's Republic of Kampuchea (PRK), effectively making Cambodia a satellite state to the SRV. But Pol Pot and the Khmer Rouge exploited the traditional Cambodian antipathy to the Vietnamese and waged a guerrilla war against the new regime and the occupying PAVN forces. As it sapped the SRV's strength, commentators referred to it as "Vietnam's Vietnam."

The PRC sided with the Khmer Rouge in its quarrels with the SRV, and clandestinely it sent arms to aid in the Cambodian resistance. Beijing also charged Hanoi with persecuting the Hoa, the Chinese minority living in Vietnam, and they amounted to about two-thirds of the 400,000 "boat people" who fled Vietnam by sea in the late 1970s. War finally broke out between the two former communist allies when on 17 February 1979 troops of the Chinese People's Liberation Army crossed the northern border of Vietnam and commenced a giant punitive raid through the SRV's five northern provinces. The PAVN resisted the Chinese invasion, and battles were fought at Cao Bang and Lang Son, battlefield sites formerly associated with the French Indochina War. But besides its forces meeting with determined Vietnamese resistance, Beijing came under diplomatic pressure from both Washington and Moscow to end its punitive expedition. In March 1979, Beijing withdrew its troops behind China's borders, but for many years thereafter relations between China and Vietnam remained strained and even hostile.

In 1989, Hanoi finally gave up on its expensive war in Cambodia and withdrew the last of its troops behind Vietnam's frontiers. But the PRK (which by then was headed by Hun Sen) continued to fight the Khmer Rouge with arms provided by the SRV, and the war was at a standoff in 1993 when Hun Sen agreed to permit free elections under the jurisdiction of the United Nations. Though the Khmer Rouge boycotted the elections, the royalists participated and received a sizable part of the vote. In consequence, the monarchy was restored under Norodom Sihanouk as a figurehead king, and the country was ruled by a coalition government under Prince Norodom Rannaridh, Sihanouk's son, as first prime minister and Hun Sen as second prime minister.

The new government continued the war against the Khmer Rouge, but the situation changed again in June 1997, when some of Pol Pot's followers made him their prisoner and opened negotiations with the Cambodian government to hand over Pol Pot for trial for the atrocities committed under DK. In return, they asked for places in the government and in the Cambodian armed forces. These negotiations ended abruptly in July 1997 when Hun Sen charged that Prince Rannaridh was actually negotiating an alliance with the Khmer Rouge in order to oust Hun Sen and his fellow communists from the government. Hun Sen's supporters carried out a bloody coup in which many of Rannarhidh's supporters were slaughtered, though the prince himself managed to flee the country with his life.

In the coup's aftermath, Hun Sen's forces drove the Khmer Rouge guerrillas to the edge of the Thai border, but there the war stalemated again until April 1998. That month the Khmer Rouge reported that Pol Pot had died while under arrest, and they resumed tentative gestures toward a negotiated peace. During the summer, Hun Sen permitted international representatives to observe all-Cambodian elections, and again the royalists received a sizable part of the vote. Eventually, Hun Sen allowed Prince Rannarhidh to return to Cambodia, and the royalists and other Cambodian political factions—save the Khmer Rouge—were given some representation in Hun Sen's government.

After the reconstitution of the coalition government, there were wholesale defections from the Khmer Rouge, and in December 1998 the last significant guerrilla group accepted the government's terms for surrender and pardon. Thus, nearly three decades after Richard Nixon's Cambodian Incursion helped to launch the Cambodian civil war, it appears to be at an end. Over the interval, and in consequence of war and genocide, perhaps more than a third of the Cambodian population has died.

Laos

Savang Vattana, the old figurehead king of Laos, died in October 1975, whereupon the Pathet Lao abolished even the façade of the Lao monarchy. In its place they established the Lao People's Democratic Republic (LPDR), headed by Kaysone Phoumvihane. Half Lao and half Vietnamese, he was already head of the Lao People's Revolutionary Party (LPRP), the core of the Pathet Lao popular-front organization, which had ruled Laos since August 1975.

The LPDR took a grim revenge on the Lao Montagnards who had sided with the United States during the recent war. It cooperated with a PAVN extermination campaign on both sides of the Lao-Vietnamese border that reportedly cost thousands of Montagnards their lives, and the Hmong population was especially hard hit. Many more thousands of Montagnards were forced to flee to the safety of refugee camps across the Thai border. Most of these people and their descendants survive in the camps today on handouts from the United Nations and other charitable organizations.

In May 1997, representatives of the Hmong living in the United States attended a ceremony near the Vietnam War Memorial in Washington,

D.C., to unveil a small monument commemorating the 25,000 Laos who died in America's service. The plaque reads in English, "The U.S. Secret Army in the Kingdom of Laos, 1961–1975." In both the Lao and the Hmong languages, it adds, "You will never be forgotten." Sad to say, most Americans, if they ever knew of the Montagnard sacrifice, already have.

The United States

The sense of relief brought to many Americans by the withdrawal of U.S. forces from South Vietnam early in 1973 was offset by the failure of Vietnamization and the fall of South Vietnam and the rest of Indochina to the communists in 1975. They were mollified to some extent when the predicted domino effect of Indochina's fall on the rest of Southeast Asia did not occur, and in fact nearly thirty years later non-communist (though not necessarily democratic) governments remain in power in Myanmar (Burma), Thailand, Malaysia, Singapore, Indonesia, and the Philippines. Moreover, the wars among the communists in Southeast Asia after 1975 largely punctured the mythic balloon of "monolithic communism" in the mind of the American public.

Vietnam vets are unique among American war veterans in that they are associated with the only war the United States has ever lost, as well as the most internally divisive American conflict since the Civil War. During the war, soldiers and veterans were often the targets of overt anti-war sentiment, but more often the veterans suffered from the public's simple indifference to their sacrifices. In addition, some veterans blamed their post-war physical ailments on exposure to Agent ORANGE (the herbicide widely used in South Vietnam and Laos), while others laid claim to the symptoms of a post-traumatic stress syndrome (PTSS) attributed to their wartime service. Despite these problems, most veterans took up productive lives after the war, and whatever the war's merits, most of them took pride in having heeded their country's call to duty. Belatedly, the United States honored the Vietnam vets in 1991 by including them in the victory parades held for U.S. troops returning from the Persian Gulf War.

For the American nation as a whole, the period after 1973 was a time for healing and reconciliation. Opponents of the late war were somewhat mollified when President Ford issued partial amnesty to those who had illegally avoided the draft, and some draft evaders who had fled the country were allowed to return without fear of criminal prosecution. On the other hand, those who supported the war were gratified when President Ronald Reagan characterized the American effort in Vietnam as a "noble endeavor." Another sign that the country had made peace with the war was the election of William Clinton to the presidency in November 1992. As a young adult, he had both opposed the war and avoided the draft, but apparently most voters did not hold his wartime behavior against him.

Perhaps the longest-lasting psychological influence of the war on many Americans was the MIA issue. After the exchange of POWs early in 1973, the Department of Defense declared that no living Americans had been left imprisoned anywhere in Southeast Asia. As explained in the previous chapter, many men listed as MIA were really in the DOD's category of "Killed in Action/Body Not Recovered," something that the DOD never made clear to the public. The DOD's confusing accounting procedures were largely responsible for creating a foundation for rumors after 1973 that nearly 2,500 Americans were alive and were being held captive in Southeast Asia.

Rumors about live MIAs languishing in Southeast Asian prisons led to public agitation for a congressional investigation, and in 1976 a select committee undertook to find evidence that the rumors had a foundation in fact. But at the end of its labors, the committee concluded that there was no credible evidence that any such Americans existed. In some cases, the supposed "sightings" of live Americans in Vietnam and Laos turned out to be the fraudulent work of unscrupulous persons offering to locate missing men for a price. In other cases, they were sightings of people mistaken for Americans. But despite these findings, several organizations in the United States, some formed during the war, put out propaganda and memorabilia in order to keep alive public consciousness on the MIA issue.

The idea that Americans were still being held captive in Southeast Asia after the war proved to be intriguing to many people, and it helped to inspire some commercial ventures, such as the movie *Rambo*. At least one private, non-profit effort was made to use force to release prisoners supposedly held in Laos, but none were located. Some conservative politicians also found the idea of Americans languishing in Asian prisons useful in mobilizing public opinion to block the normalization of diplomatic and trade relations with the SRV. But the fact remains that since 1973 only one person listed as MIA has appeared alive, and, as explained in the previous chapter, he had not been held against his will. The probability is that none of the others listed as MIA were still alive by the end of America's war.

Other carry-overs from the era of the Vietnam War were the so-called "Vietnam Syndrome" (i.e., an excessive fear of foreign military interventions on the part of Congress and the public) and the War Powers Act passed in 1973. The War Powers Act received its first major test in 1990, when a large war loomed with Saddam Hussein's Iraq following the Iraqi invasion of Kuwait. When the United Nations appealed to its member states to provide forces to liberate Kuwait, President George Bush requested congressional authority to meet the U.N.'s call for troops. By a narrow margin of four votes in the Senate, Congress authorized Bush to commit U.S. forces to the task.

The U.S. military performance in the Persian Gulf War was conspicuously different from that in Vietnam. The Bush administration put reliance on mobilizing the civilian reserves and the National Guard in order to expand the regular forces to a wartime footing, and over 200,000 of these troops went on active duty between August 1990 and January 1991. (By way of comparison, only 35,000 such troops were mobilized over the whole of the Vietnam War.) About 100,000 reserve and Guard troops reached the area of the Persian Gulf in time to join with 400,000 American regulars in the liberation of Kuwait under Operation DESERT STORM. The quick victory achieved at a small cost in American lives supposedly laid the "Vietnam Syndrome" to rest, and it helped to restore the American public's confidence in its armed forces.

The Soviet Union

The communist victories in Indochina in 1975 were of little direct value to the Soviet Union, but Moscow and Hanoi were bound together in the postwar period by their mutual hostility to the PRC. In return for Soviet economic aid, Hanoi leased Cam Ranh Bay as a naval base to the Soviet navy, but the base—nearly isolated from Soviet territory by an unfriendly China —proved to have little strategic value. More important for the future of the Soviet Union was the Soviet leadership's failure to learn from American mistakes in Vietnam.

The Brezhnev government began to repeat those mistakes when it dispatched troops to Afghanistan in December 1979 in order to prop up an inept communist government in Kabul, which was on the losing end of a civil war with Muslim rebels. Moscow soon found that it was involved in something more than it had bargained for. Like the American forces in Vietnam, the Soviet forces in Afghanistan were soon bogged down in a costly war that they could neither win nor easily abandon. The Soviet intervention also gave President Ronald Reagan's administration an opportunity to ship arms through Pakistan to the rebels and to exploit Soviet difficulties in the region diplomatically. Both Soviet prestige and power suffered in consequence.

Finally, after enduring 35,000 Soviet dead and three times that number wounded over nearly a decade of fighting, the Soviet Union withdrew the last of its forces from Afghanistan in February 1989. The communist government left behind in Kabul fought on for a few years, but the Muslim rebels finally toppled the regime. The Afghan War has been called "Soviet

Russia's Vietnam," and its strains probably contributed to the end of Soviet domination of Eastern Europe in 1989 and perhaps hastened the demise of the Soviet Union at the end of 1991.

China

Following the death of Mao Tse-tung in 1976, a power struggle took place in the ranks of the communist leadership that was eventually won by Deng Xiaoping. When it came to economics, Deng proved to be a pragmatist. Under his leadership, the PRC moved away from a doctrinaire Marxism toward a mixed socialist and open-market economy. On a growing scale, the Chinese were allowed to practice free enterprise and to seek world trade. As a result, China's per capita wealth quadrupled over the next twenty years. By the late 1990s, China was second only to Japan as America's leading trade partner in the Far East. Such a relationship could hardly have been forecast in the time of John Foster Dulles.

On the other hand, even as Deng relaxed economic restrictions, his regime showed no sign of ending the authoritarian political nature of the PRC. His attitude became clear in June 1989, when students staged a prolonged pro-democracy demonstration in Tienanmen Square in Beijing and called for fundamental freedoms under the Chinese government. Troops of the CPLA put down the demonstration ruthlessly, and its leaders were arrested and sentenced to long prison terms. The repressive political nature of the Beijing regime has continued in the decade since, and accordingly the expansion of China's political freedoms has not matched the expansion of its economic freedoms.

Deng died early in 1997, and President Jiang Zeminh succeeded him in power. Though Jiang was no more tolerant of demands for Western-style democracy than Deng, he continued Deng's economic reforms. He so favored trade with the United States that during a visit to New York City in 1998 he was given the honor of wielding the gavel to close a daily session of the stock exchange. Such a symbolic act of Chinese reconciliation with capitalism would have been unimaginable in either China or the United States a few decades earlier. Even though Sino-American relations seem likely to be troubled from time to time, and China remains as the last great bastion of formal Marxism anywhere in the world, few observers predict any return to the Cold War between the United States and the PRC.

SUMMING UP

Some commentators have argued that the United States could have avoided America's war in Vietnam altogether if after World War II its policy makers had built on the wartime alliance with Ho Chi Minh. They claim that such a policy might have prevented both the French Indochina War and the subsequent American war in Vietnam. Certainly, no other country in the world could have done more for an independent Vietnam in the period immediately after 1945 than the United States. Archimedes Patti, Ho's OSS adviser at the end of the war, claims that Ho understood that fact and that it played a role in Ho's eagerness to get U.S. recognition and support in 1945. Some advocates even argue that Ho had the makings of an "Asian Tito," a reference to the Yugoslav communist leader who broke with Stalin in 1948 and led his country to join the camp of the "Third World."

But as attractive as this theory may be, it presupposes an America with a very different perception of the post-war world than the one that developed after 1945. As Dean Acheson, the secretary of state during much of the Truman administration, makes clear in his memoirs, in the early post-war years the United States was preoccupied with restoring France to pre-eminence in Western Europe as part of its plan for European recovery. The future well-being of France's colonies took a minor place relative to that goal. By the time the Truman administration took a greater interest in the future of Vietnam, it viewed Ho and his movement through the distortions of the Cold War, as indeed did all five administrations between 1945 and 1973. They consistently evaluated Vietnam and the rest of Indochina not on their merits and their complicated internal politics, but in terms of the U.S. struggles with the Soviet Union and (after 1949) with the People's Republic of China. The American course was set as early as 1950 with Truman's decision to recognize the French-sponsored Bao Dai government as representing legitimate nationalism in Vietnam and with his further decision to fund the French military effort against Ho's Viet Minh as if it were America's war too.

But could not have the United States changed course at the end of the Indochina War and the signing of the Geneva Accords in 1954? Perhaps a change in policy would have been possible in a less stridently anti-communist era in the United States than the early 1950s, but the Eisenhower Republicans had come to power even more determined than the Truman Democrats to contain communist expansion in the Far East. The Eisenhower-Dulles perception of the Cold War as a life-or-death struggle seemed to justify even undermining the Geneva Accords, helping Ngo Dien Diem to impose his "personalist" regime on the South Vietnamese people, and then presenting Diem's Republic of Vietnam to the American people as a bastion of democracy in Asia.

American policy was even worse guided when after Diem's policies goaded a sizable part of the population into revolt, the Eisenhower administration accepted at face value Diem's claim that the trouble was caused solely by subversion from communist North Vietnam. Under Dulles's leadership in the State Department, the Cold War language of the day was harnessed to justify U.S. policy in Southeast Asia, with little concern for its accuracy or appropriateness. In consequence, another, and a long, step was taken down the slope toward a resumption of war among the Vietnamese, a war for which the U.S. government was partly responsible and one that would ultimately become America's war.

Perhaps the last chance for the United States to have avoided a catastrophe in Vietnam occurred during Kennedy's presidency. Late in 1963 Kennedy finally realized that Diem's policies were in large measure responsible for South Vietnamese discontent and the Viet Cong insurgency, and he made the decision to begin disengaging America's fortunes from the ROV's. In retrospect, that decision was the proper one, but it was undone by the seduction of a military coup in hopes of establishing a better government in Saigon. Kennedy's support for the coup, and his pledge of continuing American support to the post-Diem government, made it more difficult for subsequent American presidents to disassociate the United States from the ROV.

After Kennedy's death in November 1963, Lyndon Johnson's administration continued to prop up a Saigon government that was never much better than a rather incompetent military dictatorship. Despite increasing American aid, the ROV's situation continued to deteriorate. Johnson further complicated the problem with his notion that the DRV was the sole force behind the insurgency and that it could be made to turn off the war in the south if proper pressure was applied to the Hanoi regime. But in order to have the legal authority to wage war in Indochina, Johnson manipulated events in the Gulf of Tonkin with lies and half-truths, and his underhanded methods to get the Gulf of Tonkin Resolution through Congress in August 1964 put his administration on unsteady ground for the future.

But even more serious were the consequences of the way that Johnson chose to take the country into a major ground war in South Vietnam. Johnson would have been wiser in July 1965 to have alerted both Congress and the American people as to the military and economic implications of his decision to intervene. Instead, he downplayed the implications of his decision, and by doing so he obscured the fact that a dramatic change in policy was taking place. His lack of candor ill served him later when he struggled to keep Congress and the public behind his war policy.

Johnson committed other mistakes, of course, not the least of which was his decision to rely primarily on the draft instead of on the civilian reserves and the National Guard in order to expand the regular forces for the war. Johnson feared to mobilize the reserves and Guard because of his memory of the "political fallout" that had attended their mobilization for the Korean War, but the political fallout from the draft for the war in Vietnam turned out to be much worse. Many young men resented being drafted to fight when most reservists and National Guard troops remained at home. Moreover, the way the draft was conducted — with class favoritism at first and then imposition on the groups most opposed to the war later — fueled opposition to both the war and the draft.

Another of Johnson's mistakes was his failure to move the country to a wartime economy in mid–1965, a measure that might have reduced some of the alienation of his constituencies later. Johnson tried to avoid domestic criticism in the short run by maintaining that the demands of the war would not detract from the momentum of social spending on his "Great Society" and "War on Poverty" programs. When his "guns and butter" policy proved unworkable and he shifted spending to meet the demands of the war, many of his supporters on domestic policy felt misled and betrayed.

Johnson seemed equally insensitive to the negative attitude of America's allies to his policy in Vietnam. Administration spokesmen claimed that unless the United States stood firm in South Vietnam, America's credibility as leader of the "Free World" would be undermined. Yet friendly governments expressed no more than grudging support for Johnson's policy in 1965, and thereafter in many countries popular opposition rose as the war dragged on. When George Ball, the undersecretary of state, went on an overseas trip in 1966 in order to rally support for Johnson's policy, he was surprised to find that most of America's allies did not share the American belief in monolithic communism, the Domino Theory, or the need to defend South Vietnam. In the end, only South Korea committed substantial forces to the defense of the ROV, the real test of support.

Among the more purely military mistakes of America's war in Vietnam was the Johnson-McNamara tourniquet strategy under which Operation ROLLING THUNDER was carried out against North Vietnam. The idea that Hanoi's leaders could be bombed into abandoning their support of the insurgency in South Vietnam was never very realistic, but the prospects for success would have been increased had the air effort been intense from the outset of operations. An intense but relatively brief air effort would have tested the theory without exposing aircrews and aircraft to the effects of an attrition strategy that dragged on for years. Moreover, the "bombing pauses" that Johnson initiated from time to time not only did not lead to serious negotiations with the DRV prior to 1968, they reflected the Washington policy makers' ignorance as to the determination of the government in Hanoi. Nor did they appease the anti-war movement for very long at a time. As for the effect of aerial interdiction on supply and reinforcement via the Ho Chi Minh Trail, it slowed but could not stop the build-up of PAVN forces in South Vietnam to dangerous dimensions.

Regarding the conduct of the ground war in South Vietnam, numerous critics, both civilian and military, have attacked Westmoreland's strategy of attrition. The strategy seemed plausible enough in 1965, but its success depended heavily on the accuracy of estimates of enemy casualties and of the enemy's ability to replace them; also, the strategy took little account of the effects of its search-and-destroy tactics on the South Vietnamese population. As to enemy losses and his ability to replace them, MACV intelligence was seriously faulty by the beginning of 1968, so much so that by the eve of the Tet Offensive the enemy's capabilities as well as his numbers and intentions were seriously underestimated. Despite the fact that the Tet Offensive was finally repelled, it exploded Westmoreland's overly optimistic predictions that the end of the war was coming into view, and destroyed both his and President Johnson's credibility.

Some commentators have suggested that the U.S. Marine counterinsurgency operations, utilizing small-unit tactics and an "ink stain" strategy in the Marine zone of responsibility, should have been the model for American strategy and tactics over the whole of South Vietnam. The Marine measures seem to have been effective against the Viet Cong in the more populated parts of Quang Tri and Thua Tien provinces in terms of population and territorial control, but Westmoreland claimed after the war that he did not have enough forces to adopt such measures for the rest of the heavily populated areas of South Vietnam without effectively abandoning the less-populated Central Highlands. In his judgment, abandonment of the Highlands would have resulted in the loss of Montagnard support, the massing of PAVN forces nearer the coast, and a renewed threat even to the relatively pacified areas in the low country. Viewed in this light, MACV headquarters was faced with a strategic problem that it never really solved, namely that the conflict in Vietnam was not one war but several different wars rolled into one.

Perhaps even more fundamental to the final American failure in South Vietnam was the increasing unpopularity of the war in the United States. Growing criticism of the war put the American leaders—political and military—under the clock and steadily diminished the time needed for any strategy to work. In contrast, there was no time limit on how long the communists were prepared to wage their war and no popular pressure on the Hanoi politburo to change strategies, regardless of the cost in lives.

Under those circumstances, the communist war of attrition on America's will proved more effective than the American war of attrition on communist numbers. General Giap turned out to be correct in believing that a protracted war would wear out the American public's willingness to tolerate it before it would exhaust the communist side's will or ability to wage it.

By the time President Nixon assumed office in January 1969, the U.S. government was faced with two contradictory popular demands; one was to withdraw U.S. forces from South Vietnam as soon as practicable, and the other was to find some new and acceptable strategy by which the ROV could be salvaged. Nixon's solution to this dilemma was Vietnamization, or a policy of building up the ROV's forces while U.S. and Third Country forces were slowly withdrawn. Nixon's critics have claimed that Vietnamization only served to drag out a war already lost in South Vietnam, while it indirectly doomed Cambodia along with Laos in the bargain. Implicit in their criticism is that thousands of U.S. lives were lost uselessly after 1968.

While it can't be denied that Nixon made mistakes in the implementation of his Vietnamization policy, it is difficult to see how any American president could have ended U.S. involvement in Vietnam according to Senator George Aiken's suggestion that "we declare victory and get out." The reason is summed up by the woman who told a reporter, "I want to get out, but I don't want to give up." For despite all the anti-war agitation after 1968, public opinion polls showed consistently that most Americans opposed a policy of total and rapid abandonment of South Vietnam. Thus, for internal political reasons, Nixon's withdrawal of U.S. forces from the ROV had to be contingent on giving South Vietnam a reasonable chance of survival in the process. Vietnamization had served its chief purpose in terms of U.S. domestic politics when at the departure of the last American forces in March 1973, the ROV was still essentially intact.

Another question is the relationship between domestic turmoil in the United States and the outcome of the war. Surely the coming of age of the Baby Boom generation, the advent of the black civil rights movement, and the blooming of the youth counter-culture would have ensured a turbulent decade even had there been no foreign war involving the United States. But the war in Vietnam exercised a catalytic influence on domestic ferment by speeding up and intensifying internal conflict over the process of change. The war helped to radicalize domestic politics, and, in reciprocal fashion, instability at home damaged the war effort abroad.

On the other hand, when the influence of the anti-war movement is examined in isolation, it is difficult to prove that it hastened the end of the war. Indeed, a contrary case may be made that the behavior of the anti-war movement's more extreme elements at times was so off-putting to the general public that it diverted their hostility from the war to the war resisters. In so doing, it was actually counter-productive. Hence, Johnson's war policy would have probably survived the anti-war movement's demonstrations and arguments, and even benefited from some of its more outlandish behavior, had the war been seen by most Americans to be going well. But by late in 1967 a majority of the public were not satisfied with Johnson's handling of the war, and after the Tet Offensive in 1968 even among the war's supporters there was a broad consensus that Johnson had no acceptable solutions either for winning the war or for ending it. Thus, Johnson's massive loss of public support was not due to the propaganda and arguments of the anti-war movement, but to Johnson's inability to bring the war to a satisfactory end in a reasonable time and at an acceptable cost.

Similarly, and despite some impressive demonstrations, the anti-war movement was not very effective in influencing American policy during the Nixon administration except when it mirrored public attitudes created by events such as the Cambodian Incursion and the publication of the Pentagon Papers. Indeed, anti-war agitation seems to have had the chief effect of creating a sense of siege in the White House. Nixon sought to deal with this sense of siege through means both legal and illegal, but he did not fundamentally change his goals and methods in Indochina. Of much greater importance to Nixon's policy than anti-war agitation was the revolution in Sino-American relations in 1971–1972. Likewise, although Congress began belatedly to impose increasing limits on the President's freedom of action in regard to the war, it did so only incrementally and at an almost glacial speed until late in the conflict. Perhaps this slow pace reflected the public's very gradual loss of confidence either in the necessity for the war or in Nixon's strategy for ending it, though congressional opposition finally foreclosed any possibility of its renewal under American auspices after 1972.

Americans today may draw a measure of solace from one observation about America's war in Vietnam. Although the list of mistakes made by five U.S. administrations in regard to Southeast Asia is a long one, each of the American presidents involved made the correct decision to avoid a direct confrontation with the Sino-Soviet bloc over Indochina. Such a confrontation might have caused a localized conflict in Southeast Asia to escalate into a global conflict on the nuclear level, and such a global, nuclear war could only have brought ruin on all the parties involved, including the United States. In that sense the American policy of restraint may be said to have worked, although in a curious way: America's limited effort in Indochina could not save the area from communist domination, but it saved America from the worst consequences of its folly there.

Selected Bibliography

Adams, Sam. *War of Numbers: An Intelligence Memoir.* South Royalton, Vt.: Steerforth Press, 1994.

Addington, Larry H. "Antiaircraft Artillery vs. the Fighter Bomber: the Duel over North Vietnam." *Army.* Vol. 23, No. 12. December, 1973.

———. *The Patterns of War since the Eighteenth Century.* 2nd ed. Bloomington: Indiana University Press, 1994.

Arlen, Michael J. *Living-Room War.* New York: Penguin Books, 1982.

Artaud, Denise, and Lawrence Kaplan, eds. *Dienbienphu: The Atlantic Alliance and the Defense of Southeast Asia.* Wilmington, Del.: Scholarly Resources, 1989.

Asprey, Robert B. *War in the Shadows: The Guerrilla in History.* 2 vols. Garden City, N.Y.: Doubleday and Co., 1975.

Austin, Anthony. *The President's War.* Philadelphia: Lippincott, 1971.

Bachman, Jerald G. *The All-Volunteer Force: A Study of Ideology in the Military.* Ann Arbor: University of Michigan Press, 1978.

Bain, Chester A. *Vietnam: The Roots of Conflict.* Englewood Cliffs, N.J.: Prentice-Hall, 1967.

Baker, Mark. *Nam: The Vietnam War in the Words of the Soldiers Who Fought There.* New York: William Morrow, 1981.

Baritz, Loren. *Backfire: A History of How American Culture Led Us into Vietnam and Made Us Fight the Way We Did.* New York: William Morrow and Co., 1985.

Barnett, Richard J. *Roots of War: The Men and Institutions behind U.S. Foreign Policy.* New York: Atheneum, 1972.

Barrett, David M. *Uncertain Warriors: Lyndon Johnson and His Vietnam Advisers.* Lawrence: University Press of Kansas, 1993.

Baskir, Lawrence M., and William A. Strauss. *Chance and Circumstance: The Draft, the War, and the Vietnam Generation.* New York: Alfred A. Knopf, 1978.

Beresford, Melanie. *Vietnam: Politics, Economics, and Society.* London: Pinter, 1988.

Berger, Carl, ed. *The United States Air Force in Southeast Asia, 1961–1973: An Illustrated Account.* Washington: Office of Air Force History, 1984.

Berman, Larry. *Lyndon Johnson's War: The Road to Stalemate in Vietnam.* New York: Norton, 1989.

———. *Planning a Tragedy: The Americanization of the War in Vietnam.* W. W. Norton and Co., 1982.

Bernstein, Carl, and Bob Woodward. *All the President's Men.* New York: Simon and Schuster, 1974.

Billings-Yun, Melanie. *Decision against the War: Eisenhower and Dien Bien Phu, 1954.* New York: Columbia Press, 1988.

Bilton, Michael, and Kevin Sim. *Four Hours in My Lai.* New York: Penguin Books, 1991.

Blum, Robert M. *Drawing the Line: The Origins of the American Containment Policy in East Asia.* New York: Norton, 1982.

Bodard, Lucien. *The Quicksand War: Prelude to Vietnam.* Boston: Little, Brown and Co., 1967.

Boettcher, Thomas D. *Vietnam, The Valor and the Sorrow: From the Home Front to the Front Lines in Words and Pictures.* Boston: Little, Brown and Co., 1985.

Bond, Brian. *The Pursuit of Victory from Napoleon to Saddam Hussein*. Oxford: Oxford University Press, 1996.

Bornet, Vaughan. *The Presidency of Lyndon Johnson*. Lawrence: University of Kansas Press, 1983.

Bosiljevac, T. L. *SEALs: UDT/SEAL Operations in Vietnam*. New York: Ivy Books, 1990.

Bouscaren, Anthony. *The Last of the Mandarins: Diem of Vietnam*. Pittsburgh: Duquesne University Press, 1965.

Bradin, James W. *From Hot Air to Hellfire: The History of Army Attack Aviation*. Novato, Calif.: Presidio Press, 1994.

Braestrup, Peter, ed. *Big Story: How the American Press and Television Reported and Interpreted the Crises of Tet*. Boulder, Colo.: Westview, 1977.

Broughton, Jack. *Thud Ridge*. New York: Bantam Books, 1985.

Bryan, C. D. B. *Friendly Fire*. New York: G. P. Putnam's Sons, 1976.

Butler, David. *The Fall of Saigon: Scenes from the Sudden End of a Long War*. New York: Simon and Schuster, 1985.

Buttinger, Joseph. *A Dragon Defiant: A Short History of Vietnam*. New York: Praeger Publishers, 1972.

Caputo, Philip. *A Rumor of War*. New York: Holt, Rinehart and Winston, 1977.

Chester, Lewis, et al. *Watergate: The Full Inside Story*. New York: Ballantine Books, 1973.

Chomsky, Noam. *At War with Asia: Essays on Indochina*. New York: Vintage Books, 1970.

Clodfelter, Mark. *The Limits of Air Power: The American Bombing of North Vietnam*. New York: Free Press, 1989.

Coffey, Thomas M. *Iron Eagle: The Turbulent Life of General Curtis LeMay*. New York: Avon Books, 1988.

Committee of Concerned Asian Scholars. *The Indochina Story*. New York: Bantam, 1970.

Cooper, Chester L. *The Lost Crusade: America in Vietnam*. Greenwich, Conn.: Fawcett, 1970.

Crile, George, et al. *CBS Reports*, "The Uncounted Enemy: A Vietnam Deception." Television broadcast, 23 January 1982.

Currey, Cecil. *Victory at Any Cost: The Genius of Viet Nam's Gen. Vo Nguyen Giap*. Washington: Brassey's, 1997.

Cutler, Thomas J. *Brown Water, Black Berets: Coastal and Riverine Warfare in Vietnam*. New York: Pocket Books, 1988.

Davidson, Phillip B. *Vietnam at War: The History, 1946–1975*. Novato, Calif.: Presidio Press, 1988.

Davis, Larry. *Wild Weasel: The SAM Suppression Story*. Carrollton, Tex.: Squadron/Signal Publications, 1986.

Di Leo, David L. *George Ball: Vietnam, and the Rethinking of Containment*. Chapel Hill: University of North Carolina Press, 1991.

Drendel, Lou. *Aircraft of the Vietnam War: A Pictorial Review*. Aero Publishers, 1980.

Duiker, William. *The Communist Road to Power in Vietnam*. Boulder, Colo.: Westview, 1981.

———. *The Rise of Nationalism in Vietnam, 1900–1941*. Ithaca, N.Y.: Cornell University Press, 1976.

———. *Vietnam since the Fall of Saigon*. Athens: Ohio University Center for International Studies, 1985.

Dung, Van Tien. *Our Great Spring Victory.* New York: Monthly Review Press, 1977.

Durrance, Dick. *Where War Lives: A Photographic Journal of Vietnam.* New York: Noonday Press, 1988.

Edelman, Bernard, ed. *Dear America: Letters Home from Vietnam.* New York: W. W. Norton and Co., 1985.

Ellsberg, Daniel. *Papers on the War.* New York: Pocket Books, 1972.

Emerson, Gloria. *Winners and Losers: Battles, Retreats, Gains, Losses, and Ruins from the Vietnam War.* New York: Penguin Books, 1972.

Ethell, Jeffrey, and Alfred Price. *One Day in a Long War: May 10, 1972, Air War, North Vietnam.* New York: Random House, 1989.

Evans, Rowland, and Robert Novak. *Lyndon B. Johnson: The Exercise of Power.* New American Library, 1966.

Fall, Bernard B. *Hell in a Very Small Place: The Siege of Dien Bien Phu.* New York: Vintage Books, 1968.

———. *Street without Joy: Insurgency in Vietnam, 1946–1963.* 4th rev. ed. Harrisburg, Pa.: Stackpole Press, 1964.

———. *The Two Vietnams: A Political and Military Analysis.* Rev. ed. New York: Frederick A. Praeger, 1964.

Fitzgerald, Frances. *Fire in the Lake: The Vietnamese and the Americans in Vietnam.* New York: Vintage Books, 1972.

Franklin, H. Bruce. *M.I.A. or Mythmaking in America.* Brooklyn, N.Y.: Lawrence Hill Books, 1992.

Fulbright, William. *The Arrogance of Power.* New York: Vintage Books, 1966.

Gaddis, John Lewis. *The United States and the Origins of the Cold War.* New York: Columbia University Press, 1972.

Galloway, John. *The Gulf of Tonkin Incident.* Rutherford, N.J.: Farleigh Dickinson University Press, 1970.

Gallucci, Robert L. *Neither Peace nor Honor: The Politics of American Military Policy in Vietnam.* Baltimore: Johns Hopkins University Press, 1975.

Gardner, Lloyd C. *Approaching Vietnam: From World War II through Dienbienphu.* New York: W. W. Norton and Co., 1988.

———. *Architects of Illusion: Men and Ideas in American Foreign Policy, 1941–1949.* Chicago: Quadrangle Books, 1970.

Gelb, Leslie, and Richard Betts. *The Irony of Vietnam: The System Worked.* Washington, D.C.: Brookings, 1979.

Gettleman, Marvin E., ed. *Vietnam: History, Documents, and Opinions on a Major World Crisis.* New York: Fawcett Premier, 1965.

Gettleman, Marvin E., et al., eds. *Conflict in Indochina: A Reader on the Widening War in Laos and Cambodia.* New York: Vintage Books, 1970.

Gilbert, James W. *The Perfect War: The War We Couldn't Lose and How We Did.* Boston: Atlantic Monthly, 1986.

Gilbert, Marc J., and William Head, eds. *The Tet Offensive.* Westport, Conn.: Praeger, 1996.

Goff, Robert, and Robert Sander. *Brothers: Black Soldiers in the Nam.* Novato, Calif.: Presidio Press, 1982.

Goldman, Peter, and Tony Fuller. *Charlie Company: What Vietnam Did to Us.* New York: Ballantine, 1983.

Goulden, Joseph C. *Truth Is the First Casualty: The Gulf of Tonkin Affair—Illusion and Reality.* Chicago: Rand McNally and Co., 1969.

Halberstam, David. *The Best and the Brightest.* New York: Random House, 1969.

———. *Ho.* New York: Random House, 1971.

——. *The Making of a Quagmire: America and Vietnam during the Kennedy Era.* Rev. ed. New York: Alfred A. Knopf, 1988.

Haldeman, H. R. *The Haldeman Diaries: Inside the Nixon Whitehouse.* New York: G. P. Putnam's Sons, 1994.

Hammel, Eric. *Fire in the Streets: The Battle for Hue, Tet 1968.* Pacifica, Calif.: Pacifica Press, 1991.

Hammer, Ellen J. *A Death in November: America in Vietnam, 1963.* New York: Oxford University Press, 1987.

——. *The Struggle for Indochina, 1940–1955.* Stanford, Calif.: Stanford University Press, 1966.

Harrison, James Pickney. *The Endless War: Fifty Years of War in Vietnam.* New York: Free Press, 1982.

Harrison, Marshall. *A Lonely War.* Novato, Calif.: Presidio Press, 1989.

Harvey, Frank. *Air War Vietnam.* New York: Bantam Books, 1967.

Hemingway, Albert. *Our War Was Different: Marine Combined Action Platoons in Vietnam.* Annapolis, Md.: Naval Institute Press, 1994.

Herr, Michael. *Dispatches.* New York: Avon, 1978.

Herring, George C. *America's Longest War: The United States and Vietnam, 1950–1975.* 2nd ed. New York: Alfred A. Knopf, 1986.

——. *LBJ and Vietnam: A Different Kind of War.* Austin: University of Texas Press, 1994.

——, ed. *The Secret Diplomacy of the Vietnam War.* Austin: University of Texas Press, 1982.

Herrington, Stuart A. *Peace with Honor? An American Reports on Vietnam, 1973–75.* Novato, Calif.: Presidio Press, 1983.

Hersh, Seymour. *My Lai 4: A Report on the Massacre and Its Aftermath.* New York: Vintage Books, 1970.

——. *The Price of Power: Kissinger in the Nixon White House.* New York: Summit Books, 1983.

Herz, Martin F. *The Prestige Press and the Christmas Bombing, 1972 . . . Vietnam.* Washington, D.C.: Ethics and Public Policy Center, 1980.

Hess, Gary R. *The United States's Emergence as a Southeast Asian Power, 1940–1950.* New York: Columbia University Press, 1987.

——. *Vietnam and the United States: Origins and Legacy of War.* Boston: Twayne Publishers, 1990.

Higgins, Hugh. *Vietnam.* 2nd ed. London: Heinemann Educational Books, 1982.

Hosmer, Stephen T., et al., eds. *The Fall of South Vietnam: Statements by Vietnamese Military and Civilian Leaders.* New York: Crane, Russak and Co., 1980.

Irving, Ronald E. *Approaching Vietnam: The First Indochina War—French and American Policy, 1945–1954.* London: Croom Helm, 1975.

Isaacs, Arnold R. *Without Honor: Defeat in Vietnam and Cambodia.* Baltimore, Md.: Johns Hopkins University Press, 1983.

Isserman, Maurice. *The Vietnam War: America at War.* New York: Facts on File, 1992.

Johnson, Lyndon B. *The Vantage Point: Perspectives of the Presidency.* New York: Holt, Rinehart, and Winston, 1971.

Kahin, George McT. *Intervention.* New York: Vintage, 1966.

Kahin, George McT., and John W. Lewis. *The United States in Vietnam.* New York: Dial Press, 1967.

Kail, F. M. *What Washington Said: Administration Rhetoric and the Vietnam War, 1949–1969.* New York: Harper Torchback, 1973.

Karnow, Stanley. *Vietnam: A History.* New York: The Viking Press, 1983.

Kattenberg, Paul. *The Vietnam Trauma in American Foreign Policy, 1945–1975.* New Brunswick, N.J.: Transaction, 1980.

Kaufmann, William W. *The McNamara Strategy.* New York: Harper and Row, 1964.

Kearns, Doris. *Lyndon Johnson and the American Dream.* New York: Harper and Row, 1976.

Kiernan, Ben. *How Pol Pot Came to Power: A History of Communism in Kampuchea, 1930–1975.* London: Verso, 1975.

———. *The Pol Pot Regime: Race, Power, and Genocide in Cambodia under the Khmer Rouge, 1975–1979.* New Haven: Yale University Press, 1996.

Kimball, Jeffrey P., ed. *To Reason Why: The Debate about the Causes of U.S. Involvement in the Vietnam War.* New York: McGraw-Hill Publishing Co., 1990.

Kolko, Gabriel. *Anatomy of a War: Vietnam, the United States, and the Modern Historical Experience.* New York: Pantheon Books, 1985.

———. *The Roots of American Foreign Policy.* Boston: Beacon, 1969.

Lacouture, Jean. *Ho Chi Minh: A Political Biography.* Trans. from the French by Peter Wiles. New York: Random House, 1968.

Lansdale, Edward G. *In the Midst of Wars.* New York: Harper and Row, 1972.

LeGro, William E. *Vietnam from Cease-Fire to Capitulation.* Washington, D.C.: U.S. Army Center of Military History, 1981.

Leitenberg, Milton, and Richard Dean Burns. *The Vietnam Conflict: Its Geographical Dimensions, Political Traumas, and Military Developments.* Santa Barbara, Calif.: ABC–Clio, 1973.

Lens, Sidney. *Vietnam: A War on Two Fronts.* New York: Lodestar Books, 1990.

Lewy, Guenter. *America in Vietnam.* New York: Oxford University Press, 1978.

Lifton, Robert Jay. *Home from the War: Vietnam Veterans, Neither Victims nor Executioners.* New York: Simon and Schuster, 1973.

Lomperis, Timothy J. *The War Everyone Lost—and Won.* Baton Rouge: Louisiana State University Press, 1984.

Macdonald, Peter. *Giap: The Victor in Vietnam.* New York: W. W. Norton and Co., 1993.

Maclear, Michael. *The Ten Thousand Day War: Vietnam, 1945–1975.* New York: St. Martin's Press, 1981.

Manchester, William. *The Glory and the Dream: A Narrative History of America, 1932–1972.* 2 vols. Boston: Little, Brown and Co., 1973–74.

Mangold, Tom, and John Penycate. *The Tunnels of Cu Chi.* New York: Random House, 1985.

Marr, David. *Vietnamese Anti-Colonialism, 1885–1925.* Berkeley: University of California Press, 1971.

Marshall, S. L. A. *The Fields of Bamboo: . . . Three Battles Just beyond the South China Sea.* New York: Dial Press, 1971.

Matusow, Allen J. *The Unraveling of America: A History of Liberalism in the 1960s.* New York: Harper and Row, 1984.

Mauer, Harry. *Strange Ground: Americans in Vietnam, 1945–1975.* New York: Henry Holt and Co., 1989.

McAlister, John T., Jr. *Vietnam: The Origins of Revolution.* Garden City, N.Y.: Doubleday and Co., 1971.

McConnell, Malcolm. *Inside Hanoi's Secret Archives: Solving the MIA Mystery.* New York: Simon and Schuster, 1995.

McGarvey, Patrick J. *Visions of Victory: Selected Vietnamese Communist Military Writings, 1965–1968.* Stanford, Calif.: Hoover Institute on War, Revolution, and Peace, 1969.

McMaster, H. R. *Dereliction of Duty: Lyndon Johnson, Robert McNamara, the Joint Chiefs of Staff, and the Lies That Led to Vietnam.* New York: HarperCollins, 1997.

McNamara, Robert S. *In Retrospect: The Tragedy and Lessons of Vietnam.* With Brian VanDeMark. New York: Times Books, 1995.

McPherson, Harry. *A Political Education.* Boston: Little, Brown, 1972.

Mersky, Peter B., and Norman Polmar. *The Naval Air War in Vietnam.* Annapolis: Nautical and Aviation Publishing Co. of America, 1981.

Millett, Allan R., ed. *A Short History of the Vietnam War.* Bloomington: Indiana University Press, 1978.

Millett, Allan R., and Peter Maslowski. *For the Common Defense: A Military History of the United States of America.* Rev. ed. New York: Free Press, 1994.

Moïse, Edwin E. *Tonkin Gulf and the Escalation of the Vietnam War.* Chapel Hill: University of North Carolina Press, 1996.

Momyer, William W. *Air Power in Three Wars: WWII, Korea, Vietnam.* Washington, D.C.: U.S. Government Printing Office, 1978.

Moore, Harold G., and Joseph L. Galloway. *We Were Soldiers Once . . . and Young: Ia Drang, the Battle That Changed the War in Vietnam.* New York: Random House, 1992.

Moskin, J. Robert. *The U.S. Marine Corps Story.* Rev. ed. New York: McGraw-Hill, 1982.

Mueller, John E. *War, Presidents, and Public Opinion.* New York: John Wiley and Co., 1973.

Murphy, Edward F. *Semper Fi Vietnam: From Da Nang to the DMZ: Marine Corps Campaigns, 1965–1975.* Novato, Calif.: Presidio Press, 1997.

New York Times Staff. *The Pentagon Papers.* New York: Bantam Books, 1972.

———. *The White House Transcripts: Submission of Recorded Presidential Conversations to the Committee on the Judiciary of the House of Representatives by President Nixon.* New York: Bantam Books, 1974.

Ngo Quang Truong. *The Easter Offensive of 1972.* Washington, D.C.: U.S. Army Center of Military History, 1980.

Nguyen Cao Ky. *Twenty Years and Twenty Days.* New York: Stein and Day, 1976.

Nguyen Duy Hinh. *Lam Son 719.* Washington, D.C.: U.S. Army Center of Military History, 1979.

O'Ballance, Edgar. *The Indochina War: A Study in Guerrilla Warfare.* London: Faber and Faber, 1964.

———. *The Wars in Vietnam, 1954–1980.* Enlarged ed. New York: Hippocrene Books, 1981.

Oberdorfer, Don. *Tet!* Garden City, N.Y.: Doubleday, 1973.

Odom, William E. *The Collapse of the Soviet Military.* New York: Yale University Press, 1998.

Olson, James S., and Randy Roberts. *The War in Vietnam.* New York: St. Martin's Press, 1990.

Palmer, Bruce, Jr. *The 25-Year War: America's Military Role in Vietnam.* Lexington: University Press of Kentucky, 1984.

Palmer, Dave Richard. *Summons of the Trumpet: U.S.-Vietnam in Perspective.* San Rafael, Calif.: Presidio Press, 1972.

Papp, Daniel S. *Vietnam: The View from Moscow, Peking, Washington.* Salisbury, N.C.: McFarland, 1981.

Patti, Archimedes L. A. *Why Vietnam? Prelude to America's Albatross.* Berkeley: University of California Press, 1980.

Pike, Douglas. *History of Vietnamese Communism*. Stanford, Calif.: Stanford University Press, 1978.

——. *PAVN: People's Army of Vietnam*. Novato, Calif.: Presidio Press, 1986.

——. *Viet Cong: National Liberation Front of South Vietnam*. Rev. ed. Cambridge: MIT Press, 1972.

Pimlot, John, ed. *Vietnam: The History and the Tactics*. New York: Crescent Books, 1982.

Piser, Robert. *The End of the Line: The Siege of Khe Sanh*. New York: W. W. Norton and Co., 1982.

Plaster, John L. *SOG: The Secret Wars of America's Commandos in Vietnam*. New York: Onyx, 1997.

Podhoretz, Norman. *Why We Were in Vietnam*. New York: Simon and Schuster, 1982.

Porter, Gareth. *A Peace Denied: The United States, Vietnam, and the Paris Agreements*. Bloomington: Indiana University Press, 1975.

Prados, John. *The Hidden History of the Vietnam War*. Chicago: I. R. Dee, 1995.

——. *The Presidents' Secret Wars: the CIA and Pentagon Covert Operations since World War II*. New York: William Morrow, 1986.

Prados, John, and Ray W. Stubbe. *Valley of Decision: the Siege of Khe Sanh*. Boston: Houghton Mifflin Co., 1991.

Quick, John. *Dictionary of Weapons and Military Terms*. New York: McGraw-Hill Book Co., 1973.

Reeves, Richard. *President Kennedy: Profile of Power*. New York: Simon and Schuster, 1993.

Robbins, Christopher. *Air America*. New York: Avon, 1979.

Rogers, Robert W. *Cedar Falls–Junction City: A Turning Point*. Washington, D.C.: U.S. Army Center of Military History, 1974.

Rosser-Owen, David. *Vietnam Weapons Handbook*. Wellingborough, Eng.: Patrick Stephens, Ltd., 1986.

Rotter, Andrew J. *The Path to Vietnam: Origins of the American Commitment to Southeast Asia*. Ithaca: Cornell University Press, 1987.

Rusk, Dean. *As I Saw It*. As told to Richard Rusk, ed. Daniel Papp. New York: Norton, 1990.

Santoli, Al, ed. *Everything We Had: An Oral History of the Vietnam War by Thirty-Three Soldiers Who Fought It*. New York: St. Martin's Press, 1990.

——. *To Bear Any Burden: the Vietnam War and Its Aftermath in the Words of Americans and Southeast Asians*. New York: Dutton, 1985.

Sarin, Oleg, and Lev Dvoretsky. *The Afghan Syndrome: The Soviet Union's Vietnam*. Novato, Calif.: Presidio Press, 1993.

Schandler, Herbert Y. *Lyndon Johnson and Vietnam: The Unmaking of a President*. Princeton: Princeton University Press, 1977.

Schell, Jonathan. *The Village of Ben Suc*. New York: Vintage Books, 1968.

Schlesinger, Arthur M., Jr. *The Bitter Heritage: Vietnam and American Democracy, 1941–1966*. Greenwich, Conn.: Fawcett Crest, 1967.

Schulzinger, Robert D. *A Time for War: The United States and Vietnam, 1941–1975*. New York; Oxford University Press, 1997.

Scutts, Jerry. *Wrecking Crew: The 388th Tactical Fighter Wing in Vietnam*. New York: Warner Books, 1990.

Shawcross, William. *Quality of Mercy: Cambodia, Holocaust and Modern Conscience*. New York: Simon and Schuster, 1984.

——. *Sideshow: Kissinger, Nixon and the Destruction of Cambodia*. New York: Simon and Schuster, 1979.

Sheehan, Neil. *A Bright Shining Lie: John Paul Vann and America in Vietnam*. New York: Random House, 1988.

Simmons, Edwin H. *The United States Marines: The First Two Hundred Years, 1775–1975*. New York: Viking Press, 1976.

Small, Melvin. *Johnson, Nixon, and the Doves*. New Brunswick, N.J.: Rutgers University Press, 1988.

Snepp, Frank. *Decent Interval: An Insider's Account of Saigon's Indecent End*. New York: Random House, 1977.

Socialist Republic of Vietnam. *Vietnam: The Anti-U.S. Resistance for National Salvation, 1954–1957: Military History*. Hanoi: People's Publishing House, 1980.

Solberg, Carl. *Hubert Humphrey: A Biography*. New York: Norton, 1984.

Spector, Ronald H. *Advice and Support: The Early Years of the U.S. Army in Vietnam, 1941–1960*. New York: Free Press, 1985.

——. *After Tet: The Bloodiest Year in Vietnam*. New York: Free Press, 1993.

Stanton, Shelby L. *The Rise and Fall of an American Army: U.S. Ground Forces in Vietnam, 1965–1973*. Novato, Calif.: Presidio Press, 1985.

——. *Vietnam Order of Battle*. Washington: U.S. News Books, 1981.

Stavins, Ralph, et al. *Washington Plans an Aggressive War: A Documented Account of the United States Adventure in Indochina*. New York: Vintage Books, 1971.

Stetler, Russell, ed. *The Military Art of People's War: Selected Writings of General Vo Nguyen Giap*. New York: Monthly Review Press, 1970.

Stockdale, Jim, and Sybil Stockdale. *In Love and War: The Story of a Family's Ordeal and Sacrifice during the Vietnam Years*. New York: Harper and Row, 1984.

Summers, Harry G., Jr. *Historical Atlas of the Vietnam War*. Boston and New York: Houghton Mifflin Co., 1995.

——. *On Strategy: A Critical Analysis of the Vietnam War*. Novato, Calif.: Presidio Press, 1982.

——. *Vietnam War Almanac*. New York: Facts on File Publications, 1985.

Taylor, Maxwell. *Swords and Ploughshares*. New York: Norton, 1972.

Taylor, Telford. *Nuremberg and Vietnam: An American Tragedy*. New York: Bantam Books, 1971.

Thayer, Thomas C. *War without Fronts: The American Experience in Vietnam*. Boulder, Colo.: Westview, 1985.

Thompson, James Clay. *Rolling Thunder: Understanding Policy and Program Failure*. Chapel Hill: University of North Carolina Press, 1980.

Thompson, W. Scott, and Donaldson D. Frizzell, eds. *The Lessons of Vietnam*. New York: Crane, Russak and Co., 1977.

Tilford, Earl H. *Setup: What the Air Force Did in Vietnam and Why*. Washington, D.C.: Air University Press, 1991.

Tran Van Don. *Our Endless War: Inside South Vietnam*. Novato, Calif.: Presidio Press, 1978.

Tuchman, Barbara W. *Stillwell and the American Experience in China, 1911–1945*. New York: Macmillan Co., 1970.

Turley, G. H. *The Easter Offensive: Vietnam, 1972*. Novato, Calif.: Presidio Press, 1985.

Turley, William S. *The Second Indochina War: A Short Political and Military History*. Boulder, Colo.: Westview, 1986.

Turner, Kathleen J. *Lyndon Johnson's Dual War: Vietnam and the Press*. Chicago: University of Chicago Press, 1985.

Van Dyke, Jon M. *North Vietnam's Strategy for Survival*. Palo Alto, Calif.: Pacific Books Publishers, 1972.

Warner, Dennis. *The Last Confucian*. New York, Penguin, 1963.

Warner, Roger. *Back Fire: The CIA's Secret War in Laos and Its Link to the War in Vietnam.* New York: Simon and Schuster, 1995.

Wells, Tom. *The War Within: America's Battle over Vietnam.* Berkeley: University of California Press, 1994.

Westmoreland, William C. *A Soldier Reports.* Garden City, N.Y.: Doubleday and Co., 1976.

White, Ralph K. *Nobody Wanted War: Misperception in Vietnam and Other Wars.* Garden City, N.Y.: Doubleday, 1968.

Wilcox, Fred A. *Waiting for an Army to Die: The Tragedy of Agent Orange.* New York: Vintage Books, 1983.

Williams, William Appleman, et al., eds. *America in Vietnam: A Documentary History.* New York: W. W. Norton and Co., 1975.

Windchy, Eugene. *Tonkin Gulf.* Garden City, N.Y.: Doubleday, 1971.

Wolf, Eric R. *Peasant Wars of the Twentieth Century.* New York: Harper and Row, 1969.

Young, Marilyn B. *The Vietnam Wars, 1945–1990.* New York: HarperPerennial, 1991.

Index